The Jewish Journey Through Loss
From Death to Healing

Dr. Batya L. Ludman
Gina Junger

The Jewish Journey Through Loss

From Death to Healing

Maggid Books

The Jewish Journey Through Loss:
From Death to Healing

First Edition, 2025

Maggid Books:
An imprint of Koren Publishers Jerusalem Ltd.

POB 8531, New Milford, CT 06776-8531, USA
& POB 4044, Jerusalem 9104001, Israel
www.korenpub.com

The publication of this book was made possible
through the generous support of *The Jewish Book Trust.*

ISBN 978-1-59264-685-2, *hardcover*

Printed and bound in Turkey

In loving memory of

Rebecca Sprung z"l

רבקה חנה בת גולדה ע"ה

who was a source of wisdom, advice, warmth,
and love to our entire family,
from her sister and family.

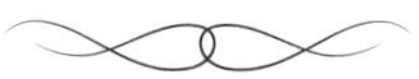

In memory of Rebecca,
she was an inspiration for so many.

Jay & Huti Pomrenze

In loving memory of our beloved David Schwartz

דוד בן שרה ויאיר ז״ל

Killed in battle כ״ז טבת תשפ״ד
defending the Jewish people and the State
of Israel at the young age of 26.
May the wisdom in this book guide and comfort
those going through the loss of a loved one.

Gitler and Schwartz Families

Dedicated to the memory of our dear mother

Seyma Lederman ע״ה

who loved Gina Junger's weekly parsha
shiurim at Protea Village
and passed her love of Torah to her children,
grandchildren, and great grandchildren.
יהי זכרה ברוך

In loving memory of

נחמה מידל בת יצחק אריה ושרה רבקה

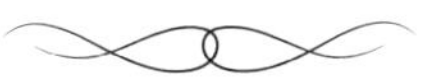

In loving memory of my sister

Marilyn Field *z"l*

who died too soon and too young.

Forever missed by her sister,

Adele Hunter

This gift to helping others cope with loss is in memory of my dear grandparents and uncle who were instrumental in guiding me as a child and shaping who I am today.

Helen Goldhar *z"l*
Samuel Goldhar *z"l*
Jack Goldhar *z"l*
Thelma Oilgisser *z"l*
Irving Oilgisser *z"l*

Richard Goldhar

Author's Dedications

This book is lovingly dedicated
to my wonderful family
who bring me great joy,
infuse my life with tremendous meaning,
encourage me to grow,
and each in their own special way,
make my journey in life complete.

Batya

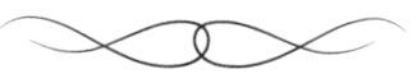

Dedicated to my parents who taught me by
example Ahavat Am Yisrael,
Ahavat Torat Yisrael, and Ahavat Eretz Yisrael.

Gina

Contents

Acknowledgments

I began this journey into the world of death many years ago, as I sought to better understand my own feelings and those of my clients as they attempted to make meaning out of their loss. I realized that while the psychological and halakhic literature each had much to offer, they were typically presented as two very distinct entities. The idea of this book was born out of the belief that Judaism has so much to contribute to our psychological (emotional, physical and spiritual) healing.

As I began to write, I was so fortunate to begin discussions with my beloved teacher and mentor, Gina Junger. What was always an amazing *ḥavruta* became the basis for us writing together. We dovetailed perfectly. With my psychological background and her perfect blend of Jewish understanding (education), working with her has been a truly great privilege. As our husbands marveled at how we could "talk death" for hours, with the deepest respect, we seemed to complete each other's ideas as well as sentences and make the sum of one and one so much greater than two. While writing a book about death seemed like such an enormous project, the topic indeed felt finite and (no pun intended), we saw an end in sight. Then along came COVID-19 followed by the multiple losses experienced during and after a horrific war, and we suddenly had infinitely more we needed to say. We have already started talking about the next edition!

There are so many people whom I would like to thank. I would be remiss in first not thanking my beloved husband Mark, among other things, always my editor, technology expert, and secretary extraordinaire. While dreading hearing me call to him from the computer, he always knew exactly which questions needed to be asked and just how they should be answered. Thank you for always being there for me, day and night and challenging me to try to be the best I can be. To our three wonderful children and spouses, my true guiding lights, Benjamin and Danielle, Aaron and Einat, and Shayna and Barak, and our precious grandchildren, Mia, Emma, Yehonatan, Noam, Ora, Yishai and Itamar. You have grown up in difficult times, and yet with open conversations around both life and death, you just assume that all of this is normal. To my beloved parents of blessed memory whose contribution to community and the *ḥevra kaddisha* , opened my eyes to the importance of giving at a young age. Also to my wonderful parents-in-law *z"l*, who along with my own parents loved me unconditionally and were always so supportive of my work.

Thank you to Marianne Ferguson *z"l*, Mindy Jacobson, and Rabbi Saul Aranov, my teachers of *ḥevra kaddisha* , and Carol Lee Loebenberg, who helped facilitate my growth around death education, to Rae Brown of Riverside Memorial Chapel and Edward Yarmus of Plaza Jewish Community Chapel, of New York who graciously shared their feelings about funeral practices and why this book was so important.

To my dear friends and family who are always there for me, in spite of my never seeming to manage my time better, I am truly grateful. To my beloved patients who taught me so much over the years with their incredible insights, as they allowed me to accompany them on their journey in both life and death, through loss and through healing. You guided my thinking and helped bring this book to fruition.

Thank you above all to Hashem, for enabling me to be in the right place at the right time. I am deeply grateful to and in awe of our amazing country which strengthens both my heart and soul and teaches me the real meaning of resilience. With Your blessing, Israel has shown itself to be the true light unto other nations. As we continue to guide the world in showing humanity and deep respect after one of the worst massacres in history, may You help guide us in caring for the deceased and for those left behind to rebuild their lives. May You bless and protect us and shine Your light upon us as we face the many challenges that lie ahead. Please help us to grow with integrity and find true meaning as recipients of your tremendous love.

Batya L. Ludman, Psy.D. F.T.

*****

I want to take this opportunity to thank several people without whom this book would not have been produced.

Thank you to my husband Abie for his constant love and support. He has always been my greatest cheerleader and he believed in the value of this project from the beginning. He had tremendous patience during the writing and editing process but was also invaluable in his insights and advice regarding the content. I couldn't have done it without him.

Thank you to my wonderful daughters and their amazing partners. You have supported me and this book throughout the process. You bring us such joy and *naḥat*.

Mikol melamdei hiskalti: From all my students I have become wise (Ps. 119). I am so grateful to all my students both past and present – young and old. They continue to ask wonderful questions that make me a better teacher and they inspire me on a daily basis.

Thank you Batya for being my partner in this very important project. I couldn't have wished for a better match. My respect for you as a professional has only grown from working closely with you and I value our friendship and your advice. May Hashem give you strength to continue to do the important work you do and to help those who need *refuat hanefesh*.

Thank you to the *Ribbono shel Olam* for giving me the opportunity to learn Torah and teach Torah in *Eretz Yisrael*. May this book be a tool for people to find comfort in their grief and help them on their journey of healing.

Gina Junger

******

The authors would like to express their gratitude to the staff at Koren Publishers. To Aryeh Grossman, who helped us get the project moving; Caryn Meltz, our wonderfully professional and responsive managing editor, who dealt with our endless questions; Leah Goldstein, Debbie Ismailoff, and Ita Olesker, for their editorial expertise and skillful proofreading; Marc Sherman, our very thorough indexer; Tani Bayer, art director; and Taly Hahn, our graphic designer, who produced a beautifully designed book.

We are deeply appreciative of our sponsors who believed in the need for this book, and especially Jack Berman, whose efforts brought together many of these generous contributors. We are honored that this book has been dedicated in memory of their loved ones, and we hope it brings them comfort.

Finally, we would like to thank our family, friends, and colleagues who shared their feelings and stories with us. Many of these exchanges are the basis of vignettes in the book.

Introduction

The final moments of life draw to a close with death inevitable, and yet no matter how prepared you may think you are, whether death was long anticipated or has happened suddenly, you are never truly ready. How can you be? The final moments, as in all else, are in Hashem's hands, and your focus, as it should be, has been on living and on life. You never quite know just what to expect with respect to what lies ahead in the next moment, let alone the days, weeks, and months that follow.

As you exit the room of your beloved, you begin on your own path of grieving. For some, this journey may have been long anticipated, and your grieving felt – and perhaps even acknowledged – even before the actual death itself. For others, the death is sudden, and the grieving process has not yet started. Many of you, when confronted with the inevitable, may speak with a rabbi or consult books on halakha to gain a greater understanding of just what has to be done around and after a death. Procedural guidelines notwithstanding, few of these books tell you what to really expect at each stage, and as such, how you might feel.

Just as each pregnancy and entry into the world is unique, so, too, does each person exit the world in their own way. With no two deaths being the same, and each differing in the set of issues it presents, your response also will vary. Each loss is different. No two people grieve in the same way – even for the same loss – and no one person grieves the same way for different individuals. Your thoughts and feelings that accompany each stage of grief are dependent on a multitude of factors, and each of these variables alone could fill a book. As such, no one can truly prepare for the emotional roller-coaster ride that lies ahead. In part, no matter how prepared you think you are, no one can fully anticipate the emotional ups and downs that will ensue over the coming year. What you think will upset you may not, and what you don't really think about may catch you off guard and feel devastating. It may be as simple as a trip to the grocery store, a sight, or a smell.

As is true in birth and beyond, so too are you surprised and unprepared for what follows after death. Yet the physical, cognitive, emotional, and spiritual feelings that surface at two very different ends of the life cycle have many similarities. Grief, and the mourning period, can be a time of growth. Just as you may have no idea what to expect when expecting a baby, this book was written on the premise that you may have no idea what to expect in your grieving process. If you can be at all prepared psychologically for the myriad of feelings you may face, or at least understand their origin, you may weather the storm that lies ahead just a bit differently.

Some of you think about death, some fear death, some run from death – yet in the end, death is inevitable, and in its wake it may leave behind a beloved partner, immediate family members, other loved ones, an entire social circle, and a community all with no roadmap to navigate in the months ahead. One of the most beautiful aspects of Judaism's approach to death is its focus on ritual. This prescribed structure, filled with incredible wisdom, lovingly embraces the mourner, moving you forward, step by step, through your pain. As you transition through the process of shiva, *sheloshim*, the first year and *yahrzeit*, this book provides a framework to guide and enable you to grieve, all at a pace that parallels and promotes your own psychological healing. Judaism's beautiful traditions give you a much-needed sense of balance and bring honor to your loved one's memory, while offering consolation and a meaningful path forward to those left behind.

Knowledge is empowering. The intent of this book is to help you attain a better understanding of what to expect during this potentially tumultuous period. Through achieving greater insight and clarity of your own thoughts and feelings, it is hoped that you can begin your own personal journey of healing in a way that best meets your needs at each stage of the grieving process.

The need for this book was driven by the authors' own stories, both in the recent past and with previous experiences of loss, as well as by the stories of others – clients and friends. This book began with a difficult year, individually and within our own little community, here in Israel. Both authors lost close family members, one more suddenly, and the other anticipated. Shortly thereafter, our beloved rabbi became very unwell, and after what felt to many people like a short illness, passed away, leaving close family, friends, and a community bereft and alone to mourn both individually and collectively, pick up the pieces, and move forward. Loss is cumulative, and the sudden shock of such a serious illness, when the community was already shaken by horrific events such as terrorist stabbings, lengthy power outages, destructive hail, and horrific floods, made coping all the more tenuous in the early days, as some remarked that they felt rocked by plagues. While the first chapters of the book had been written, so intense and all-consuming was the topic that, as in life itself, it was put aside for other life events – both wonderful and painful. These events, including COVID-19, a real-life plague that shockingly caught all of us off guard and had a devastating impact on the Jewish community, became our impetus for returning to the book and the subject matter we thought was so very important.

Just prior to going to press, the unthinkable happened. War broke out in Israel. This has been a traumatic event of epic proportion that has impacted not just Israel, but also the entire Jewish world and beyond. We felt that above all, we owed it to our readers to stop, begin to examine its impact, and try as best as we could to share what we have seen and what we anticipate in the coming months and years.

Some day we will write a revision to this chapter, but for now, as we attempt to look at what is almost unimaginable in this Jewish journey from death through healing, we pray that all who have been impacted by this tragedy will be comforted.

In order to best examine the grieving process, we felt it essential to first look at the very foundation on which the loss itself occurred. So, to move forward more easily, you may find it helpful to briefly take a peek into the recent past. This book therefore takes you, the reader, through the year of mourning that officially starts when death is declared, but unofficially begins with the anticipatory grieving you might feel if you are in a situation when you first hear that a loved one has become unwell.

The authors, a clinical psychologist/thanatologist and a Jewish educator, hope that you will find the support you need through reading this book to help you on your own personal path of healing. We recognize that there is much you don't anticipate or think about until you are actually in the situation and are confronted by so many unknowns. This, too, often comes at a time when you may already be feeling quite fragile and confused. We know through experience that there is definitely more than one way to feel. We have learned that there is no one "right" way to feel, just your way, and that this is very much okay. It may differ from how other family members feel, or from your friends' experiences, or even from what you have read. Your feelings are yours and whatever they are, they hold personal meaning for you.

While at times we may raise more questions than we answer, we hope that in doing so, we give you food for thought – and that this in turn helps both direct and comfort you as you begin this challenging and unfamiliar journey. Our goal is to make your thoughts and feelings during this difficult period and the various transitions throughout the year of mourning easier to comprehend.

We have attempted to do this through our own personal experiences, as well as illustrative vignettes and stories that were shared by others. Some have chosen to remain anonymous, while others have given permission to use their names. We have tried, when we thought it was appropriate, to offer helpful tips and biblical sources as well as other Jewish references to highlight our text.

This book is not a halakhic guide per se but is very much guided by our understanding of the halakhot. We felt that books on the halakhic guidelines of mourning address the laws, but not necessarily the thoughts and feelings you might experience, and that this understanding is indeed an important aspect of the grieving process. As such, this is a book about feeling and not simply about doing. Should you have halakhic questions, we urge you to discuss them with a rabbi. We ask for your forgiveness if we don't always anticipate correctly just how you may be feeling. We also recognize that your feelings may change quickly, at times with little or no warning, and that this, too, may temporarily increase your level of discomfort and emotional pain.

While we are unable to take away your pain, we sincerely hope that through this book we will "walk" alongside you as you take your journey forward into the land of healing.

Sincerely yours,
Batya and Gina

Chapter 1

From Illness Until Death

We have chosen to delineate the period of time from illness until death into two time periods – the first, from when your loved one felt unwell up until a diagnosis was made; and the second, from diagnosis until death. These are in many ways arbitrary, as determining an actual diagnosis may come at just about any point along the timeline continuum, from recognition that your loved one is unwell until they ultimately die. Depending also on the situation, one may never receive an actual diagnosis, but only a tentative or working diagnosis. The time from diagnosis until death can vary greatly, being short or more protracted, given that in general people are now living much longer and with life-threatening illnesses that were once considered fatal.

HEARING THE NEWS

How you hear the news around death, and when you hear the news, will have a great impact on how you deal with the issues at hand. If you are reading this book now, it is possibly because you know of someone very ill, but it is far more likely that someone you know has recently died. If you didn't read this book when your loved one was sick, you will not be alone. You see, we often don't think about death. We may not want, or be able, to face the realization that someone is very sick. Yet we all will face loss and we all will grieve. It is one hundred percent certain that all of us will die someday – hopefully *ad me'ah ve'esrim*. In theory, as with Moses who lived until the age of 120, we, too, would like to be blessed with a good, long life. For some, in the prime of their lives, death comes too early. Others, who have been unwell, may be more than ready for their life to end.

Perhaps we are jumping a bit ahead of ourselves with the title, "hearing the news," because in actuality, if there is an illness, it may precede death by weeks, months, or even years. It may come with grace or as a shock, with worries, fears, anxiety, and distress. Although it is important to live in the moment, we will go back to the period of time leading up to the death and explore this in detail. This phase, as well as the nature of the death, is important in understanding and coping during the post-death period.

WHEN DEATH IS SUDDEN

It is hard to imagine, without going through it, that your whole world can change literally within a minute. Death rarely occurs at an opportune moment; there is rarely a good or right time to die. We may initially understand the time of death as the time on the clock when our loved one took their last breath, rather than try to ascribe meaning to the sudden loss because this comprehension cannot come now, during a period of initial shock.

With time, part of the healing around the "suddenness" of the death may come with a greater understanding of how the loss itself is interpreted. Coming to terms with such a dichotomy, where everything feels so "normal" before a death and so "not normal" afterwards, is a huge challenge. The unforeseen war in Israel and our experience with COVID-19 has shown this to be the case, with so many people dying unexpectedly.

SUDDEN VERSUS ANTICIPATED DEATH

When your loved one is extremely ill over a period of weeks to months and begins to deteriorate, you may find yourself thinking about and even anticipating their final days on earth. Sometimes, that last breath will come quickly, and at other times, the end will take place over a prolonged period of time, giving both you and your loved one time to prepare. For some, even with a prolonged illness or with no apparent illness at all, death may be very sudden and unexpected.

Whether as a result of an accident, suicide, or other misfortune, when the call comes, you may be in a state of disbelief. Sudden death can feel confusing, complicated, destabilizing, and traumatic. With so much uncertainty and no time to prepare, you may feel quite helpless.

No one can compare one person's loss or pain to another's. How can one say who experiences more pain: one whose loved one died suddenly, or one whose loved one was unwell and suffered for a prolonged period before succumbing to death? Whether you expected the death of a loved one, or it was completely unexpected, all losses are painful, with each having its own very personal and profound effect. No one can compare their pain or their loss to that of anyone else. Your grief is your own, just as someone else's is theirs. While no person's grief is worse than yours, many people may try to tell you otherwise. As you will learn, if you have not already, people can and will say the darndest things.

It has been said that if one is going to die, a four-to-six-month period of illness preceding death might be the most optimal. Less time than this may feel too sudden and make it more difficult to put affairs in order. A protracted period of being unwell or acutely sick may require a change in coping strategies at some point, as you cannot easily maintain the same degree of vigilance in caregiving that you were once able to provide when your loved one first became unwell. The longer they are unwell, the greater your stress may become; you may feel less equipped to deal with an acute illness that has now become chronic in duration.

If one is "fortunate enough" to have a window of time to put important issues in order and also achieve some form of closure, there is often a tremendous amount of physical and emotional "work" to be done. Much has been written on both sudden and anticipatory death, because how your loved one died and the circumstances around their death, along with your own life experiences, will surely have an impact on your ability to cope.

> *Our trip of a lifetime that we had anxiously been waiting for got canceled because my wife had a debilitating stroke. I realize I am grieving for the fact that we didn't get to go – and now probably never will. I am grieving for past losses as well as future losses, not to mention the ongoing and very painful daily losses. I am feeling totally overwhelmed. I am feeling so sad and angry now at what was taken away from me – from us.*

Given that you might be first picking up this book only after your loved one has died, we hope that this chapter will help serve as an attestation to all that you may have just been through. We hope that we can provide a framework for understanding what the past weeks or months may have been like, as well as how this may have influenced your thoughts and feelings. Hopefully, it will now serve to guide you as you navigate the next stages of the grieving process.

Initially upon hearing of the sudden death of your loved one, you may feel absolutely jolted – punched in the gut with no time to prepare for the blow. Blindsided, it grabs you when and where you least expect it, sucks out your air, and leaves you shaken and in a state of disbelief as you attempt to figure out what just happened. You are left speechless, stunned, in shock, and with little thought about what will happen next. Caught off guard and totally unprepared, feeling as if the ground has crumbled beneath you, as you attempt to gain equilibrium, you will likely be left with far more questions than answers.

> *In many instances, we were forced to make immediate decisions, and because we were in shock, we relied on the dear, close people who surrounded and supported us.*
>
> Smadar Shir, *Miriam's Song: The Story of Miriam Peretz,* p. 144

An unanticipated loss may often feel very senseless and difficult to comprehend, with your capacity to cope being challenged to the core. As you attempt to put one foot in front of the other and move forward, you are left wondering how your world could change so dramatically, literally from one minute to the next. With no warning or ability to predict what has happened, there may be a strong sense of disbelief and denial, a feeling that this is not and cannot be happening now, that this is not real. You may feel totally overwhelmed.

> *No, it can't be, I'm not hearing it, I'm walking out. If I don't hear it, then it can't be happening. It can't be true.*
>
> A teenager's response to the death of his mother

We are here to tell you that you *will* get up and you *will* go on. You may not care, know how, or even want to move forward, but it *does* happen. You are more resilient than you ever could have imagined. You may feel that with each step forward, you take two steps back, but even with your baby steps, like others who have walked a similar walk, you will continue on your journey because life around you goes on.

When something so traumatic as an unexpected death happens, your world gets turned upside down. However, through looking to make sense out of the situation so that you can understand it, you ultimately will put order and meaning back into your life. It does not happen overnight. In fact, there is no timetable, and it takes place only gradually. It will take much longer than you and others think – and perhaps longer, too, than it took someone who had time to prepare for the loss. Your shock and disbelief will be greater, and trying to understand just what happened while simultaneously coping with the loss places an additional burden on you, leaving you exhausted, anxious, and overwhelmed. It is so difficult to be patient. So difficult to have faith. So difficult when you are in such great pain. Repetition of the details of the events doesn't necessarily provide you with logic, clarity, or insight, but it is hard not to review them, hoping that this time, finally, when you ask yourself "why and how could this have happened?" something will have changed, and answers will finally be forthcoming.

> *Sometimes, I look back and ask myself, how did we get to this point?… an illusory thought crosses my mind – maybe it didn't really happen?... Imagination is deceptive and coming down to earth is painful. I put aside the question of why because there's no answer to it. Even faith and Judaism have no explanation for this, and so I have to move forward, look ahead. Until the next time my imagination overcomes me and tries to sell me an illusion.*
>
> Smadar Shir, *Miriam's Song: The Story of Miriam Peretz*, p. 247

With a sudden death, you may feel robbed by the inability to say goodbye to your loved one, tell them how much you loved them, put their affairs in order, apologize for things left unsaid, and more.

You may not *ever* be able to make sense of what happened, but may have to learn to live with the fact that there are not always answers and that life can be very unfair. With great difficulty, you may have to acknowledge and accept that it "just is," which may be an ultimate test of your faith and challenge your religious beliefs to the core. The deeper your faith, the easier this may be, but this, too, is not a given. It is never easy. Learning not to try and make sense of the situation, accepting that it just is, and allowing yourself to live with this uncertainty will help lessen your pain and enable you to slowly start to rebuild your world.

TIP: While at times you will be exhausted, at other times, you may find yourself overthinking things. Try to give yourself a break and just "be."

Footprints in the Sand
The story is told of a man walking along the sand. As he took stock of his life, he noticed that most of the time he was able to discern two sets of footprints. He understood this to represent the presence and support of God in his life. But then he noticed that there were times when there were only one set of footprints.

Could it be that at the lowest and saddest times of his life God had abandoned him?

He questioned God. How could You leave me when I needed you the most?

God responded: "I didn't leave you. During those times of hardship and suffering, I was carrying you."

Psalm 23 – "The Lord is my shepherd" expresses the feeling that even in difficult times not only is God with us, but also His presence is comforting. "Though I walk through the valley of the shadow of death, I will fear no evil, for You are with me. Your rod and Your staff, they comfort me." King David spoke about two different sticks – a *mishenet* (walking cane for support) and a *shevet* (rod for hitting) – "*shivtekha umishantekha hema yenaḥmuni* – they [both] comfort me." These two sticks are a metaphor for the two different ways God relates to people. The reason that they are both able to comfort is "*ki atta imadi* – because You [God] are with me." The awareness of one's constant connection to God, whether that connection happens to be pleasant or difficult at the moment, is the key to being able to cope with painful difficulties and challenges.

Sometimes, our deepest spiritual experiences come when we least expect them, when we are closest to despair. It is then that the masks we wear are stripped away. We are at our point of maximum vulnerability – and it is when we are most fully open to God that God is most fully open to us. "The Lord is close to the brokenhearted and saves those who are crushed in spirit" (Ps. 34:18).

We find God not only in holy or familiar places, but also in the midst of a journey, alone at night. "Though I walk through the valley of the shadow of death I will fear no evil for You are with me" (Ps. 23:4). The most profound of all spiritual experiences, the base of all others, is the knowledge that we are not alone. God is holding us by the hand, sheltering us, lifting us when we fall, forgiving us when we fail, healing the wounds in our soul through the power of His love.

Though we may fall, we fall into the arms of God. Though others may lose faith in us, and though we may even lose faith in ourselves, God never loses faith in us. And though we may feel utterly alone, we are not. God is there, beside us, within us, urging us to stand and move on, for there is a task to do that we have not yet done and that we were created to fulfill. Leonard Cohen wrote, "There is a crack in

> everything. That's how the light gets in." The broken heart lets in the light of God and becomes the gate of heaven.
>
> R. Jonathan Sacks, "How the Light Gets In," in *Studies in Spirituality*, pp. 31–32

> TIP: Giving yourself as much guilt-free time (without self-judgment) is a gift that you may now need to learn and then practice. Perhaps a close friend can help you with this.

THE INITIAL CRISIS PERIOD

During this initial crisis period, when first informed that your loved one is unwell or perhaps very ill, you may experience a momentary sense of shock and disbelief and wonder how it could be true. This is especially so when your loved one is young, appears healthy, if details have been kept private, or if the revelation of information has come as a surprise to you.

Their illness may herald the beginning of a decline that may be short lived (under six months) or be part of a chronic debilitating condition (greater than six months). Each presents its own set of issues and timeline. The situation may deteriorate slowly with time, or may change suddenly, resulting in only hours, days, or weeks to prepare for the inevitable. You may be very aware of what is going on, or for many reasons be in denial. Your loved one, too, may be aware or unaware of just how sick they are. They may suspect something is wrong or be caught off guard. The period before death itself may therefore be fraught with tremendous uncertainty, upheaval, and change in daily routine. It may be a roller coaster ride of emotions with lots of decision-making or, if you are well prepared and very lucky, a period of relative calm as each issue is attended to.

How you and your loved one experience this period immediately after they become ill or get diagnosed will indeed have an impact on the many challenges you'll ultimately face. Again, no two people or illnesses are alike. Your (you and your loved one's) responses and ability to cope during this initial crisis and after a death will be impacted by various factors, such as:

- your age and stage in life
- the nature of your relationship
- your proximity to each other
- your fears and level of comprehension
- your communication style
- your preparedness and readiness for death
- how well you and your loved one have worked through past hurts and issues around forgiveness
- your philosophy of life and personal worldviews
- your previous and current physical, emotional, and cognitive abilities
- the onset, timing, nature, and general understanding of the illness
- your preparedness in terms of diagnosis, course, and prognosis
- the goals of your loved one's care
- the support network of family, friends, and medical team
- your living and household arrangements
- your financial situations and work responsibilities
- your religious and spiritual beliefs
- your social issues and cultural expectations
- your ongoing stressors
- your history and management of previous losses

Each one of these factors has relevance throughout the illness, death, and post-death period, and together could be the subject of an entire book on their own. They will impact how you grieve for both your physical and symbolic losses, as you attempt to work through and come to terms with your personal situation.

While there may be many demands at such a difficult time, you may find yourself using this opportunity to redefine your relationship in new ways. How, for example, can you now spend your time together in a more meaningful way, make different life choices, and even resolve past issues?

In recent years, you may have had the opportunity to think about your own mortality and the eventual death of those you hold dear. Simply understanding the trajectory of the aging process, however, does not mean that you are focused on death; rather, like most people, you concentrate on life and only when you are faced with the inevitable, might you allow your mind to go there. Death is frightening for many: unknown events in uncharted territory, unfamiliarity with what lurks around the corner, a frightening lack of predictability, and overwhelming fear.

No matter how prepared you think you are, you are unlikely to be as fully prepared as you would wish. Therefore, a diagnosis may feel in itself traumatic, leaving you shocked, vulnerable, and at a loss for what to do next. It is not at all uncommon to feel overwhelmed and out of control. You may feel as if you're in the midst of a bad dream. Your body is thankfully designed to attempt to make your world feel right and so, after this initial shock and immobility, the fog does begin to lift. Slowly you will begin to plan for what comes next as you respond to both the physical aspects of the crisis and take steps to cope with the illness itself, its symptoms, treatments, and side effects, as well as other ongoing demands of life that face you as you absorb the reality of the situation.

While you may be very busy taking care of both the mundane and important aspects of your loved one's care, it is important as well to spend some time addressing your own thoughts and feelings as you go through this very difficult period. You should ask yourself what you can do to prepare for the inevitable. This may include exploration of what you may need to say or tell your loved one, and what you would find helpful to hear from them. You may, for instance, need to ask their forgiveness or have them ask this of you. You may ask yourself what stories you need to hear again, or what details you need to fill in that may be otherwise lost. You may want to ask how your loved one wants to be remembered, and what wishes you may be able to fulfill now or after they are gone. This can be an important learning opportunity: a time to share history, to fulfill wishes, to become even closer, and to reestablish what is really important as best as you are able. There might also be priorities that may or may not involve you, such as relationships in need of repair. Perhaps there are things that need to be told to your loved one or to other family members – parents, siblings, and children. Given this gift of time, how can you best use it and how would your loved one choose to use it?

Giving your loved one a sense of dignity when they are sick, enabling them to have a positive attitude, and instilling hope are all valuable gifts at this very difficult time, as are small things such as a particular food or even a picture that brings pleasure. Your role may be to interface with the medical personnel and notice how they treat your loved one. Are they attuned to their special needs – be it a sign over the bed to ask people to speak loudly in case of a hearing impairment, or particular dietary preferences? How do people talk to or with your loved one? Do they talk to them or to you if you are in the room, and is it respectful? Do they talk about your loved one as if they are not there? Do they talk loudly enough so that your loved one can hear, or do they whisper inappropriately or chat just outside the room? A sick patient may hear more than you think and may not want others to talk as if they are not there. Your loved one may be very sensitive to sound and there may be a role for music in their care. They may also be more responsive to other senses, such as touch or smell. You may want to explore with the staff if they have addressed this as well. As you can see, your role may be quite varied, but of infinite help.

Sitting in the hospital or at your loved one's bedside for hours at a time and for many days or weeks, even with breaks, is both difficult and exhausting. In addition, any routine that you once had may feel nonexistent, with responsibilities for other family members perhaps ignored. The list of things that you feel you "must" or "should" do may feel like it has grown exponentially, with nothing crossed off the simple but ever-growing "to do" list. Knowing, too, that the situation may change at any moment only increases everyone's level of stress. It is important to take time to eat and drink, get out and go for a walk, and take care of some of the many errands that come up. As hard as it may be for you, you will need to ask others to share your "burden" or help out in order to keep your own energy level up. What you initially believe will be a short-term situation can easily become longer and more difficult than you may have anticipated. As a result, while it is easy to neglect yourself, it is very important not to do so. Your needs, too, will change over time, so be prepared to reevaluate the situation and ask for help when necessary. By enlisting others, who themselves may feel quite powerless and are just waiting to be asked to help out, you are making them feel better. Remember, too, that what is comfortable for one person may be stressful for someone else.

It will be up to you to help determine how information is relayed about your loved one and the current situation, so that when you finally leave them at night and are yourself ready to collapse, you do not have to then spend hours on the phone.

TIP: It is often best to "designate" one family member to liaise with the medical community and another person to liaise with friends and family. In this way, calls and any updated information can go through them, and you can protect yourself from the constant bombardment of people who mean well, but who may inadvertently exhaust you. This "spokesperson" can take responsibility for relaying information about your loved one's health, prayer requests, food needs, and help with errands. This frees you up to "just" care for your loved one.

You may split visits with other family members, so that you each visit at separate times and report back to others while maximizing time with your loved one. This will allow you time for other things such as work and family obligations. You will have to be selective in screening visitors and visits. From one day to the next, you may not be able to anticipate whether your loved one is having a difficult day; and even when you do give permission, people may arrive unwell or overstay their time, exhausting both you and your loved one. As we have intimated previously, it is not at all selfish to take care of yourself at this very difficult time, but rather a gift that you can give to everyone involved. You have to do what is right for you, regardless of what others say. As you will discover, people will have their own opinion and ideas with respect to how to best help – much of which you do not need to hear or will not be at all helpful.

TIP: No one ever said on their deathbed that they wished that they had spent more time at the office. If you are prioritizing time spent with your loved one, you don't have to apologize for this precious time spent together.

DEALING WITH TERMINAL ILLNESS

Coming to terms with terminal illness and eventually the actual death is challenging on many difficult levels for both you and your loved one, emotionally, physically, and even on a spiritual level.

It is a process that takes time. Quality end-of-life care is essential for your loved one, and critical for your family. While advance knowledge of an impending death can help diminish the shock, no death is ever easy. In general, when you think about dying, you may fear being in horrible pain, being alone, or perhaps you worry that you will not be heard or understood. In reality, none of these need to be the story of your loved one. When you are given the opportunity to face death head on, you give yourselves and your loved ones some ability to plan for your future – even if that future may be death.

While you may not be able to change the outcome, you often can help your loved one prepare to move on in a way that enables everyone to experience the death in a positive way. This, in part, evolves when your loved one and you are able to see that you both can have your needs met. These needs, for example, might range from ensuring appropriate and adequate pain management to discussions about important decision-making from the onset of the illness, through treatment at each stage of the illness and ultimately through the end-of-life choices and the dying process itself. Our Jewish values can truly guide us through this uncharted territory.

We all have a lifetime to prepare for death. How that lifetime may be defined, however, often escapes us. One often describes a good life as both a long life lived, and one containing good events. A life cut short by illness or tragedy can be devastating, but how one defines a good life differs from individual to individual. One person may think that living to the age of eighty-five is enough, or more than enough. Another may feel that this is the prime of their life. So, whether your loved one was taken from you after mere hours, or after many years, one's interpretation of that loss is very personal, and one cannot compare one person's pain to another.

Even if you anticipate that death is imminent and feel that you are emotionally prepared for the loss, you won't know how you are actually going to feel until you are in that moment. How much time you will have with your loved one, how these waning hours will be, or even when the actual moment of death will occur are in Hashem's hands alone.

While you may know, for instance, that your loved one has been sick for a long time, and on some level, you know they are dying, when death actually occurs, whether unexpectedly, or if seemingly unrelated to their illness, you may react as if the death was sudden, and be in a state of shock. It is important to remember that estimates from the medical team are at times just that. Might there be days, weeks, or months? We are only able to guess, and one never knows what issues may come up at any time.

> *When my mom was first diagnosed, the doctor stated rather emphatically that she had forty-eight hours to live. His words created quite a frenzy. She did not die after two days. She died eight weeks later, having had time to settle her affairs and gain some peace of mind. Ultimately, only Hashem is in charge. Life has been described as a huge tapestry. On one side we see the whole picture, but on the other side, there are many knots – we don't know where and how they are tied together. Things are not always as they seem. Hashem has a hand in it all, and only He sees the whole picture.*

Sometimes, there is a very fine line between emergent and urgent. We just don't know what someone's final days will look like or even how many there might be. When your loved one is living far away, and with work and family commitments, you actually may not be able, or want, to travel twice – to come both when your loved one is sick and then again for the funeral and/or shiva. The decision to come, and when, may be a difficult one, and is not always in your hands. It may additionally be influenced by the medical condition of your loved one, your relationship with them as well as your siblings and other family members, the costs involved, and a myriad of other relevant factors. You may feel that you have said your goodbyes and want to remember your loved one as you last saw them and choose not to be there for the death or funeral; or you may want to be there in the final stages and when your loved one dies. It may also feel that your loved one is holding on and waiting for you to arrive before they allow themselves to die. What may become the final visit is very much a personal decision and even if given the option, not necessarily an easy or rational one to have to make at such an emotional time.

> *When my father was in the hospital in Israel, I asked the doctor whether my sister in the States should come. His response was, "It would be good for her to come." During shiva for my father, I told the doctor I would always be grateful to him for his suggestion. My sister was able to spend two weeks with my father before he died. Actually, many times it is important for the family to take initiative and ask the doctors these difficult questions.*

END-OF-LIFE DECISION MAKING

Prearranged burial

Prearranged burial or advance funeral planning has become more commonplace in recent years. People have chosen to purchase a burial site in anticipation that someday, hopefully many years from the time of purchase, they will leave the surviving family with less to do at the time of death – as well as with greater peace of mind. Advance purchase of a burial plot can also enable the deceased to have a role in the process, thereby taking both the decision-making and financial burden off the family. This will help minimize the stress at a very emotional time. Preplanning also consists of sitting down with someone at a predesignated funeral home and delineating the wishes with respect to burial, possibly picking out in advance a casket and/or burial location, and attending to other personal requests.

It is an age-old desire of Jewish people, wherever they reside, to be buried in the Land of Israel because of its sanctity. If a person living abroad chooses to be buried in Israel, this is a conversation that ideally will take place when end-of-life decisions are being discussed.

When Abraham purchased Maarat HaMakhpela, it was to provide a burial place not only for his beloved wife Sarah, but also for himself and his family members. "And Abraham expired, and died in a good old age, aged and satisfied, and was gathered unto his people. And Isaac and Ishmael his sons buried him at the cave of Makhpela, in the field of Ephron, son of Tzoar the Hittite, which is before Mamre" (Gen. 25:8–9).

The Sages of the Midrash advise us to purchase a burial plot while we are still alive and well. It is commonly said that doing so will actually bless one with a long life. Perhaps it brings this blessing (a *segula* for longevity), because by doing so one contemplates their own mortality and uses their time on this earth in a more meaningful way.

My father was on the ḥevra kaddisha of our small Jewish community. It was always very important to him that perpetual care was set up to look after the cemetery and all of the graves when the community would no longer be self-supporting financially, or when there were no longer any members. His tremendous foresight has enabled the cemetery to be maintained at all times. As a child, I grew up knowing that he was the one who arranged this, but had no realization of the importance. Now as an adult, I see how so many families have benefitted from his advanced planning both then and now. I have also come to recognize that while I may not want to face my ultimate demise, I do want to plan for it so that my children can rest assured that my wishes were taken care of, and they don't have to worry.

TIP: If you have a pre-arranged burial plot and for some reason have moved and will no longer require it, consider donating the burial plot to a synagogue or funeral home who, at your request, can use it to provide burial for someone in need.

Planning for the worst, hoping for the best

Death is a natural course of life. Nonetheless, adopting a philosophy of planning for the worst while always hoping for the best is one we advocate as a way to be focused on what is important while still living in the here and now. Making the time, if it is at all possible, to discuss with your loved one their wishes, goals, values, and concerns both currently and for the future is critical before situations deteriorate further and you may lose out on a valuable opportunity. This may be a time when one considers the completion of advance-care directives or a healthcare proxy, as well as a discussion of end-of-life care options. Now may be the time to begin a discussion about end-of-life wishes. This may involve a conversation between your loved one, the family, healthcare providers, your lawyer, a rabbi, and anyone else deemed relevant.

Medical concerns

With advances in medical care, people in general are living longer. Nonetheless, aging is often accompanied by illness, and many people are living with chronic yet serious issues. Many are unprepared for the waning stages of life, and few choose to have discussions with their families and physicians about their prognosis, what to expect, and the goals of care. However, a shared decision-making process which includes a discussion of end-of-life options for care can be meaningful for both you and your loved one.

An example of this might be the creation of a plan for hospitalization or home hospice at some stage in the future, and discussion of this with all of the relevant people. While some issues may seem far off and a discussion of them may feel as though the focus is on the inevitable, planning will often bring a sense of calm to you and others.

Emotional care

This is a time that, due to uncertainty, can be fraught with tremendous apprehension. Making decisions, having conversations that may involve forgiveness, creating an action plan for going forward, and letting family and friends know of any final wishes may all help decrease anxiety. These will also help you and your loved one feel more in control at a time when life feels so very tenuous.

Given the nature of the situation, it is important to have these difficult end-of-life conversations frequently, as the feelings and needs of you and your loved one will change over time. Determining your loved one's preferences also enables them to feel heard through their own personal requests, and affords them the dignity they deserve.

While it may be difficult to have any discussion that focuses on the time near the end of your loved one's life and beyond, these discussions will hopefully give them and you closure, calm, and peace of mind. Your loved one may need reassurance that regardless of what happens, you will be okay. Now is the time to let your loved one know how much they mean to you, and share whatever it is that you feel is important to you. What, too, would your loved one like from you? What do they worry about? What are their personal wishes, and how can you empower them to achieve them? It is important to speak from your heart and resolve any unfinished business. Now may be the time to express your love and appreciation, and ask for their forgiveness as well as offering yours. This may also be a time in which you can get a better sense of how they feel they are doing, as you give them the opportunity to seek out reassurance, voice their fears and concerns, or simply share their thoughts about having their needs met, managing their pain, and being alone as they continue to decline. This may lead to a conversation about what they and you would think of as a "good death."

It is important for both your loved one and you to try and resolve as many unanswered questions as possible in order to reduce and to potentially alleviate any physical, psychological, social, and spiritual stress.

> TIP: With regard to end-of-life decision making, there are many questions that should be asked. "Who needs to be called?" "What family members need to be involved?" "Who needs to be told what?" and "What financial, medical, and personal issues need to be attended to?" Addressing these concerns will help reduce stress and enable as much control as possible.

Legal and financial issues

This also is the time to make sure that your loved one has an up-to-date and legal will. This helps to ensure that their assets are properly distributed in the manner in which they choose.

> Maimonides wrote that a person who puts their affairs in order before their death and leaves a written request (a will) gives themself peace of mind and lengthens their days.

If there are joint bank accounts, it is important to make sure that relevant forms are signed so that someone else will be able to access the account if need be (to pay a caregiver, for instance). In Israel, an "*Arikhut Yamim*" document ensures that in the event of the death of your spouse, your account will not be frozen, denying you access to the accounts until the estate is probated. Probating the will could take time, leaving you with an additional emotional and financial burden.

Other legal issues that may clearly depend on your loved one's place of residence are the creation of an advanced healthcare directive – a living will or an Enduring Power of Attorney (EPOA) (in Hebrew this is referred to as *Yipui Koaḥ Mitmashekh*). This is a personal end-of-life directive describing the actions that should be taken by a proxy, an appointed person (*yipui koaḥ*) should your loved one no longer be able to make everyday medical (but not end-of-life), financial, personal, or legal decisions for themselves due to physical illness or cognitive decline. In Israel, a separate document regarding end-of-life decisions, medical wishes, and management can be downloaded from the Ministry of Health.[1] These documents should be reviewed with a lawyer and filed with the Ministry of Health. In the United States, you can contact the EMES program which promotes Halakhic Living Wills and end-of-life preparedness through the National Association of Chevra Kadisha (NASCK). You will need to find out what the requirements are and what the law says with respect to similar documents in your own country or state.

TIP: Set up a file with important phone numbers and contact information of your loved one's lawyer, accountant, and financial advisor if relevant, bank account details and a recent statement, insurance and health information, credit-card particulars, a copy of the will, and anything else you feel is important. This file will be invaluable for those who ultimately will need to sort out any paperwork left undone by your loved one's departure. Remember, getting online access to information may not always be possible.

1. www.health.gov.il/English/Services/Citizen_Services/Pages/Dying Patient Request.aspx.i (to learn more about this in Israel please go to ad120.tzohar.org.il/en/about/).

Spiritual legacy

If not previously conveyed during their lifetime, now is a perfect opportunity for creating an ethical will, a spiritual legacy of instructions, values, and wishes your loved one would like to pass on to the next generation. This also enables your loved one to address their final wishes to those they care deeply about. Some people have chosen this time to impart words of wisdom and stories for the future generations by leaving a letter or a recorded voice message behind for each child or grandchild to read or listen to at some future date.

Assessing priorities

During this period both around and following diagnosis, your goal will become one of assessing your priorities – and of course, those of your loved one. They may very well not be the same. You, and many around you, need to determine what actually *must* be done (and not just what you think may need to be done) in an attempt both to introduce order into the chaos, and to bring a sense of peace and as much predictability as possible into the environment of your loved one.

This period may enable you to settle into a routine, albeit of undetermined time. This in itself may be stressful, but it is of major importance to attempt to make the most of this time together, while accomplishing whatever needs to be done both medically and otherwise.

> *I was told that my mother had forty-eight hours to live, my father-in-law in another country had just had a failed cardiac procedure, and our son was diagnosed with pneumonia. I could not eat, and I felt depressed. Thankfully, it didn't last. Finally I realized that while I couldn't change any of this, I could make the last few days as meaningful as possible for my mom, my son would improve, and my husband could travel briefly to his*

> *father. The feelings of helplessness and hopelessness started to shift, and rather than feel "done to," with things happening to me that I could not control, I felt grateful and believed that I was able to control some of the little things in these small acts. That helped me give strength and support to these three people who were so important to me.*

TAKING CARE OF YOURSELF

While you address both the medical and emotional concerns of your loved one, it is also essential not to neglect your own needs. These may be very different from those of your loved one, and will change over time, depending on so many variables previously cited above.

Dealing with your own issues while trying to be available for others is not easy, especially when the illness is protracted. It is important to be aware of just how your loved one's situation might affect you. An illness, for example, might be chronic in nature, but the end may come suddenly, and with little or no warning.

At times you may find it almost impossible to balance your own needs with those of your loved one. It can be very difficult when you feel that you cannot be there for them physically and emotionally in the way that you, or they, would like. Added to this is the guilt that you may have "missed" the signs of illness, were not attentive enough, or should have addressed your loved one's concerns sooner, better, differently, and more lovingly. It is natural to have regrets, but at times an illness may require a superhuman response, and you will have other demands and prior commitments that you cannot neglect. With time, as well, as the illness goes on, you will sadly recognize that your loved one is less available to you physically and emotionally. As your expectations begin to shift, it is a normal part of anticipatory grieving to be both present in this moment but also begin to prepare for a future without them. This in itself is exhausting. Feeling thrown off-balance and trying to swim in a sea of disequilibrium is a hallmark of this initial period of illness. It is so easy to lose sight of all that you do and have done for your loved one. Finding a place for forgiveness is crucial at this time.

TIP: Try whenever possible to remind yourself of all the positive contributions that have made your loved one's life so much easier, better, happier, and more meaningful. Focus on all that you do and did do, rather than looking back with guilt on what you didn't, or couldn't, do.

With time of the essence – and for many other reasons – your priorities may change very quickly and unexpectedly. While perhaps it is difficult to make changes and go with whatever takes precedence at the moment, this is a time that will require great flexibility on everyone's part. It is okay to just "be" and spend time with your loved one, but you may also need to take a brief time out from caregiving to look after your own needs and those of your family.

> *I was truly running on empty. I was looking after our three children at home, and trying to see my mom in hospital every morning before going to work. I realized that she would be in hospital for a while, and parking, which was prohibitively expensive, would be discounted if I got a special pass. I arrived at the office to get the pass, and the clerk told me she only gives out passes at eleven a.m. and I would need to come back. But we were both there now, and she was available, I tried to argue. She continued to say "no" and demanded that I return later, which made no sense, and I got angry. I started crying while raising my voice. I told her how senseless it was, and she called security. I told her my mother was dying and I had no time. She ultimately gave*

> *it to me "just this once." Reflecting back years later, I realized that my behavior was very uncharacteristic of me. I was under tremendous stress, and they were being completely inflexible.*

The initial crisis period of illness and arrival at a diagnosis typically leads to treatment planning. This phase may vary from minimal to intense medical intervention, with varying degrees of success. The goal is to make the most of this time – whether it is days, weeks, or months. In addressing your loved one's needs, as well as your own and those of other family members, hopefully this will be achieved.

> TIP: When others offer their assistance, just say yes. It will benefit you most if you can give them specific tasks. Delegate non-essential tasks, such as laundry, dinner, carpooling, preparing for Shabbat, making phone calls, and completion of paperwork so that you can attend to other things. If someone offers and it is appropriate for them to visit your loved one, this too may give you a brief respite.

DIFFICULT CONVERSATIONS: END-OF-LIFE DISCUSSIONS

End-of-life discussions are never easy. You will have to see what you are physically and mentally able to cope with, how much time you can give, and what the other demands are in your life. If indeed you are unable or don't feel that you are the right person to have these discussions, you can help find a suitable person to be there for your loved one. You may want to begin a conversation separately or together with various professionals – the medical team, a clinician skilled in death education, a rabbi, a lawyer, or anyone else who can be of assistance during this difficult transition.

You can start by trying to get a sense as to what your loved one understands about their illness as well as their prognosis. Are they able to weigh the risks and the benefits, and help make medical decisions? This will help you get a better sense as to whether they are aware that they are dying, and what is important for them that you know for the future. What are the values that are guiding principles in their life, and what do they want their family and medical team to know to better enable them to be taken care of as they would wish? Your loved one, for example, may want to know everything about their health and be an active participant in decision making. Others want to be on a "need-to-know" basis, and prefer their relatives look after them and take responsibility – or stay out of these issues entirely. The more one has thought of these advanced-care directives, the easier it will be to make difficult decisions, take ownership for them, and help ensure that they are implemented.

One may want to have the discussion, for example, about life-prolonging treatment and the short- and long-term impacts on quality-of-life issues. Perhaps you will talk through what constitutes a "good death," and who you would like to have present in the waning days and hours. As you can see, while these are not easy discussions to have, they are very important; it is critical to find and make the time to have them, as they can have a huge impact on your loved one's understanding of what is going on and their feeling calm and heard.

Their quality of life will have a direct impact on yours as well. We cannot judge the wishes and desires of our loved ones, but rather need to be present for them and hear them with as much care and understanding as we can. This is a process that can take place over time, or simply evolve. Hopefully it will not be a one-time conversation if there is time, it is started early enough, and your loved one is ready to go deeper into the discussion as the medical situation may warrant. So many people want to have these conversations, but sadly many do not, and therefore many do not know what their loved ones want for their end-of-life care.

We recommend reading a truly excellent document entitled, "A Conversation That Can Change Your Whole Life" put out by Life's Door.[2] It is part of "The Conversation Project" founded by Ellen Goodman. We encourage you to use this as your basis for empowering your loved one in decision making.

End-of-Life Lessons from Jacob and King David

Parashat Vayeḥi (Gen. 47) opens with, "When the time drew near for Israel (Jacob) to die, he called for his son Joseph." The *haftara* for the *parasha* (I Kings 2:1) begins with the verse, "David's days drew near to die." Both figures instruct their children before their death. Final words are very important, and their messages are significant to those left behind. Regarding Jacob, the Torah relates, "And it came to pass after these things that Joseph was told: 'Behold, your father is sick.'" This is the first time in the Torah that someone is described as ill. The Midrash teaches us that it was actually Jacob who prayed to God for sickness to descend upon a person, and that they not suddenly die – so that they would have the time and ability to put their affairs in order before departing for the next world. Jacob came and asked for compassion from God. He said, "Master of the World, when one falls ill, one becomes aware of oneself. One charges one's household (about the future), one's iniquities are cleansed, and one engages in *teshuva*." The Blessed One responded, "You have asked well. By your life, I will begin with you first." We then read a detailed scene of Jacob's deathbed and individual blessings and instructions given to each of his sons. In this light, sickness can be seen in Jewish life as the almost necessary reminder of one's mortality and of the obligation to use one's time and gifts wisely while we are alive.

2. Conversation Project, Conversation Project Kit, www.lifesdoor.org.

King David leaves Solomon to deal with his "unfinished business," giving Solomon instructions on how to deal with what David thought would be the greatest threats to his throne, and also rewarding those who had been steadfast in their loyalty to the royal family. But perhaps the most important message that David gives his son is to follow the path of Torah and mitzvot: "Be strong, and show yourself a man, and keep the charge of Hashem, your God...." We don't get to choose how we leave this world, and we hope to be spared suffering, but Jacob and David teach an important lesson about taking stock of our lives and the conversations we need to have with our children and those close to us about the values we hold dear and the legacy we wish to leave behind.

ANTICIPATORY AND AMBIGUOUS LOSS

The process of beginning to grieve for your loved one may start years to months before their physical loss. As a result, you may neither recognize the early stages of grieving as your loved one deteriorates, nor know how you would even define the onset of your loss. If your loved one had a chronic illness, or was physically present but psychologically absent due to dementia, brain injury, cognitive impairment, mental illness, or other disorders where one turns inward, a feeling of anticipatory loss may have clouded your relationship long before their actual death. You may have felt your loved one beginning to disengage or turn away from you, showing signs of "leaving" and focusing inward, to the exclusion of you and your relationship. This may have felt extremely painful without you being able to put into words just what has happened.

When the actual death does occur, you may find yourself further along in your grieving than you could have imagined, as in some small way you have had the opportunity to begin to start preparing for the separation. Don't be surprised if initially you briefly feel a sense of relief that the stress over your loved one's health as well as your concern for their pain and suffering is over. It may also be that the stark reality of the loss itself, or the cumulative losses you have experienced over time, was not apparent until much later – and most likely, not until after the actual death itself.

At any time during your loved one's illness, and certainly as the time towards the end draws nearer, it is not at all uncommon for you to grieve in anticipation of their impending loss. We don't grieve just for the physical loss itself, but rather for the many things we have enjoyed within the relationship with our loved one in the past, and which we will be denied sharing in the future. There are also losses around financial security, the idealized person you once knew, the loss of social connectedness, the loss of an imagined shared future, a loss of freedom, and so much more. In situations where your loved one has been severely cognitively incapacitated for a long period of time (and possibly no longer even recognizes you), you may begin to grieve for the loss of this person, and who they once were, long before the actual death. This loss, which affords no closure, is known as ambiguous loss – given your loved one may be physically present, but mentally or emotionally unavailable.[3]

> *I mourned the loss of my mother twice. My mother was diagnosed with Alzheimer's and slowly started to slip away. At first, she didn't remember events, but then it got worse. Towards the end, she didn't recognize me or my family. I felt that I was grieving the loss of my mother even though she was still alive. She was no longer the funny, vibrant, active person who had come to all my school plays and concerts. She was no longer the wise and experienced mother whom I asked for advice. She was no*

3. A more in-depth discussion of ambiguous loss can be found in the writings of Pauline Boss, 1977, 2000.

> *longer the attentive grandmother my children loved. When I sat shiva for my mother, it was a different grief. Admittedly there was some relief, as her care was taking an increasingly greater toll on our family. While I felt I had already lost my mother as such years ago, now I had to acknowledge the finality of it all when I would no longer have her physical presence.*

Talking with others who have been through similar situations and have some understanding of what you are going through can be helpful in giving you strategies for coping.

PRAYER INSTILLS HOPE

Although we have spoken about some very difficult areas that you may wish never to address in your lifetime, it is important to recognize that Judaism encourages hope. This is a gift you can offer to your loved one. There is positivity in just about any situation; others may need your help to focus on this, especially when all else seems bleak. Situations can change and even improve, even in small ways, and it is always important to keep this in mind. Prayer can be a powerful conduit for instilling hope and helping you when all else seems so difficult.

THE ROLE OF PRAYER

Each person approaches prayer in their own individual way. For some, the structured prayers, the daily routine, and the familiar words of the *siddur* bring comfort; for others, prayer is more spontaneous, and involves choosing one's own words. Both are equally acceptable. When your loved one is in a difficult situation, your prayer is often more heartfelt and sincere.

When your loved one is unwell, you may find the recitation of *tehillim* (psalms) to be therapeutic, having both a calming and stress-relieving effect. Psalms contains verses that can help you articulate your feelings. In addition, praying and saying psalms can make you feel proactive, and bring comfort at a time when you are feeling helpless. Most editions of Psalms include prayers to be said for an ill person. When people know that others are "praying for them," it gives them hope and *can* make a tangible difference in people's lives. You may feel strange asking people to pray for you or for someone close to you, but keep in mind that it gives others support when they hear "You are in my *tefillot* (prayers)."

Prayer may not change the outcome, but it can change you and the way you view a given situation. Prayer may help you find a way to be more useful, more understanding, and even more accepting, therefore benefitting both you and the sick person.

> *Less than prayer changes the world, it changes us.*
>
> R. Jonathan Sacks, "When the 'I' Is Silent," in *Covenant and Conversation: Genesis*, p. 192

If someone asks you to pray for them or their loved one, and you are uncomfortable or unable to take this upon yourself, there are many other ways in which you could respond. Instead of "you are in my prayers," you might say "you are in my thoughts." This conveys your desire to be there for them and offer emotional support in other ways that they would find beneficial.

> *A few years ago, we hired an amazing man to help us do the carpentry work for our new apartment. He was secular, from the north, and our conversations were for the most part work related. Due to a family illness, he had to postpone work for a few weeks. I wrote to him and asked for the Hebrew name of the person involved so that I could include her in my prayers. He was so very grateful and asked on two separate occasions over the next six months after he had finished working with us if I*

could pray for two other people. I felt honored that he entrusted me to add the names of his loved ones to my tefillot.

The Hebrew text of the prayer for a sick person mentions both physical and spiritual healing. We ask that Hashem send a "complete" healing – recognizing the connection between body and soul. "*Shelaḥ lahem refua shelema min hashamayim, refuat hanefesh u'refuat haguf* – May He hasten to send from heaven a complete recovery, a healing of spirit and a healing of body." When praying for an individual who is unwell, it is customary to use their Hebrew name, along with their mother's name. If only the mother's non-Hebrew name is known, it can be used – or the father's name, if the mother's name is unknown.

The source for mentioning the name of the individual's mother is King David's entreaty (Ps. 116:16): "*Ana Hashem ki ani avdekha ani avdekha ben amatekha* – Please, O Lord, for I am Your servant; I am Your servant the son of Your maidservant," wherein he specifies his mother.

In Jeremiah 31:15, we have the image of Rachel weeping for her children, and this in itself elicits God's mercy. Perhaps we, too, are seeking God's mercy by evoking the image of a maternal figure.

According to the Talmud (Bava Kama 92a), when a person prays for another person, that prayer is considered to be on a higher level. This is because the individual is putting their own interests aside and instead concentrating on the needs of another. Many of our *tefillot* are worded in the plural, which suggests that we always have others in mind when we pray. When a *refua shelema* – a complete recovery – is no longer possible, or when hope for recovery is no longer probable, you can pray that your loved one not suffer. Sometimes, prayer is something we do when we feel there is nothing more that can be done on the physical plane.

When we are low or feeling desperate, and have no other place to turn, we often turn to God. We pray that God be compassionate, kind, caring, and provide an end to any suffering. And, while we don't count on them, Hashem can make miracles happen.

The Talmud (Berakhot 32b) records various statements of the sage Rabbi Elazar with regard to the potency of prayer. Rabbi Elazar tells us that prayer is always effective to a certain degree. To support his position, he points to the biblical episode in which Moses beseeched the Almighty to allow him to enter the Promised Land. This request was denied, yet due to his heartfelt prayer, Moses was granted the opportunity to see the land from afar.

There Are No Wasted Prayers

After Nachshon Wachsman, a corporal in the Israeli army, was kidnapped by Arab terrorists in October 1994, his captors demanded the release of hundreds of their compatriots by nine a.m. the following Friday morning. Nachshon's family asked the Israeli public to pray and say psalms for Nachshon. Women were also asked to light Shabbat candles on Friday night, making sure to do so at the proper time. It was hoped that in the merit of the prayers and performance of these mitzvot, Nachshon would be saved. Unfortunately, Nachshon was murdered during the rescue attempt. During the shiva, in response to a reporter's question about how he felt about all the prayers that people said for Nachshon that were apparently ignored, Nachshon's father famously said that sometimes Hashem says "no." We cannot understand Hashem's ways. Often, we daven for things and our requests are denied. While it seems like we are not getting what we want, it may very well be that Hashem, our Parent, has another plan. In fact, Nachshon Wachsman's father followed up his famous statement by saying that from what he heard about the rescue attempt, many more Jewish soldiers could have been killed. Perhaps the tefillot were not going to save Nachshon but instead saved someone else's son. There is no such thing as a wasted prayer.

CAN I PRAY WHEN I AM ANGRY WITH GOD?

As you and your loved one face difficult times ahead, you will each determine the role and importance of faith and prayer in your life. Perhaps there are people to whom you would like to reach out or speak to who can address your concerns.

> Anger is a legitimate emotion. The Talmud (Berakhot 31b–32a) tells us that a number of great individuals spoke quite harshly to God, either out of their personal pain, or for the sake of the Jewish people. It refers to this as "flinging one's sharp words upward towards God." Chana, Eliyahu, and Moses all directed their great pain and frustration towards God.

People must bring to prayer the fullness of their experience – including doubt, disappointment, or even anger – in order for their prayers to be meaningful. Some people who read my first book, Night, were convinced that I broke with the faith and broke with God. Not at all. I never divorced God. It is because I believed in God that I was angry at God, and still am.

Nobel laureate and Holocaust survivor Elie Wiesel,
in a lecture entitled "Why Pray?" 2005

Sharing our pain with God, particularly when we don't fully understand it, can form a bond of trust, and bring Him into our lives much more deeply than we ever could by intellectual

means alone. We need to direct questions to God, not against God. We can try to see that although challenges in life are painful and difficult, they are given to us by God, and we have the opportunity to learn and grow from them.

Adapted from R. Yitzchok Kirzner,
Making Sense of Suffering

RELAYING BAD NEWS TO YOUR LOVED ONE

You can say just about anything to anyone, but how you choose to say it will determine how it is heard. You need to be sensitive when relaying bad news, as a person's physical and emotional well-being go hand in hand. One can have an impact on the other. When relaying bad news, it is very important to be cognizant of this and find the right time and way to have such a conversation. Generally, you will want to express yourself in a factual and straightforward manner. Too many words can be very confusing. This is especially true when speaking with children. There is a fine line between being gentle and open and being overly dramatic or dismissive. It might help to ask yourself in advance how you would like to be told this information, and would the person to whom you are speaking value the same approach? There may be times when it is best not to share bad news with your loved one, because it may cause more harm and suffering. Sometimes, it may be better to have the physician or rabbi, and not a family member, speak with the patient. This is especially true when your loved one may have questions that you won't be able to answer or if it is too difficult for the family to discuss.

AS ILLNESS PROGRESSES

At some point, and this can happen quickly or with little warning, your loved one will start to deteriorate, and you will be called upon to reevaluate the current treatment plan. While much depends on external factors, one decision that you may both have to consider at this end-of-life stage is whether your loved one should remain at home or be hospitalized.

If your loved one remains at home, you may look after their every need, or have home palliative care assistance with various options for additional care. Your loved one may be in a residential or assisted-living facility, where they have the option to receive increasing degrees of medical attention as needed. If your loved one is in the hospital, there may be several options: a regular ward with visiting hours; an Intensive Care Unit (ICU), where perhaps you can visit very briefly a few times a day; or a palliative care or hospice unit, typically with open visitation.

PALLIATIVE CARE

Palliative care in the hospital, hospice, or at home is designed to provide comprehensive care for your loved one's physical, emotional, and spiritual needs. While attempting to reduce pain and suffering, it sees death as a natural process. Its goal is to provide empathetic, informed decision making and quality end-of-life care, neither hastening nor postponing death. It provides appropriate pain management as well as other symptom relief within a supportive family-centered care approach.

Home palliative care or home hospice offers tremendous support for the caregiver as well as for your loved one in the comfort of their familiar surroundings. Depending on where your loved one will spend their dying days, and your ability as the caregiver to be present and/or cope, your role may change to become more or less involved in the decision-making process and/or in their direct care.

Rabbi Dr. Shlomo Brody of Ematai (2023) suggests that Judaism very much believes in the value of life. That being said, it is sometimes seen as appropriate to forgo intervention that will only prolong a life of suffering. Halakha recognizes that sometimes the patient or the family can make these decisions.

If not discussed previously, now is the time to explore, if possible, your loved one's feelings about resuscitation and other life-prolonging interventions. These are issues that should be addressed with the medical, palliative care, or home hospice team, and possibly your rabbi. In theory, one would hope to have this discussion and paperwork in place and your loved one's wishes known long before they are in a critical state. This information, such as a DNR (do not resuscitate) or DNI (do not intubate) order, should be made available and clearly displayed in a medical chart if hospitalized, possibly directly above their bed, or as part of a notarized document if your loved one is at home. This enables medical first-responders to take the proper action (such as performing or refraining from providing CPR or assisted ventilation) should the situation warrant it. It is less complicated to withhold or not initiate life-prolonging treatment, (such as CPR, dialysis, chemotherapy, or intermittent feeding) than it is, for example, to withdraw or stop treatment (such as disconnecting from a respirator or stopping tube feedings once they have been started).[4]

> *There were many times when it was challenging to watch our little girl at home. We knew she had a terminal illness, yet we wondered every time she got sick if she would get better, or if this time would mark the beginning of the end. How would we know? We did not want her to suffer, and after talking with many professionals who could tell us what the end could be like for her, we made the decision for her not to receive CPR or be intubated and potentially prolong her suffering. However, if we saw her struggling, how could we not call the Emergency Medical Service; and if we*

---

4. For more information on this topic, please see ad120.tzohar.org.il.

did call them, would they not want to do something? Why else would they come? It can be very difficult to watch your loved one suffer and not intervene. Perhaps our greatest gift, when she was dying, was in being able to cradle her in our arms, let her know how deeply we loved her, and tell her that we were there with her.

Looking after your loved one, regardless of where they are, may signify a time of letting go and change. They may withdraw from the world around them, turn inward, and be either more calm or more fearful; they may be more or less interested in sharing their thoughts as they prepare to separate. They may also become more aggressive, and say some very painful things to those whom they always cared deeply about. They may seem bothered by the noises of young children, appear less responsive to conversation, not want to be touched, complain, yell out, curse, or act out of character. They may be extremely irritable, agitated, restless, paranoid, delusional and even slip in and out of consciousness. You may see profound mood swings and times when you feel your loved one's personality has changed. This may leave you feeling helpless and questioning who they are, and who they have become. Added to your pain, you may feel that, at times, your loved one prefers a stranger or other family members to you.

This is at a time, too, when the various body systems may be shutting down, organs are beginning to fail, and fluid buildup in tissues may increase and become extremely uncomfortable, further increasing agitation. Depending on the type of illness, medication, closeness to death and other factors, your loved one may have a diminished need to eat or drink, and may start to excrete less urine. They may experience swelling, their skin may feel cold or clammy to the touch, and their breathing may begin to change – becoming more shallow, irregular, and labored. While your loved one may at times be less responsive and not speak, it is still possible that they can hear – so feel free to talk to your loved one as if they do hear you.

> *When Mom was dying, she had no energy to get out of bed, and then her appetite began to wane until she turned down my dad's offers of her favorite pudding. He felt rejected in that he could not nourish or nurture her, and that she wouldn't eat "for him." The more he tried, the angrier and more despondent she seemed. These were not easy times in a marriage of forty-three years. She was letting go, she was leaving regardless of what he tried to do. He felt so helpless.*

In spite of some of these difficulties, which are not present for everyone, the final days of your loved one's life will hopefully bring a sense of acceptance of the dying process, and an acknowledgement that the ultimate decisions of life and death are in Hashem's hands alone.

ORGAN DONATION

Although it may be a difficult discussion, now may be the time to speak with and hear the wishes of your loved one with respect to organ donation. Depending on the cause of illness or death, one can choose to donate one or several tissue types or one or more organs. Many people have considered organ donation at an earlier time in their life, and may already carry a donor card (in Israel, this is the ADI card issued by the Ministry of Health), which speaks to their desire to donate their organs after death. (People living in other countries need to check on the relevance of an organ donor card in their area.)

At the time of death, when emotions are all over the place, organ donation is ultimately in the hands of the family members. It will be up to them to make a final and very quick decision, which is why knowing your loved one's wishes are so important. Organ donation is encouraged by Jewish law and supported by many rabbinic authorities, because it is considered a mitzva to help save another person's life. With advances in medicine and the success of organ transplantation, donating organs can also be seen as a way of continuing to give life to others through your loved one.[5]

In April 2023, Lucy Dee and two of her children were murdered in a terrorist attack. In acting quickly, Lucy's husband, Rabbi Leo Dee, was able to donate her organs, which gave new life to five recipients. Lucy Dee lost her life tragically, but was able to save several others. Organ donation not only saves lives, but can also provide the family consolation for their loss.

The Mishna (Sanhedrin 4:5) says: "*Kol hamekayem nefesh aḥat, me'alim alav ki'ulu kayam olam maleh* – Whoever saves a single life is considered to have saved an entire world."

NEARING DEATH AWARENESS

As people near death – in the final hours, days, or weeks – they may report premonitions, or seeing or hearing the voices of their deceased loved ones. They may also use euphemisms to describe moving on themselves – traveling, going to see their loved ones, getting ready to die, etc. One senses that they view their death as imminent, and if things seem as settled as they can be in this world, that they are very much looking forward to connecting with those they love in the next. This is a relatively foreign topic for many, and in fact is often mistaken by family and medical staff as patient confusion or a result of medication. What is often witnessed is a sense of readiness and peace.[6]

---

5. Please see the Ematai website for more information about Jewish perspectives on organ donation – www.ematai.org.
6. Callanan and Kelley, *Final Gifts*, 1997.

The closing days of your loved one's life may be marked by ups and downs. One day they may seem to be doing better, and both you and they may feel hopeful; the next day the situation may worsen, and your loved one deteriorates further. That said, at times, a day to hours before death, especially if one knows that a loved one is arriving from far away, a person may appear to rally. It is indeed a shock when someone in a coma opens their eyes, or if lying in bed suddenly sits up for a moment. This all adds to the emotional upheaval, making it potentially even more difficult to make basic decisions that now seem all the more complex and impossible. This may be before or at the time that more family is called in to begin saying their final goodbyes. At some point, the medical team will be able to guide you with respect to indicators that suggest that your loved one's body is beginning to shut down and help you know what to look for. Nonetheless, as we stated earlier, no two deaths are the same. One death may be calm and peaceful, and another may be suddenly filled with trauma and drama in the last minutes, leaving little opportunity to prepare for the loss.

Hollywood has given us a skewed perspective of death: a loving bedside scene as the patient slowly fades away. While this may happen, often as time draws near, there will be those who could not imagine being with their loved one as they take their final breath, and others who feel they very much want to be there. There is no right answer, as being with someone at the time of their death is an individual decision, and as such each decision must be respected as being right for that person.

> *I was blessed to be with each of my parents when they died. I was quite surprised at how peaceful it seemed, all things considered. Both were receiving palliative care and, as deaths go, I know they, and by extension our family, were very fortunate. It does not work out this way for everyone, and the end can feel very painful after already going through so much suffering. Not everyone wanted to*

be in the room as the end approached. It was as painful for some to be present as it was for others who chose not to be – they chose to remember the soon-to-be deceased as they had last seen them.

As a caregiver, you too may feel that your emotions are all over the place. You may be the one who is guiding and being strong for others, or there may be someone else taking this role and your role may now be very different. As difficult as it is, you may ask yourself if you are ready to say goodbye. To do so means that you are willing to accept and acknowledge the impending death.

You may never really be ready to part from your loved one, nor be able to imagine being without them. Nonetheless, if you see that they are suffering and that the end is near, telling them that it is okay to die, that they can go to their final resting place and that you will be okay and will take care of things, is often a "gift of permission" that you give them in order to enable them to let go and move on. Granting them this gift may precede the actual death by mere minutes to hours, if your loved one is ready to depart.

While we think that no one wants to die alone, so many times I have heard stories in which, in the few minutes when someone walked out of the room for something and returned, their loved one had died. Initially this is very upsetting to the family member, who feels that had they not left they would have been there at the moment of passing. While we will never know, it often feels as if the person dying chose that very moment when their loved one would *not* be present so they would not feel the pain of their passing. Perhaps they need the family member to step out so they can cross over into the next world. Viewed in this way, it can feel comforting to have actually helped the process along.

No matter how ready we think we are, we are never really prepared. The period around the waning of life and the moment of the last breath, and thus death itself, often catch us off guard. There may be lots of commotion, but if you are lucky, those who are not afraid of death can make the last moments of your loved one's life truly beautiful to witness. You may pause as the time in between breaths gets longer, awaiting the final breath. This may be the time, if the situation feels appropriate, to softly sing or play the music and prayers that your loved one finds comforting and calming. This may also be a time to do nothing, other than to be there with your loved one in this quiet, calm, and sacred moment – as if time has stood still. There is no need to rush or panic, but rather appreciate the transition of your loved one out of this world. There will be time to organize details and call people. This may be your last moment with your loved one.

Letting People Go If They Are Suffering

Ketubot 103b–104a

Rabbi Yehuda HaNasi was very ill, and the Sages decreed a fast, and begged for divine mercy so that he would not die. And they said: Anyone who says that Rabbi Yehuda HaNasi has died will be stabbed with a sword. His maidservant ascended to the roof and said: The upper realms are requesting the presence of Rabbi Yehuda HaNasi, and the lower realms are requesting the presence of Rabbi Yehuda HaNasi. May it be the will of God that the lower worlds should impose their will upon the upper worlds. However, when she saw how many times he would enter the bathroom and remove his phylacteries (tefillin), and then exit and put them back on, and how he was suffering with his intestinal disease, she said: May it be the will of God that the upper worlds should impose their will upon the lower worlds. She had compassion on him and didn't want him to suffer.

This is a very significant issue regarding end-of-life ethics. Do we pray for people to live if they are suffering?

The Sages, meanwhile, would not be silent, and would not refrain from begging for mercy to let Rabbi Yehuda

HaNasi live. The maidservant took a jug and threw it from the roof to the ground. Due to the sudden noise, the Sages were momentarily silent and refrained from begging for mercy, and Rabbi Yehuda HaNasi died.

On the website "Torah in Motion," Rabbi Jay Kelman explains that based on this gemara, many authorities[7] note that while one may not actively end a person's life, we may, and perhaps at times should, pray for someone to die. Making a *misheberakh* is inappropriate when there is realistically no hope and much pain. This story has huge ramifications for end-of-life issues.

Gesher Haḥaim, by Rabbi Yechiel Michel Tuchazinski, suggests that life is a bridge, beginning with birth and ending with death. When a child is born, we witness the birth of a body, and when a person leaves this world, we witness the birth of a soul. We don't know the exact moment a baby will be born. There is a period of waiting. Likewise, the same period of anticipation occurs as we wait for the moment of death, the birth of our soul.

Rebbetzin Shira Smiles, "Life and Death,"
Mishpacha Magazine, Nov. 29, 2022

END-OF-LIFE *VIDUI*

Jewish law developed many laws and customs that help us. One of them, known as the last confession, is *Vidui.*

The talmudic Sages (Shabbat 32a) teach: "One who became ill and tends toward death, they say to him: 'Confess.'" The

7. E.g., *Iggerot Moshe, Ḥoshen Mishpat* 2:74:4.

rationale for this ritual is readily apparent. Once people die, they cannot confess or make amends.

The *Vidui* recited at the end of life is very different from the *Vidui* on Yom Kippur. Firstly, it is personal rather than communal, and it acknowledges the past mistakes of the dying person themselves, and seeks a final reconciliation with God. It is not a deathbed "confession of sins," but rather an opportunity, in our final moments of life, to express our regrets and our hopes. It is a chance to seek a sense of closure for both finished and unfinished business.

Parashat Ki Tavo (Deut. 28) contains the "blessings and curses." Among the blessings we find: "*Baruch atta bevoekha uvarukh atta betzeitekha* – Blessed are you when you come and blessed are you when you depart." The simple meaning of the verse is that a person should be blessed when they leave their homes every morning and when they return in the evening. Rashi explains that this verse refers to when a person enters and exits life. As you entered life free from sin, so should you be blessed to exit life. Perhaps Rashi's message is not only a call to *teshuva* (repentance) before death, but also to make amends with people before it's too late.

The *Vidui* prayer is said when death seems imminent; it may be said by the dying person, family members, or a rabbi. As in all matters concerning the dying, the dying person should be the one to decide whether they want to say or hear this prayer. *Vidui* should never be imposed. The central element of the *Vidui* is the *Shema*. The *Shema* is the last thing a Jew is supposed to say before death. After *Vidui*, some people add "Master of the Universe, may it be Your will that my passing be in peace."

Rabbi Eliezer taught, "Repent one day before your death." His students asked him, "But how do you know when you will die?"

To which he replied, "Indeed. Therefore, repent each day so you will live a repentant life."

Given the frailty of life, we should always aspire to have our physical and spiritual affairs in order. This is certainly the case when there is a concern that one may be dying. This talmudic ritual was codified in the classic books of Jewish law.

THE CHALLENGES OF A LAST CONFESSION

Despite its meaningfulness, the *Vidui* ritual is not always possible to implement. In some cases, a person does not have the ability to verbalize the prayer. It is also difficult for people to face the probability of their upcoming death. For this reason, the traditional *Vidui* includes a prayer for recovery.

It may also be difficult emotionally to suggest to someone that it might be time to recite *Vidui*. Many classic rabbinic sources contend that if such a suggestion will "break the spirit" of the person, it is best not to mention the idea. However, withholding the discussion of the "last confession" is to deny them a critical tool for their spiritual preparations for death.

Moreover, some patients may find solace in the ability to confess and repent, while finding meaning in an opportunity for reconciliation. Through the recitation of *Vidui*, Jewish ritual has thus provided an important spiritual and emotional tool for critically ill patients.

Adapted from R. Shlomo M. Brody,[8]
"Judaism Should Bring the 'Last Confession' (Vidui) Back,"
Jerusalem Post Magazine, March 11, 2023

8. Rabbi Brody is executive director of Ematai, dedicated to helping families navigate healthcare choices about aging and end-of-life care, www.ematai.org.

DEATH

Kissed by God

"*Vaya'al Aharon hakohen el Hor HaHar al pi Hashem vayamat sham* – And Aaron the priest went up onto Mount Hor at the commandment of the Lord, and died there" (Num. 33:38).

"*Al pi Hashem*" can mean by the word of God, but also by the mouth of God. Rashi explains that we learn from this that Aaron died with a kiss.

The midrash *Yalkut Shimoni* describes the death of Aaron. First, Aaron removed each of his priestly garments, one by one, and placed them on his son, Elazar. At that point, Moses said poignantly to Aaron, "Just think Aaron, my brother, when Miriam died, you and I attended to her. Now that you are about to die, I and Elazar are attending to you. But when I die, who will attend to me?" The Almighty said to Moses, "As you live, I will attend to you." Moses was trying to tell Aaron that at his moment of departure he was surrounded by loved ones, and God tells Moses that when it is his time, He will accompany Moses. Moses will not die alone.

What will that final moment be like? We all fear painful death, so the Talmud holds out hope that we will die like Moses, Aaron, and Miriam – with a gentle kiss from God.

The Malbim (Meir Leibush ben Yehiel Michel Wisser, 1809–1879), explains this beautifully: "Aaron was not killed by the angel of death; [rather] he died with a kiss. Rather than being struck down by external causes, his soul gradually extended beyond him, moved by joyful anticipation of being freed from the prison of the body and being allowed to be gathered up into the state of eternal life with God.... That is why instead of saying 'Aaron died,' the Torah reports, 'He was gathered to his people,' meaning that his soul departed

> the material world in order to return to its 'people,' the place, that is, where the souls of all the Righteous dwell."
>
> This model of meeting our death without despair is itself a gift to those we leave behind. When their time to go arrives, they may be able to see, as we did, that death is not the end of our impact upon the earth; and – who knows? – it may be just the gateway to another stage of being that our tradition describes as beyond and better than what we now know.
>
> R. Lawrence A. Hoffman, "Kissed by God,"
> *New Jersey Jewish News*, June 16, 2010

> The Zohar explains that all of one's mitzvot (good deeds) come to escort a person to their place in the spiritual world. Just as the *Shekhina* is present at the birth of a baby, the *Shekhina* is present as it escorts the soul to its next level of existence, unencumbered by the physical constraints of the body.
>
> Rebbetzin Shira Smiles, "Life and Death,"
> *Mishpacha Magazine*, Nov. 29, 2022

WHEN DEATH CANNOT BE CONFIRMED: AMBIGUOUS LOSS

Ambiguous loss, a term coined by Pauline Boss (Boss and Yeats, 2014) describes a complicated type of grief when a loved one's body is not found. It is a loss that is said to be ongoing, without any closure or resolution because the person is physically absent.

A person may, for example, be missing and their whereabouts unknown, and therefore the finality not verified. With the person's status or whereabouts unknown, there is always a hope for a return – as is seen with hostages and prisoners-of-war, and those missing after a downed airplane or a terror attack. Without actually being able to identify a person or having a body to bury, one may feel immobilized. It is harder to accept the death as permanent, and religious rituals such as a funeral and shiva may be absent, leaving the grievers without support.

With loss being both physical and psychological, the lack of clarity and ambiguity complicates and delays the grieving process.

Ambiguous Loss in the Torah

After Joseph had been sold into slavery, his brothers dipped his coat in blood. They brought it back to their father and said: "Look what we have found. Do you recognize it? Is this your son's coat or not?" Jacob recognized it, and replied, "It is my son's coat. A wild beast has surely devoured him. Joseph has been torn to pieces." We then read: "Jacob rent his clothes, put on sackcloth, and mourned his son for a long time. His sons and daughters tried to comfort him, but he refused to be comforted. He said, 'I will go down to the grave mourning for my son'" (Gen. 37:34).

Why did Jacob refuse to be comforted? In his discussion of the portion of *Vayeshev,* Rabbi Sacks suggests that there are laws in Judaism about the limits of grief – shiva, *sheloshim,* a year. There is no such thing as a bereavement for which grief is endless. The Midrash explains Jacob's behavior. "One can be comforted for one who is dead, but not for one who is still living." Jacob refused to be comforted, because he had not yet given up hope that Joseph was still alive.

That, tragically, is the fate of those who have lost members of their family (the parents of soldiers missing in action, for example), but have as yet no proof that they are dead. One cannot go through the normal stages of mourning, because one cannot abandon the possibility that the missing person is still capable of being rescued. The bereaved person's continuing anguish is a form of loyalty; to give up, to mourn, to be reconciled to loss – are all forms of betrayal. In such cases, grief lacks closure. To refuse to be comforted is to refuse to give up hope.

R. Jonathan Sacks, "Refusing Comfort, Keeping Hope," in *Covenant and Conversation: Genesis*, pp. 253–254

Personal Reflections after the Crash of Swissair Flight 111 Off the Coast of Nova Scotia

On September 2, 1998, Swissair Flight 111, on its way from New York to Geneva, crashed over Nova Scotia, killing all 229 people on board.

Those of us who were part of the ḥevra kaddisha on site were put on alert to be available to prepare bodies as they were recovered, only to discover that as time passed, our services would unfortunately not be needed. Due to the difficulty in retrieval of the bodies and in making identification as as result of the magnitude of the destruction, and because there were-several Jewish people on board, many important and difficult questions arose with respect to burial and mourning rituals. People with expertise from previous mass disasters were brought in from as far away as New York and Israel in order to expedite the search and rescue, and ultimate retrieval process. Not being able to observe rituals such as a funeral, or to have shiva visitation by friends and relatives, or even to have a gravesite to visit, would deprive the families, at least temporarily, of places to seek comfort and feel near their loved ones. Needless to say, this delay in the mourning process made it that much more difficult for the families to deal with their own loss and to move on with their lives.

Batya. L. Ludman, "A Month since the Swissair Disaster: Some Brief Personal Reflections," *The Nova Scotia Psychologist* 12, no. 4 (1998): 18–19

Chapter 2

From Death Until the Funeral

The moment of death and the last breath drawn signals a rupture between the world of what once was and the world of what is now. Your world as you once knew it is forever changed. How can it not be when someone you loved is no longer with you? You pinch yourself, as you cannot believe that it is true.

Everything has changed, but your loved one, and the relationship you had with them, will forever remain in your heart. Now you will need to learn to "be" with them in a different way than ever before. While a link to what was part of your life "before" has been in some ways severed and the historical bond between you and your loved one frozen in time, your job will become one of making meaning out of your loss. This is a process that takes time and tremendous energy, perhaps much more than you could ever imagine having, especially at this moment. This will become your mourning, and each person will grieve in their own way. For now, though, in this moment, your job will simply be to do whatever needs to be attended to before the funeral.

Your first task may be to tell other family members that your loved one has died. You may be the one to do this in person, or ask someone to go to the house to be with a parent or children so that they are not alone when hearing the news. Children, as well as other mourners, will need to get an idea as to what will happen over the next twenty-four hours and the days ahead, so that plans can be made for someone to look after them if necessary, as you will most likely be preoccupied with funeral arrangements. Putting one foot in front of the other, you will deal with one small task and then another. Judaism recognizes that at this time, when you are sad, confused, overwhelmed, and have a myriad of other feelings, you need as few demands as possible placed upon you because now, at this moment, you need time – time to process, to do, to follow, to care for others, and to be cared for yourself.

Right now, you may want someone to be with you for emotional support: a family member, a friend, and perhaps your rabbi to be there to guide you with logistics, to help you sort out what you would like or need to do next, and simply be there to provide assistance.

> *Seemingly within minutes after my dad passed away, our rabbi appeared at the hospital. He sat in the waiting room and was simply waiting for us to emerge from the hospital room. Just his presence and the sense that he had all the time in the world for us brought so much comfort. I don't even remember what he said when he saw us, but I do know that he brought order to our confusion, and gave us guidance and direction with respect to what we needed to do next. His tremendous sensitivity to all of the needs of various family members was the cradling we needed to begin to move forward and make plans. His calm, reassuring,*

> *and tender demeanor spoke volumes at such a difficult time. These are the kindnesses that we reflect back on years later. We never know how something seemingly so small can have such a great impact and be a source of tremendous strength.*

This time after death and before the funeral is so important and distinct, that Judaism refers to you as an "*onen*." Because of the need to make and conclude the funeral arrangements, you are released from the obligations of prayer and many other specific positive observances, such as reciting the blessing over bread or the Grace after Meals. Jewish law recognizes your distress, grief, disbelief, and psychological state, and because of that, you, the "*onen*," are not obligated to fulfill positive mitzvot. A prolonged period of *aninut* can be extremely stressful, as one is neither here nor there, so for this reason we try to minimize this time period and hold the funeral as soon as possible. Please seek out a halakhic authority for more discussion on this topic.

WHO ARE THE MOURNERS?

Judaism obligates seven people to mourn: child, brother, sister, husband, wife, father, and mother. For most of you reading this book, your first loss as an "official" mourner will be that of your parents. As difficult as it may be, this is the more typical order of loss, as they are older than you. Whatever age our parents are when they die, it may feel too soon for us, who are left behind to carry this generation into the future. The loss of a first parent may also mean that we are now helping to care in some way for the second parent – with respect to their loss in the present as well as their and your losses into the future. If it is the death of a second parent, you now find yourself an "orphan," and this, in itself, may raise a different set of issues.

If the death is of your sister or brother, you may now grieve for the past history that you have had in common, as well as the loss you now feel as you go on alone. If your parents are alive, you might have to shoulder some of the grief they feel for the horrific loss of their child, as well as come face to face with your own mortality as you grieve someone close to you in age.

If the death is of your spouse, your grief is for the years you shared in the past, a life you made together, and a future you will no longer share. You are dealing with your loss as well as that of your children, and maybe that of your in-laws as well as your parents.

When you lose a child, your assumptive world is challenged in every possible way. The natural order of parents predeceasing a child has been altered, and you are forced to live with daily reminders as you see children of your child's age grow up into adulthood, marry, and have children. Sometimes, it may be an adult child who predeceases you, which is as difficult, although perhaps in different ways.

All losses are difficult, and one can never measure whose pain is greater. The year ahead will have moments that are better or worse, depending on the loss. In many ways, the best gift you can give yourself now is to not have any expectations. Rather, you will need to take life one day – and when necessary, one hour or one minute – at a time.

DISENFRANCHISED GRIEF

There may be others who are grieving over a loss, but the halakhic laws of mourning do not apply to them. These mourners are referred to as "disenfranchised grievers." They may include sons- and daughters-in-law, grandparents or grandchildren, girlfriends or boyfriends, fiancés, ex-spouses, same-sex partners, step-parents, close friends, co-workers, or even foreign caregivers. It may also be someone who experienced a pregnancy loss, or the death of a family member to suicide (some people have difficulty openly acknowledging a suicide).

Disenfranchised grief[1] is grief that is experienced when one incurs a loss that is not or cannot be openly acknowledged, publicly mourned, or socially sanctioned. Typically observed by those other than the seven traditionally recognized (first-degree relatives) in Judaism, it is loss or grief that is often seen as "less significant." Disenfranchised grievers are often not "seen" as grieving, and are therefore not included or only minimally participate in rituals that enable meaning. It may feel deeply painful, and result in the isolation of the griever. The lack of support by family members or society at large for those dealing with disenfranchised loss can prolong their emotional pain and make the grieving process itself more difficult.

> *I heard a new expression that was coined to describe disenfranchised mourners in Judaism. These people are "standing shiva [omdim shiva]" instead of "sitting shiva." This describes the fact that they don't have an official seat among the mourners, yet they are still grieving and are usually the ones standing to serve and provide for the official mourners. These are often the spouses, children, grandchildren, and others closely connected to the designated mourners.*

BETWEEN DEATH AND *ANINUT*

Not everyone will want to see their loved one at the time of death or afterwards. Some may want to do so only momentarily, whereas others may find it very difficult to tear themselves away and leave. If the death occurred in the hospital and your loved one was pronounced dead by a physician, all medical equipment will be removed,

1. See Doka, *Disenfranchised Grief.*

the body will be washed and, depending on the timing, you may again be able to spend a few precious moments with your loved one in their hospital room before they may be taken to the morgue or funeral home. Whereas for you, it may all feel very surreal, the hospital will eventually want to reassign the room and, while trying not to rush the family, will be in a "life goes on" mode. Once you walk out, you will not see your loved one until the funeral, and this sense of finality may leave you feeling very torn. With that said, after a certain time, staying won't make it any better and leaving does psychologically help to begin move the process forward.

When a death has taken place at home, an emergency medical service (EMS) may or may not have been called in, depending on the end-of-life request of the deceased or their family. An attending physician who is part of this team or may have also been called in separately will typically examine your loved one and "declare" or "pronounce" death. There will be a formal written report. As with a death in the hospital, your loved one's eyes will be closed, extraneous medical equipment removed, and their body covered. Candles, as per Jewish custom, may be lit and placed at the head of the deceased. Afterwards, because the death has occurred at home, the police will typically meet briefly with the family to ensure that there has been no foul play, issue a report, and then, depending on location, the *ḥevra kaddisha* or funeral home will arrive and remove the body.

There is tremendous reverence for the deceased in Judaism, and therefore it is customary to hold the burial as quickly as possible. In Israel, the burial is generally conducted within twenty-four hours of death, even if this means that the funeral is held late into the night. Only under special circumstances, such as waiting for close relatives coming from distant locations, would the funeral be postponed. Outside of Israel, there is often more leniency with respect to time of burial, as one may have to deal with non-Jewish authorities, state regulations, and weather conditions.

Notwithstanding these delays, it is still considered respectful to the deceased to try and facilitate a burial as soon as possible.

For the mourners, the longer the time from death until burial, the more difficult it is due in part to lack of closure, and the ability to begin to move on. This holding pattern can feel very disconcerting.

> *My father-in-law died on the west coast of the United States early Wednesday morning, Israel time, and was going to be brought to Florida for burial next to my mother-in-law. We flew from Israel to New York right away to be on the same continent, and planned to spend Shabbat with our children as we could not be certain when the funeral in Florida would be held. Due to logistics in sending a body to another state, the tremendous amount of paperwork, Shabbat, and a weekend, it meant that the funeral could not take place until Sunday afternoon at the earliest, east coast time, assuming the body was actually released and would arrive on time. Imagine, five days of being neither here nor there. Without a funeral, there is no outward acknowledgement of the loss. You are not officially a mourner and so don't recite Kaddish but you can attend Shabbat services. Many other things, too, are different – it was surreal.*

Until the actual interment, the primary concern is very much for the deceased and all of the many preparations that need to be completed. Only afterwards can the real focus be on the mourners. Despite this, Judaism appreciates the tremendous difficulty of grieving while simultaneously being asked to make some very difficult yet important and timely decisions. You will quickly become involved in relaying the news, perhaps writing a eulogy or obituary, helping to make funeral arrangements, determining shiva logistics, speaking with a rabbi, and dealing with many other details – all the while with a likely sense of disbelief that this is actually happening to you.

> TIP: Don't be afraid to ask others to help you with the logistics. There is so much to do, and people who are close to you will want to help out in whatever way it is that you need them.

A TIME AND A PLACE FOR SILENCE

Jewish tradition teaches the power and beauty in taking time to pause and reflect. Silence is an integral part of the process of grief and mourning.

> In *Parashat Shemini*, we read that on the day of the dedication of the *Mishkan*, the Tabernacle in the desert, Aaron's two sons, Nadav and Avihu, were slain by a fire that came from heaven. When Aaron was informed of his sons' deaths, the Torah records: "*vayidom Aharon* – And Aaron was silent."
>
> There is a talmudic tradition that Aaron's silence expressed his acceptance of the Divine decree. As painful, and perhaps inexplicable, as his sons' deaths may have been, Aaron deferred to God's greater wisdom. Rabbi Isaac Abrabanel explains that Aaron was silent because "Aaron's heart turned to lifeless stone. He did not weep, nor did he accept Moses's attempts to console him, for his soul had left him and he was speechless." Rabbeinu Bahya teaches that silence is one of the ways in which people express mourning. Aaron's response to his sons' deaths reminds us that grief can take many forms. Whether Aaron's silence meant he was in an inner process of reconciliation, or that he was heartbroken, what is clear is that he was in the process of grieving. The Torah highlights Aaron's silence to model for us that sometimes silence, and not words, are what we need at a painful time.

Bad news often travels quickly. With good intentions, we often feel we have to rush over to the home where there has been a loss, thinking "I have to be there for them." Wait! Only very close family or friends whose assistance is required in making arrangements for the funeral or helping with other matters should visit at this time. This might be a difficult thing to do – to stay away. You may need to ask yourself if you are going for the mourner, or if you are going for yourself. If it's the former, your role may be very task-oriented, because this is really not a time to sit and give comfort. There is a reason why no formal condolences should be extended at this time. Before the burial a person is not able to "receive or hear" condolences as they could still be in disbelief and denial, and may not have actually begun to process the loss.

> The mishna in *Pirkei Avot* 4:23 records the opinion of Rabbi Shimon ben Elazar, who counseled that one should not console his friend "at the time when his deceased lies before him [i.e., before burial]."

PREPARATIONS FOR THE FUNERAL: FOR THE MOURNERS

From the time of death until the funeral, there is a lot that must be done by the immediate mourners, other family members, and close friends. A funeral cannot take place without first obtaining a burial permit and, depending on where the death took place, a death report from the doctor or ambulance service, several copies of which will be needed for later. In addition, if the death took place at home, a letter from the police is usually also required. You may find yourself dealing with this and other bureaucratic details that need to be done quickly.

This is all at a time when you are often feeling fragile and exhausted. It may be helpful to have a friend or family member with you. Other things that have to be done right away include speaking to a rabbi, choosing someone to officiate at the funeral, and securing a time for the ceremony. The funeral time may depend on availability of the rabbi, *ḥevra kaddisha,* the funeral home, or cemetery scheduling, family members coming from far away, and other factors, such as weather and traffic conditions. If the death took place outside of Israel, you may need to speak with the funeral home to make financial arrangements regarding the funeral, as well as deal with the logistics around retrieval of the body from the place of death, choose a casket, burial plot, arrange transportation for both the body and family to the funeral service, decide the location of the funeral, among other details. The rabbi (or whoever is officiating) will want to meet with the family and explain what the funeral will look like, as well as hear details about your loved one that will enable them to write an appropriate eulogy. You may also want to eulogize your loved one or choose others to speak or be pallbearers. You will have to decide how many you would like or need, and who they will be. Will they have to lift and carry a heavy casket or wheel a gurney?

Regardless of whether the funeral is held the same day as the death or later, it may feel like there is much to do in a short period of time. Shiva times and place need to be discussed, who to inform and how to tell people through printed death notices, synagogue lists, social media, email, and other lists of friends and family, are all tasks that can be designated to those who want to help. The community or *ḥevra kaddisha* may arrange for the mirrors to be covered, bring low chairs for the official mourners as well as chairs for visitors, supply prayer books and a weeklong memorial candle, and organize food for right after the burial, all of which will need to be arranged before the funeral. If the shiva is expected to be large, someone may want to arrange for a water cooler, cups, disposables, and even a tent to house the visitors. In short, there is lots to be done, and now is a good time to delegate and assign roles to others who have offered to help. You may also want to write an obituary for the local or out-of-town newspaper or other news sources. Finally, you will want to choose a garment that you will wear to the funeral which will be torn, and you will continue to wear for the week of shiva (with the exception of Shabbat).

> TIP: You may want to bring water, tissues, a change to non-leather footwear if you will be starting to sit shiva at the cemetery, and any other useful item, such as sunglasses, a hat, a folding chair, a fan, or an umbrella.

SHEMIRA

There is a Jewish tradition of watching the body after death and before burial referred to as *shemira* (guarding). Although the soul has separated from the physical body, we believe the body should be treated with respect and care. We try not to leave the deceased alone from the moment of death until burial. The person doing the watching is referred to as a *shomer* (if male) or a *shomeret* (if female). In many instances, the *shomer/et* is a family member or a personal friend of the deceased. If this is not possible, the family may turn to the *ḥevra kaddisha,* or to the local synagogue to find individuals who perform *shemira.* The *shomer/et* must remain awake at all times, and ideally should be reciting from the Book of Psalms (*Tehillim*). In the past, the *shomer/et* had the responsibility of guarding a body against thieves and animals. Today, when this is no longer relevant, not leaving the body unattended is a way that family and the community can show respect for the deceased. It is not necessary for the *shomer/et* to be actually watching the body. The body may be covered or in a closed casket already, but there should be someone present in the room at all times. In some cases, this may extend to the next room, provided that the door to the room of the deceased is left open. The act of serving as a *shomer/et* is seen as a great mitzva.

PREPARATION OF THE DECEASED

The next stage for your loved one will be a *tahara*, the ritual washing, dressing, and preparation of the body prior to burial. Their body will be taken from the morgue and brought to the funeral home or room at the cemetery where this preparation will take place. Often this is done just before the funeral.

TAHARA EXPLAINED

Judaism has such tremendous respect for the deceased, but also for the simplicity of life. Simple burial shrouds allow everyone to be treated equally, and ensure that those who cannot afford fancy clothing are not embarrassed. We all come into the world free of the trappings of society and so when we exit we are dressed alike, in a shroud made of cotton or linen. Shrouds have no pockets, which symbolizes that we cannot take our material wealth with us. We don't make up or adorn the body, but in fact remove all jewelry, nail polish, and makeup before burial.

> *Many years ago in our small Jewish community, after the death of my beloved mother, the female head of the ḥevra kaddisha made a shiva visit to our home. Speaking so warmly about my mom, she described what they did and how beautiful she looked at the end. She was so comforting that I asked her if I could join the ḥevra kaddisha. The woman asked that I wait six months and if I was still interested, to contact her. I did and I continued to serve on the ḥevra kaddisha for the seven years before we made aliya. My father was a long-standing member of the ḥevra kaddisha, and my memories of him leaving the house at night to perform this very private and mysterious mitzva always filled me with reverence and left me intrigued.*
>
> *Each call I received to go and perform a tahara was very special. There was a men's and women's ḥevra kaddisha. In the*

women's unit, four or five volunteers at any one time (coming from all walks of life within the community) met at the funeral home. We lovingly combed the deceased's hair, cleaned her nails, and then ever so gently washed her entire body, all the time being so careful to protect her privacy and showing her the deepest respect imaginable. We each asked for forgiveness if we had in any way offended her in the process as well as in life if we had known her. We spoke in hushed tones and discussed only what was relevant to our work at the moment. We dressed her carefully in a clean white linen shroud, similar to that of the kohanim (priests), which consisted of several vestments (shirt, pants, booties, hat, and a belt). These are known as takhrikhim.

During the entire tahara, a male member of the ḥevra kaddisha stood outside the room saying psalms and from then until the funeral, a shomer, a person assigned to "watch" the body, prayed nearby. This process is similar for a man, with the exception that on top of his shroud, he may be then covered with a tallit (a ritual prayer shawl), which is made pasul (non-kosher) by cutting off some of the fringes. In Israel just before the burial, the tallit is usually removed.

As we, the ḥevra kaddisha ladies left the building, we washed our hands ritually before heading home. On arriving home, I put my clothes in the wash, showered, and kissed each of my sleeping children and husband. Never did life seem so precious.

Adapted from B. L. Ludman, "Life-Death Passages: Jewish Burial – A Study in the Psychology of Healing," in *Life's Journey*, 248–252

Chapter 3

From Funeral to Burial

The Jewish funeral or *levaya* (accompanying), reflects the interactive process of burying your loved one. Neither the rabbi nor the *ḥevra kaddisha* buries the dead; rather the mourners, with the participation of the community, perform this mitzva. At this time, the purpose is not to comfort the mourners, but rather to pay final respects to the deceased. Judaism recognizes that in this moment there is little comfort to be achieved while standing before the deceased. Healing can only start after the burial has been completed.

IDENTIFICATION OF THE DECEASED

Prior to, or at the same time that family and close friends arrive for the funeral, a family member will be asked to identify the body to ensure that the correct person is being buried. The face is uncovered, and the process is generally short. If other mourners request to be there as well, permission may be given. It is very much a personal decision as to whether you choose to see the deceased.

While you may prefer to remember them as they were the last time you saw them, or feel that seeing them in this state now would be upsetting on many different levels, you may also want to see and even speak to your loved one one last time. This is especially true if their death was sudden, and you did not get to say goodbye. Of course, seeing them may not give you the comfort you hope to achieve. Only you can decide if it is the right thing for you.

> *People are often very afraid and anxious about what they might see when they view their loved one. As a member of the ḥevra kaddisha, my experience has been that when we placed the body in the coffin at the end of the tahara, we always drew comfort in the fact that they looked very much at peace.*

A death can feel very disorienting. Things may all be happening very quickly. Everything that you know has been turned upside down, often suddenly or with minimal preparation. You may be at a loss with respect to what to do or how to act – or you simply may be in shock. Judaism's rituals provide a supportive framework and a focus to help ground and orient you as you move through your loss. There are different rituals and customs with regard to various aspects of the mourning process. As such, you may see differences in terms of viewing the body, performing *kriya,* saying *Kaddish,* sitting shiva, and more. In general, these mourning rituals may seem harsh, and burial may feel as if it happened too quickly to process, but they are designed to help the mourner face the loss and begin the healing process.

KRIYA

Those considered mourners (parents, children, siblings, and the spouse of the deceased) will then perform *kriya,* the tearing or rending of their garment. *Kriya* can be very painful emotionally, given that it is usually done in the presence of the deceased. Seeing the actual form of the body on a metal gurney (in Israel) or the casket (abroad) may evoke a flood of emotions. As the mourners stand together, the rabbi or another individual begins *kriya* with a knife, and the mourner further tears the garment or ribbon. Outside of Israel, and in some communities, mourners are offered the option of rending a separate piece of black cloth, which is then pinned onto the intact clothing. Immediate family members will make the blessing, *"Barukh atta Hashem Elokeinu melekh ha'olam dayan ha'emet* – Blessed is the True Judge" as the garment is ripped. Death is an unexplained concept. We are left with so many questions. There is no way for us to comprehend. At the moment of pain and confusion, we acknowledge that God is ultimately the True Judge.

Kriya is seen as a permissible and safe way to express grief in place of physically hurting oneself – as was practiced as part of some mourning rituals in the ancient world. The garment, typically a shirt or jacket for a man, and a blouse, dress, or cardigan for a woman, is torn just below the neck and above the chest on the left side when the deceased is a parent, and on the right side for all others. This rending may feel very real – it is an outward sign of a painfully broken heart and visual reminder of the loss of your loved one. The mourners then join other family and friends who have come to the funeral. The rent garment is now worn throughout the entire shiva period with the exception of Shabbat, when all outward signs of mourning are suspended. If shiva is delayed, *kriya* is also delayed.

> *When my father died it felt like a rip in the fabric of my world, and no matter how hard I tried, I couldn't hold the edges together. Even now, four years later, when I am going about my day, sometimes I brush up against that seam and it hurts like hell.*
>
> J. Picoult, *Wish You Were Here*, p. 160

The *kriya* ceremony is a traditional custom in which the mourners rend (tear) their clothes as a symbol of a broken heart or the empty space created in their souls by the pain over the death of their relative. The source of this custom is in the Torah, when Jacob rent his clothes in mourning for his son, Joseph, who he thought was dead (Gen. 37:34). During the talmudic period, mourners customarily rent their garments themselves immediately upon seeing or hearing of the death.

THE FUNERAL SERVICE AND BURIAL

After *kriya*, if not already present, the deceased is wheeled into the room or outside area where the funeral service will take place, and all mourners gather around. If a funeral is performed at the graveside, *kriya* is often performed at the time of the burial.

The deceased is typically placed in the front or center of the space where the funeral service is held, unless the entire funeral takes place at the graveside. Depending on the country and the cause of death, the deceased, dressed in a shroud, or tallit and shroud, is placed directly onto a metal gurney or will be in the casket on top of a table with wheels.

At the beginning of Jewish funerals, we recite this passage, "*Hashem natan veHashem lakaḥ yehi shem Hashem mevorakh* – The Lord has given and the Lord has taken away that which He has given. May the name of God be blessed" (Job 1:21). This verse is understood as Job's acceptance of God's decree.

The deceased is now typically eulogized by a rabbi, family members, and/or friends.

THE EULOGY: *HESPED*

A eulogy, known as a *hesped* in Hebrew, is a speech given in honor of the deceased. It gives us the opportunity to look back on a person's life and recognize their achievements, good deeds, and values.

Jewish eulogies are customarily given during the funeral service, prior to the burial. When our matriarch Sarah died, the Torah says that her husband Abraham cried and eulogized her. Judaism takes the obligation to eulogize the deceased appropriately very seriously. The Tanakh tells us that the Jewish people were punished with famine for not giving King Saul a sufficiently respectful eulogy. We make an effort to mention the good character traits of the person and praise them for who they were and what they did, with stories told to exemplify their character and with a recognition that their values will live on in others.

However, we also try to be honest and respectful and not exaggerate a person's good qualities or faults. Some of the themes in a eulogy may include the deceased's life story, legacy, accomplishments, values, positive and unique character traits, love of family and friends, and devotion to community, Judaism, and the Land of Israel. As with all the elements of the funeral and burial, the focus is on giving respect to the deceased and not on the eulogizer. This is accomplished by keeping one's words brief and appropriate, bearing in mind that the goal is to honor the deceased, while comforting the mourners.

The Talmud (Sanhedrin 46b) debates if the purpose of a eulogy is to honor the deceased or if it is intended to benefit the mourners. While the eulogy should serve both purposes, Jewish law prioritizes the deceased, and so if they had requested not to be eulogized, that preference should be respected. Often a rabbi will deliver the *hesped* but family members and close friends are invited to speak if they wish to do so. For some mourners, it is a way to recall good memories of the deceased and also say their goodbyes. If the mourner finds it too difficult to deliver the eulogy, it is perfectly acceptable to share their notes with someone else who can read it on their behalf. They can also share memories with the officiating rabbi, who can include their words. When delivering a eulogy, one should be very careful not to reveal details that might be embarrassing to the deceased or their family. It is best to ask family members directly before sharing information if there is a concern that it might not be appropriate. The tone of a eulogy should be serious and respectful, though when appropriate, some gentle humor can be acceptable and sometimes even comforting. It is important to keep eulogies relatively brief, especially if there are many speakers. It is also important to consider the weather conditions and that people will often be standing for a long time.

It is customary not to eulogize on *Erev* Yom Kippur, Ḥol HaMoed, Rosh Ḥodesh, Hanukka, Purim (and *Purim Katan*), Tu BiShevat, the whole month of Nisan Lag B'Omer, *Pesaḥ Sheni*, Tisha B'Av, Tu B'Av, and *Isru Ḥag*. Exceptions are made if the deceased was a Torah scholar.

We have personally attended funerals where the officiating rabbi or member of the *ḥevra kaddisha* said, "Today is Rosh Ḥodesh (or Hanukka, etc.), and it is customary not to eulogize, so we will keep the *hespedim* brief." This shows great sensitivity to the mourners, who may find it difficult to bury their loved ones without sharing memories or speaking about the good qualities of the deceased. The accepted custom seems to be that we refrain from giving an intensely emotional eulogy during these holidays, but we praise the good deeds of the deceased and inspire others to follow in their footsteps.

Sometimes these *hespedim* will be printed up and available at the shiva, or even posted online, for those who were unable to attend the funeral. This gives the visitors greater insight into the life of the deceased. Modern technology also allows those who were unable to be present to participate and eulogize their loved one from afar.

It is customary for *kohanim* to refrain from contact with the dead, because such contact would render them ritually impure.

However, for their next of kin – parents, spouse, and children – not only is it permitted for them to attend their funerals and burial, but it is also a mitzva for a *kohen* to attend and pay his final respects. *Kohanim* often have their own respective place off to the side as they are not typically in the same room or near the grave of the deceased. They might attend the eulogy, but not proceed to the gravesite. If they attend the actual burial, again they often stand off to the side.

In *Parashat Shemini,* Moses inquired about the meat of the sacrifice that had been burned, not consumed. He was upset: "Why did you not consume these in the holy place as commanded?" Aaron responded, "On a day that this occurred (his sons' death), should we offer the offerings and eat them? Is that proper in God's eyes?" Moses heard, and agreed. Moses was upset that the offerings had not been consumed by Aaron and his other sons. Aaron, struck speechless by the death of his two sons, now challenged Moses. Does our role as Divine servants eliminate our human feelings of tragedy? Is a holy person angelic – or holy while remaining a person? Am I not entitled to mourn at least today? This brief, very brief, confrontation expresses a universal theme of the holy man. Does holiness squash our humanity, our emotions, our desires, our hold on this world? Does the religious leader, the holy man, float untethered to normal human feelings of grief? Does he continue serving God sublimating the pain he is suffering?

Religions of the world come down differently on this question. Aaron sets the Jewish view, agreed to by Moses. The holiest person we have, the *Kohen Gadol,* cries like anyone else on the death of his children. Normal service does not continue as if nothing happened. However holy the holy man is, he is also a person with legitimate feelings. Holy men are holy, but men they remain.

R. Reuven Tradburks, https://tinyurl.com/yc8p2dsy

> "*Vayavo Avraham lispod leSara velivkota* – Abraham came to eulogize Sarah and to weep." The Talmud has a fascinating discussion over the nature of eulogy, of *hesped*. "Is a eulogy designed to benefit the dead?" asks the Talmud. "Or is it for the benefit of the living survivors, the mourners?" The Talmud has its own conclusion, but there can be no doubt that from a psychological perspective, the eulogy does both. It honors the dead, and it provides the mourner with the opportunity to give vent to his grief and to achieve a degree of catharsis. Perhaps this is why Abraham both "eulogizes" Sarah and "cries for her." In his "eulogy" he honors her person, her character, her achievements in life. By "crying for her," he gives voice to his profound sense of the loss of his life's partner.
>
> R. Dr. Tzvi Hersh Weinreb, "Chayei Sarah: To Eulogize and to Weep," https://outorah.org/p/3051/

A selection of psalms are then said. *Kaddish* is recited by the mourners. The procession then follows the deceased, assisted by pallbearers (friends and family members), from the place where the eulogies were given to the grave for burial. Although this is emotionally difficult to do, it's also considered a mitzva to accompany the dead to their final resting place. Outside of Israel, sometimes only family and close friends travel to the cemetery, which is often quite far away.

BURIAL IN THE LAND OF ISRAEL

When burial occurs in any country other than Israel, the *ḥevra kaddisha* traditionally places a packet of earth from the Land of Israel in the casket in order that the deceased is buried "in holy soil." Often, a person requests that after their death, their body be transported to Israel for burial. Many Jewish communities and individuals in the Diaspora have pre-purchased plots in cemeteries in Israel in order to accommodate those who have expressed their wish to be buried there. Purchasing a plot and being buried in Israel is a custom that links the person to the Jewish people and its ancient homeland. Though exhuming the body is normally not accepted by Jewish law, one exception that is made is for reinterment in Israel.

> *I once joined a couple in their car for a ride to Beit Shemesh to visit a friend sitting shiva. After the visit, the driver of the car asked me, "Do you mind if we take a few minutes to visit my parents who are nearby?" As I was the "hitchhiker," I of course agreed, assuming that his parents lived in Beit Shemesh. Imagine my surprise when we pulled into a cemetery near Beit Shemesh to "visit his parents." They had lived in the United States and had both been brought to Israel for burial. As we walked among the graves, we saw signs with the names of different Jewish communities in the United States, Canada, and the United Kingdom.*

Abraham purchased a burial place for his wife Sarah in the cave of Makhpela, starting a tradition of families being buried together. Even when famine prevented Jacob from living in the Land of Israel, he did everything possible to ensure that his remains would be taken there for burial. Jacob made Joseph swear to bury him in the Holy Land. We find that Joseph followed in his father's footsteps, asking his brothers to swear to have his remains brought to Israel. The Torah describes that at the Exodus from Egypt, Moses took the bones of Joseph with him. The word *etzem* (bone) in Hebrew also means "essence." We could therefore suggest that the phrase *atzmot Yosef* (Joseph's bones) is also hinting to *atz'miut Yosef* (Joseph's essence). Although Moses literally carried Joseph's remains out of Egypt, he also took along Joseph's essence – his deep connection to *Eretz Yisrael.*

The rabbis of the Talmud spoke of the greatness of living in Israel, adding that one who could not live in Israel should do their best to be buried there. Burial in Israel is the way that we connect to thousands of years of Jewish history, to the "Promised Land," and to the Jewish people. While in the past, this was a difficult wish to fulfill, modern travel and communications have made it much easier. Rabbi Nahman of Breslov said, "*Kol makom she'ani holekh, ani holekh le'eretz Yisrael* – Wherever I go, I am always going to the Land of Israel."

MAN'S RETURN TO THE EARTH

"Earth you are, and to earth you will return" (Gen. 3:19) were God's words to Adam.

According to Jewish law, at the end of human life the body should return to the earth, as the first human being was initially formed from the earth. The name Adam is symbolic of his connection to the *adama,* the earth. Jewish law prescribes that the body be returned to the earth, in a way that allows for the natural process of its decomposition. As human beings are "created in the image of God," in the period between death and burial, the integrity and dignity of the body must be respected and preserved. For this reason, halakha doesn't support embalming the body, displaying it, or cremating it. Autopsies are generally not carried out unless required by law or if it serves to save the lives of others. If an autopsy is performed, the body is, according to Jewish law, buried in its entirety.

> In the words of King Solomon: "And the dust returns to the ground as it was, and the spirit returns to God, who gave it" (Eccl. 12:7).

Outside of Israel, the custom is to bury a person in a plain and modest casket. The idea of a simple coffin is to focus on a person's good deeds and good name, and not on the outer trappings of life. This casket is made entirely from natural material (usually pine or another wood) that will decompose in the ground and allow the body to return to the earth as quickly as possible. The casket typically has many small holes drilled across the bottom to enable the earth to come directly into contact with the body, thereby hastening the decomposition process. The use of metal nails or bracing in a wooden casket is discouraged, because metal is considered the material of weapons and war. The casket interior should also be plain and unadorned.

In Israel, the body is dressed in a shroud and buried directly in the earth. A coffin is used only in exceptional circumstances. Jewish burial in general is noted to be eco-friendly, because the body decomposes and returns to the earth without causing additional damage to the environment.

INDIVIDUAL IN-GROUND OR FIELD BURIAL (*KEVURAT SADEH*)

With in-ground burial, a member of the *ḥevra kaddisha* may climb into the grave to assist with the burial of the body, while typically outside of Israel, the casket is mechanically lowered into the ground. The body or casket is gently lowered feet first and face up in the grave. In Israel, if a tallit is covering the shroud, it is usually removed at this time. Concrete cinder blocks are placed above the body, Psalm 91 is said, and a pile of fresh earth that was removed when the hole was made is now placed by members of the *ḥevra kaddisha* and funeral attendees in the grave. Family and friends then shovel additional earth into the grave, covering the body in its entirety.

This is another very heartfelt moment, as the sounds of earth being shoveled on the grave provide a very stark reminder that the death once again is indeed very real, and you and your loved one are now separated. As one person so aptly described it, "My loved one is now lovingly enveloped like a blanket and embraced by the earth of the Land of Israel," and this in itself is comforting.

We return the body to the earth that is its source. This is our final act of caring, and it is considered a great mitzva to physically participate in the burial.

The back of the shovel is sometimes used for shoveling earth into the grave during burial. The shovel is also not passed from person to person, but is instead stuck back into the pile of earth after each person helps shovel so as not to transfer pain from one person to the next. The reason for these unusual customs is that at this moment nothing feels normal, especially this final act of saying goodbye. Burial is seen as a true act of *ḥesed,* lovingkindness, as those who choose to assist in shoveling are seen as sending the deceased to their final resting place. We learn the importance of this mitzva from God Himself, who buried Moses.

ḤESED SHEL EMET (TRUE KINDNESS)

When Jacob summoned his son Joseph before he died, he requested that he transport his remains from Egypt and bury him in the Land of Israel. He referred to this as doing "*ḥesed ve'emet,*" kindness and truth for him (Gen. 47:29). Our rabbis explain that kindness for the deceased is referred to as "true kindness," and is the highest form of *ḥesed* that there is. The reason is that when we do a kindness for a living person there is always the possibility that the recipient of the favor will repay us somehow. However, when doing something for the deceased, there is no expectation of receiving anything in return.

The term *ḥesed shel emet* is also applied to the preparation of the body for burial as well as the involvement in the burial itself. It also includes any acts of kindness done by a member of the community or the *ḥevra kaddisha* for the deceased.

I came to the funeral, but I was not sure what my role should be. Am I here to just stand back and watch as I pay my respects to the deceased? I feel uncomfortable and wonder if it is my place to be involved further. In the discomfort and the not knowing, halakha directs us step by step just how to be there, first for the deceased and then afterwards for the mourners, in this time of great sadness and loss. Having something to do is so important, especially at a time when you don't know what to do. Judaism directs me to be an active participant in the burial process which, like other aspects of accompanying the deceased, is considered a great mitzva and also the greatest kindness – ḥesed shel emet. It's the highest form of ḥesed because it cannot be "paid back." So, I pick up the shovel and then afterwards I help make the line that the mourners will pass through, and offer them words of comfort, reminding them that at this time they are not alone.

OTHER FORMS OF BURIAL

Due to lack of space for standard in-ground (side-by-side) burial, the shortage and costly purchase of land, and concern for the environment, cemeteries now offer other burial options.

Double burial (kevurat makhpela)

This involves two people who wish to be buried next to each other in a double plot where one person typically predeceases the other. In this paired burial, there is often a joint headstone.

Layered tier burial (kevurat komot)

This involves multiple burials of two or more family members in a single in-ground grave, one above the other, each separated by earth and stone. There is typically a single common headstone, divided into dedications for each person buried there.

Multi-tier above-ground entombment (kevurat kukhin)

The deceased is placed onto a platform or shelf that is inserted into a burial niche or alcove in the wall. This above-ground burial may contain up to four bodies, each separated by earth and in their own niche. The opening is then caulked closed, and a bronze or stone external headstone embedded on the front wall. This burial may be noisier than you may have anticipated.

> *I arrived at my neighbor's funeral to discover that the burial was not as I expected. After the eulogies, we followed the funeral procession and found ourselves in front of a wall. The rabbi and the mourners spoke lovingly again of the deceased. Instead of the customary burial in the ground, the deceased was removed from the gurney and placed into a shelf in the wall. It was strange to hear the sound of the metal as my neighbor was literally put into the wall, and the wall was then sealed closed, a sight I had never seen before. It somehow seemed to take longer than I expected as I watched the ḥevra kaddisha perform this task and then step down off the ladder onto the ground. The whole experience reminded me of the shock I felt when I attended my first funeral in Israel and discovered that there was no casket, but rather just the form of the deceased on the gurney. I was comforted by being able to put a stone on the shelf in front of the grave. In this day and age, where land here in Israel is so scarce, this type of burial is becoming more commonplace, more*

affordable, and definitely saves precious space that can be used to build for future generations.

Bone gathering (likut atzamot)

Another method that has been proposed is referred to as bone gathering. This involves collecting bones approximately a year after a temporary burial and then reinterring the remaining bones into a much smaller ossuary. This is then placed in a family plot or multi-tier alcove, thereby enabling many more burials. While this space-saving idea was carried out in Second Temple times, and has recently sparked much interest, it is not yet supported by all.

BURIAL *KADDISH*

A specific version of *Kaddish* recited only at the time of burial, says: "The Lord has given, and the Lord has taken. May the name of the Lord be blessed."

At the very moment when our faith is most shaken, when we might feel angry at and distanced from God for the death of someone dear to us, we rise to recite the praises of the Creator: "*Yitgadal veyitkadash shemeh rabba* – Magnified and sanctified be He who created the universe." The *Kaddish* prayer is found in ancient sources bracketed by the *Tzidduk Hadin*, the prayer justifying God's decree.

The *Kaddish* prayer dates back to the first century B.C.E. It was written mostly in Aramaic, as that was the spoken language of most Jews at the time. Aramaic was used so that every individual would understand the prayer. By the sixth century, *Kaddish* was part of the synagogue service. There are five forms of *Kaddish* that are recited. "Mourner's *Kaddish*" is not a prayer for the dead, but rather a prayer that praises God, which is evident from the key words: "*Yeheh shemeh rabba mevarakh* – May His great name be blessed."

PLACING A STONE ON THE GRAVE

At the end of the funeral, the Mourner's *Kaddish* and *E-l Maleh Raḥamim* (Prayer for the Deceased) are recited. Stones are then placed on the grave as a personal marker by family and those in attendance. This custom is typically repeated whenever anyone visits the gravesite in the future – a reminder that we have been there and that our loved one is not forgotten.

> *"Grass withers and flowers fade" (Is. 40:6–7). Flowers, though beautiful, will eventually die. A stone will not die, and can symbolize the permanence of memory and legacy. In moments when we are faced with the fragility of life, Judaism reminds us that there is permanence amidst the pain. While other things fade, stones and souls endure.*
>
> Adapted from D. J. Wolpe, "Why Stones Instead of Flowers?" in *Wrestling with the Angel*, p. 129

> *When my daughter was in the Israeli army, she served in the Educational Corps, teaching Jewish history and Zionism to soldiers in the process of converting to Judaism. The army included a trip to Mount Herzl, the military cemetery in Jerusalem, as part of the curriculum. My daughter heard from her commanding officer that the idea of placing a stone (even in Hebrew) on the graves stands for aleph – av or em (father or mother), bet – ben or bat (son or daughter), nun – nin or nina (grandson or granddaughter). Although this life has ended, there is continuity from generation to generation, which helps keep that person's memory alive. When we, too, visit the cemetery, we frequently visit others whom we have lost and continue to hold dear in our heart, leaving a stone behind.*

PREPARING TO LEAVE THE GRAVESITE

Following the completion of the burial, it is customary for the funeral attendees to form two parallel lines, making space for the mourners to pass through the rows and receive support and words of comfort from the community.

There is a custom for people leaving the *kever,* the gravesite, to take a different route from the one in which they came, in order not to retrace the steps that were directed towards death and burial. This metaphorically describes what we experience at a funeral, in that we do not return the same way in which we came. We are hopefully touched by the words of the eulogy we just heard, and are encouraged by the achievements and good traits of the deceased. We make a decision to improve our lives and cherish our days.

As people prepare to leave the cemetery, the mourners may remove their leather shoes and put on non-leather ones, especially if close to sunset. The mourners may sit down so that they can be comforted right there in the cemetery – allowing this day to conclude the first day of shiva.

This is a very important transition period, as the focus now shifts from the deceased to comforting the mourner, a change in status from *aninut* to *avelut.*

WASHING YOUR HANDS

The interment has taken place, the funeral is over, all attendees wash their hands as a symbol of ritual purification, and the mourners now leave for the place in which they will typically sit shiva for the next seven days. If you do not have the opportunity to wash, upon returning from the cemetery, someone may have placed a bowl, a washing cup, and a towel outside your door.

There are different reasons for the custom of washing your hands upon leaving the cemetery. Washing our hands is a symbol of purity. Today, the *kohanim* wash their hands before blessing the congregation. When leaving the cemetery, we symbolically "wash away" the ritual impurity associated with death. Washing our hands can also be seen as a life-affirming ritual. After an encounter with death, we wash our hands as we do in the morning – when our "souls" are returned to us – alternating pouring water from one hand to the other as we do in preparation for a new day.

In addition, the Torah (Deut. 21:1–4) describes a ritual carried out by village elders when a dead body was found outside the city limits and the cause of death was unknown. The elders would wash their hands and say, "Our hands did not shed this blood, nor did our eyes see this crime." Washing our hands at the cemetery symbolically affirms that we did not shed innocent blood.

Many people don't dry their hands afterwards but rather shake off the water and allow them to air dry. This may symbolize the ambivalence around wanting to "wipe away" our sadness while keeping the memory of the deceased with us even as life moves on.

> *Today in Israel is Memorial Day for fallen soldiers and victims of terror. A grieving brother who wishes to remain anonymous wrote me as follows:*
>
> *When we leave the cemetery, we observe two customs. It's one moment before we get into a hot car that was standing in the sun, one moment before looking at our cell phones, one moment before getting back to the world.*
>
> *The first custom is to place a stone on the grave. A stone symbolizes building. It symbolizes our taking the legacy and the spirit of the one who passed away and building the world in their light. A flower fades but a stone endures.*
>
> *But there is one more custom: On leaving the cemetery, we wash our hands. We take a vessel and fill it with "living" water*

that symbolizes blossoming and growth. We pour the water over our hands that represent creative work.

I once went on a group tour of Mount Herzl and happened to meet Miriam Peretz there. She lost two sons to war and, turning to our group, spoke as follows: "Stones and living water are not just meant as customs. They incorporate a perspective that we must take with us as we venture forth from this holy day."

In the memory of my brother, in the memory of them all.

Sivan Rahav-Meir,
"The Daily Thought," April 25, 2023

Chapter 4

Shiva

When you walked out of your house to attend the funeral, your focus was on burying your loved one. When you return, hours later from the funeral and cemetery, the focus will have gradually shifted to now be on you, the mourner. One of the most healing traditions that Judaism offers to mourners after a death is that of shiva. One literally "sits shiva" – sits on a low chair and receives visitors for seven days, with the exception of Shabbat, when there are no outward signs of mourning.

The day of the funeral will count as the first day of shiva as long as the burial takes place before sunset. (In Jewish tradition, the day begins and ends at sunset.) Shiva ends on the morning of the seventh day (after the burial). After the mourners have completed the morning prayers (Shaḥarit) on that day, they sit for a few minutes, and then they "get up."

The first reference to a seven-day mourning period is in Genesis, when Joseph spent seven days mourning for his father Jacob. (Gen. 50:10) According to the Jerusalem Talmud,

> Moses enacted seven days of rejoicing after marriage (*sheva berakhot*) and also seven days of mourning. The Talmud (Moed Katan) explains that just as the rejoicing on the holidays of Passover and Sukkot are seven days, so too, when it comes to mourning we mourn for seven days. Mystically the number seven is seen as a complete unit of time, as in the seven days of a week.

Jewish law considers the bereaved to be those who have lost any one of these close relatives: a father or a mother, a wife or a husband, a son or a daughter, a brother or a sister.

During shiva, people come to give comfort and offer their condolences to the family of the deceased. Shiva provides the opportunity not only to deal with the death of your loved one, but also to remember the life of a person who is no longer there.

You may be sitting shiva at the home of the deceased, your home, or elsewhere, depending on the situation. You may choose to sit with the other mourners or be in a different location. Some family members spend the entire shiva in one house and sleep there, others spend the day together but go home at night, and some may even "split" the shiva between two or more locations, depending on the circumstances.

CLOTHING OF THE MOURNER THROUGHOUT SHIVA

Regardless of where you sit shiva, your clothing will identify you as a mourner and will reflect your somber mood. It is customary not to wear leather shoes during the shiva period. You may change out of your leather shoes at the cemetery if that begins the first day of shiva, but otherwise you might change shoes as soon as you get to the place in which you are sitting shiva. During the shiva, mourners often wear slippers, non-leather shoes, or just socks. Leather shoes are considered comfortable, and their removal demonstrates again your disinterest in vanity or physical comfort at this painful time. There is a biblical basis for this, too, as the prophet Ezekiel was told to remove his shoes while he was in mourning. With respect to the clothing you tore (*kriya*) at the funeral, you'll wear this throughout the entire week of shiva, with the exception of Shabbat.

THE MEAL OF CONSOLATION

A meal of consolation, *seudat havra'a* is typically provided for the mourners by friends, neighbors, or a synagogue committee. It is the first meal after returning from the cemetery, and begins the shiva process. The meal generally includes "round" foods, such as lentils, hardboiled eggs, and bagels, to symbolize the cyclical and continuous nature of life. Being the recipient of a meal provided by neighbors or relatives is very comforting, reminding mourners that they aren't alone in their grief.

Another, deeper psychological reason lies behind this gesture, for it recognizes that mourners, having just returned from the trauma of the burial, may not want to go on any more without their loved one. A person may ask themselves, "How can I eat at a time like this?" Eating, however, is very life affirming, and a significant part of Jewish custom. As a recipient of the meal of consolation, you are given a strong message that you have a responsibility to continue living, and you need to be strong for others and for yourself. It's significant that this meal is prepared by others and that it is almost as if the mourner is being "fed." The mourner does not want to think about trivial questions like, "What do you want to eat?" "What are you in the mood for?" Most probably the answer to both those questions would be "nothing" or "I don't care." As the mourner, you are spared the need to make a decision about something as mundane as eating, which at this time is already so difficult.

Throughout the week of shiva, you will be taken care of and served by family members or community members. It is a very strange feeling to have other people wait on you, especially if you are accustomed to taking care of others. It also feels uncomfortable not to get up when a guest enters or to accompany them to the door at the end of a visit. All of these behaviors that are generally deemed as appropriate are suspended at this time, when you should not have to be bothered with social courtesies.

TIP: It is beneficial if someone who is close to the family, but not one of the mourners, "runs" the shiva house. There are many logistics that need to be attended to, such as receiving food, serving the mourners, as well as keeping the house in order. This task can be shared by a rota of people, each responsible for taking care of the house and mourners for a period of time. This enables the mourners to sit and not have to be concerned about the mundane activities in the functioning of the house. This may be a way for the "disenfranchised mourners" – sons- or daughters-in-law, grandchildren, close friends, or others – to have a role and be included in an important part of the shiva process, even though they are not actually sitting shiva.

My mom died twenty-seven years ago. The funeral was enormous – so many people, and yet I only remember a few in attendance. I do remember the police escort to the cemetery from the funeral. And I do remember returning home. Outside of my home was a pitcher, a wash basin, and a cloth. This was the first sign that something had changed from when I left that morning. We washed our hands and entered to the sight of covered mirrors, a reminder that this is not a time of focusing on your own appearance, when inside you feel such pain. In addition, there was a large candle that would burn for the entire week, a box of prayer books, chairs for all of the mourners, and a few wonderful women from the sisterhood – angels who had prepared the house to make it ready for a week of visitors.

I removed my leather shoes and was guided over to sit in a shiva chair and handed a plate with a bagel and a hardboiled egg. This meal was bland, and did not taste good. Nothing at this moment could have. I can close my eyes and still remember chewing – just going through the motions, a feeling I had many times throughout the entire week of movement through a sea of numbness, or reduced feeling. Where was I and how did I get here? I asked myself. It all seemed so surreal. The moment passed and I somehow moved into a state of being taken care of, and for the next many days our house was full – full of people, so many people, and yet in my own house, I was the one being taken care of.

Additional angels showed up to prepare and feed us meals each day, and somehow organize the house at night before the early arrival the next morning of men for minyan. Such a strange feeling. Such tremendous compassion. But these were the men and women, arriving early in the morning for minyan and leaving as the doors finally closed around ten p.m., who were there for us lovingly and seemed to mourn alongside me during this ever so strange period called shiva. These were the people who literally moved me through the period following the death of my beloved mother, back into the world of the living. They brought themselves and their stories and their love and their wonderful cakes and meals and laughter and tears. I know more than anything that I could not have imagined getting through the week without them. In the same way that I wonder now, how as a Jewish woman I could survive my week without Shabbat, I cannot imagine surviving my losses without the wonderful customs of shiva and the people who embraced me at such a difficult time in my life.

CUSTOMS IN A SHIVA HOUSE

There are many customs (*minhagim*) around shiva, but very few hard and fast rules (halakhot). You need to do what is right for you. Sometimes you will know just what that is, and at other times you may only know it in hindsight. Each shiva may feel different. You'll need to give yourself time and self-compassion, neither of which is easy.

In the house where the shiva is being held, the door is often left unlocked or ajar to allow visitors to enter quietly without the distraction of doorbells or knocking. The door left slightly open is also a reminder that this is not a "social call," and the mourner is not your host. You have come to comfort them.

You may have a seven-day memorial candle, which burns throughout the duration of the week. This is called a *Yizkor* candle or *ner neshama*. The symbolism comes from the book of Proverbs: "*Ner Hashem nishmat adam* – The person's soul is a candle of the Lord." Although the body is gone, the soul of the person continues to "shine" and give light forever.

The mirrors throughout the home are covered, as during shiva, your concerns are not with physicality and vanity regarding how you look, but rather on your personal loss. Generally, mourners do not leave the home during shiva. Nor do they shave, use makeup, or attempt to "look their best." Intimate relations between a husband and wife are suspended during the week of shiva.

The custom of covering mirrors conveys to the grief-stricken individual that personal appearance simply does not matter now. Frequently, too, prayer services are held in the shiva house. Since one is not supposed to pray in front of their reflection in a mirror, your focus again is not on yourself, but rather on God.

> *I heard another reason for covering the mirrors. When we see our reflection in the mirror, we often see "our father's eyes" or "our mother's smile" or are reminded of people saying, "you and your brother look so much alike." These memories may be especially painful during the intense shiva period, so we cover the mirrors and for the time-being, spare mourners from this added pain.*

During shiva mourners will often sit on a low chair, sofa (without cushions), a cardboard or wooden box, a mattress, or even on the floor with or without pillows. This position of being "low" is said to reflect your feelings at this time. This also distinguishes you, the mourner, from others in the house. If you are elderly or have health issues, you might want to consult with a rabbi about sitting on a regular chair.

> The friends of Job "sat with him on the ground for seven days and seven nights" (Job 2:13).

After losing someone, it is often comforting to focus on giving to others. It is customary to have a *tzedaka* (charity) box in a shiva house so that people may donate money in memory of the deceased. Some may give *tzedaka* when they visit, and others may make a donation to charity or give money towards a gift to the synagogue in your loved one's name as a way to honor their memory. You may be receiving acknowledgements of this for many months after your loss.

> King Solomon proclaimed, "*Tzedaka* can save people from death" (Proverbs 10:2). We also recite in the High Holy Days liturgy that repentance, prayer, and charity can ward off the evil decree. For this reason, people give *tzedaka* in the name of the deceased to hasten the redemption of their soul.

MINYAN IN A SHIVA HOUSE

It is customary, especially if there are mourners who are reciting *Kaddish,* to hold services in the shiva house. Someone may need to arrange for a Torah scroll and prayer books. Some people hold three services a day, others only one or two. If services are being held, usually one of the mourners will lead the service. If you do not feel comfortable doing so, another community member may lead the prayers.

You may feel that the daily minyanim are comforting and give the days of shiva some structure. It may also give you the push to get out of bed (when you don't want to), knowing that people are coming for early morning prayers. If prayers are held in the early afternoon or evening, it may also provide a welcome respite for the mourners to get up, go to the bathroom, stretch, and take a break from conversation. The minyan times should be both convenient for you as well as for those who are coming to support you. In some communities, the attendees split themselves between synagogue attendance and the shiva house. This requires coordination to ensure that the shiva house is assured of a minyan so the mourners can recite *Kaddish*. Some visitors may choose to participate in the services, while others may choose not to.

PRAYERS THAT ARE CHANGED OR ADDED IN A SHIVA HOUSE

The *Shulḥan Arukh* (OC 131:4) rules that we do not recite *Taḥanun* (Supplication) in a mourner's house. Also called *nefilat apayim* ("falling on the face"), *Taḥanun* is a prayer unit containing confessions of sins as well as petitions for God's grace and mercy, which is recited immediately after the reader's repetition of the *Amida* in the weekday morning and afternoon services (Shaḥarit and Minḥa). It is usually omitted on holidays and happy occasions. The Levush (Mordecai ben Avraham Yoffe) writes that there is no *Taḥanun* in a house of mourning, since it is not appropriate to bring up Hashem's attribute of justice in the mourner's house, as a death has just occurred. We do not want to add to the mourner's grief by highlighting God's judgment.

In Israel, the Priestly Blessing, *Birkat Kohanim,* is usually not recited, but it depends on Sephardic or Ashkenazi custom. There are different customs regarding the recitation of Hallel, and a rabbi should be consulted.

Psalm 49 is recited after the morning and evening service and in some *nusaḥim* (versions) at Minḥa instead of Maariv. At certain times, Psalm 16, *Mikhtam leDavid* is recited instead.

Psalm 49 acknowledges death as part of life. Our time on this earth is short-lived. It is too valuable to waste. In verse 17, the author says: "*al tira ki ya'ashir ish* – Don't be troubled by envy when you see that a man grows rich [while you remain poor]." "*Ki yirbbeh kavod beito* – When he increases the glory of his house." Such concerns are mistaken, "*Ki lo vemoto yekaḥ hak-kol* – For upon his death, he will not take anything with him." "*Lo yered aḥarav kevodo* – His glory and all his possessions will not descend [into the grave] after him."

The psalm looks at the role of material possessions in a person's life. We were put on this earth for a higher purpose, not simply to accumulate and enjoy material possessions. In the end "we can't take it with us." We should not take pride in our money and possessions, but rather in the good we have done. The psalm asks: "[What does the rich man think?] "*Viḥi od lanetzaḥ* – That he will live forever," "*lo yireh hashaḥat* – never to see the pit." "*Ki yireh ḥakhamim yamutu* – When the rich man sees that even wise men die," does he still think that he can cheat death? "*Yaḥad kesil vava'ar yovedu* – When he sees that the fool and the boor both perish,"

> "*Ve'azvu la'aḥerim ḥeilam* – And leave their hard-earned wealth to others," does he still think he will live forever?
>
> R. Yitzchok Kirzner, Nafshi Project: Tehillim (https://nafshi.org/category/tehillim)

Having sat shiva personally gave me insight that, as a visitor coming to a minyan in the shiva house, I never had previously. Wondering if people would show up early in the morning, waiting as people slowly arrived and hoping we would have a minyan, filled me with anxiety and a sense of dread. I realize how important it is for people to show up on time and not be late, especially as others need to leave to go to work. I so much appreciated all those who made an effort to come daily and ensure that we had a minyan.

Suddenly when there is a death announcement, a sign on the fence and the door, you realize your neighbor who you hardly knew had a loss. You may not be at all close, but you bake muffins and off you go. It somehow completely changed the relationship we had with each other. Not a religious family, they were so happy that my husband joined in when it was time for Minḥa prayers.

TORAH STUDY IN A SHIVA HOUSE

The study of Torah is not permitted for the individual mourners during shiva, as it is considered a source of joy. As it is written in Psalms 19:9: "*Pikudei Hashem yesharim mesamḥei lev* – The laws of God are righteous and rejoice the heart." However, a mourner may read about the laws of mourning and study books on ethical behavior.

Nevertheless, in a community setting, words of Torah are encouraged, and thus it is common for someone to speak after the *tefilla*. It is considered an honor for the soul of the departed when Torah is studied in their memory. It is appropriate to connect the words of Torah to the *middot* (good character traits) of the deceased. It is also customary to study sections from the Mishna (משנה, Oral Law) on each day that *Kaddish* is recited. Sometimes, chapters of Mishna whose initial letters comprise the Hebrew name of the deceased are chosen. One reason is that the word Mishna has the same Hebrew letters as the word *neshama* (נשמה, soul). Many people have the custom of dividing the study of all the tractates of the Mishna amongst friends and family, completing it by the *sheloshim*.

THE WEEK OF SHIVA

The first three days of shiva are in many ways considered to be more intense, given the rawness of the recent burial. Some feel that only very close friends and family should be in the house of mourning, because the mourner is so bereft at this time and not as open to the comfort provided by others. This depends on many factors, not least of which is the nature of the death.

It is also important to take into consideration whether the mourner has a support system available in the form of family and friends. Comforting the mourner is an important mitzva, and if there is a chance that the mourner will be alone with no visitors, or that you will not have an opportunity to visit another time, it is acceptable to visit during the first three days.

SHIVA FOR THE MOURNER

You needn't be alone with your loss. On the contrary, it is important to share grief with others, and surround yourself with family, friends, and fellow mourners. Shiva can be a time to gather and strengthen each other through stories, prayer, viewing photographs, food, and just about anything else. Children and grandchildren can participate by printing pictures to pass around. It is a time to be there and support each other as individuals and within the family. This is a time of reflection, healing, and even growth. Tears of joy and tears of sorrow may at times go hand in hand, and this, too, may feel so strange. Daily life is in no way the same. There is no "business as usual," as for the moment, every single thing has changed. There are periods where it can feel very intense, and just the sight of someone who knows you or your loved one can bring back a painful reminder of a time of past connection. Seeing people you haven't seen in many years, or contemporaries of the deceased, may also bring mixed emotions. You may experience tears of joy, and even laughter, for memories that were once shared; and while this might feel inappropriate, it may indeed provide great comfort for you.

There are quiet times, too, when you can attend to logistics with other family members. There are also times when you wish that the last visitor for the evening would soon depart. Shiva is so much more exhausting than one could imagine, especially if one has spent days before sitting in a hospital with the loved one or has flown in from far away. Often by the end of the day you feel talked out, your voice is strained, and you are long past ready to fall into bed. Then, when you finally lie down to sleep, you may discover that you are preoccupied with all kinds of thoughts and concerns. Shiva is for the mourner, and it is always important that visitors take their cue from you in every way with respect to the timing of the visit and even what to say or not say. The shiva period is a gift. Given permission to talk about your loved one and having a dedicated time to mourn is very therapeutic, albeit exhausting in every way.

You may want to have a guest book (at the funeral home or shiva house), where people can offer condolences, write stories, or share memories. These may be read at a later time, and are often very comforting to the family. For those who are unable to visit, letters, emails, and other messages are often sent. These may be read by the mourners at a quiet time during and after shiva.

> *When my mom died, my dad wasn't sure how he felt about sitting shiva. I think he questioned if it would be too much for him. He knew I was sitting, and we agreed to take it one day at a time. At the end of shiva, he expressed such gratitude that we had had this time together to honor my mom. I think he was shocked by all the people who came to be there for him. He talked and talked, often retelling the same stories to all who came; he played with the young grandchildren who brought life to the shiva house; and he "greeted" the men who came to make the minyan each morning. It almost felt as if he looked forward to it each day, as it provided him with a framework in which to place his grief. It kept him focused and busy, and allowed him to be with his loss in a safe place surrounded by those he cared for. Without a doubt, he found it incredibly therapeutic, something he definitely did not anticipate.*

> *During the shiva for my father, I had the opportunity to spend time with my uncles, my father's younger brothers. After morning prayers and before visitors started to come, they would tell me stories about their childhood in Mexico and in Israel, during the early days of the state. I had heard many of their stories over the years from my father. It was fascinating to hear the same stories from a different storyteller, providing it with a different perspective. Those early morning chats were very special. I learned things about my father from his brothers that I never would have heard otherwise.*

When my Dad died at the age of eighty-three, I was already living in Israel and was fortunate to be there with him for his last few days in the hospital and then for the week of shiva. Shiva is an amazing thing, and when I think of the people who put themselves in a place of discomfort to actually come and visit me, I am deeply touched. Yes, there was the woman who, within minutes of arriving home from the cemetery, I overheard telling a friend in a very loud voice that she came now as it was convenient for her. (Without a doubt, someone grieving is far more sensitive to the nuances of conversation and actions, and this felt painful.) But more importantly were the two women, younger than I, who came to see me during the middle of the day, in the middle of shiva when the house was quiet, not necessarily a time someone might choose to come because it's more difficult to slip in and out of the house unnoticed. With each of us having young children, and not having known them well as I had lived in another country for the past six years, I was surprised but so very touched and honored that they came to see me. Would I have gone to see them had they lost a parent? I am not sure, but their visit to me taught me a very important lesson. Even though you may not have known the deceased at all, or the mourner well, your very presence can go such a long way towards helping someone else heal. They gave me an opportunity to talk about my dad, a stellar member of the community, and they listened and asked questions with tremendous interest. As such, their visit stood out more than any other, was a real gift to me from the heart, and strengthened me for my return to Israel – where I then received my friends who had over the years become my "family," even though many did not know my dad.

On a personal level, there may be intense times filled with emotion, and other times when you may be surprised at how little you actually feel. You may not have shed a tear, and perhaps wonder why.

The tone of shiva will in many ways be determined by the nature of the loss. The sudden and unexpected death of a young person in the prime of their life will feel very different from the death of someone in their nineties who has lived a full life. In situations where one has experienced anticipatory loss for a long period, shiva, too, may feel very different. This is especially true after a prolonged illness or advanced dementia (with lack of memory and recognition for a loved one), and where it has been clear that the situation would continue to deteriorate. Tremendous sadness for all that was lost even prior to the death, accompanied by mixed feelings of guilt and relief that your loved one's suffering is finally over, make grieving more complex. The process of self-forgiveness, as well as giving yourself permission to let go of any guilt, acknowledging what can't be changed, and exploring regrets as well as forgiveness towards the deceased and other family members, are tasks that will likely not be addressed during shiva. While worthy goals to explore, the week of shiva may not allow enough time or energy for you to be emotionally or physically ready to begin this process. There will be plenty of time later on.

You do not grieve with just your heart and soul. You grieve with your entire body. Although you may have been resilient, and possibly carried the burden of your loved one's illness as well as their loss, you probably have dealt with tremendous emotional and physical upheaval for some time, especially during this period in which your eating, sleeping, and just about everything else has been totally disrupted. Sooner or later, your body feels the stress you have been under, and it is not unusual to suddenly discover seemingly unexplained symptoms starting to emerge. These aches and pains may be new, or ones you were previously unaware of or ignored. It is a reminder that there is no one way to grieve, and everyone's response, both emotional and physical, will be very individual. As strong as you may be, you won't necessarily know how you will respond until you are in the situation. Grief often carries with it such a sense of overwhelming sadness, shock, and distress. It is hard to imagine beyond today, and even thinking about the here and now of today and this moment can be very stressful. The tightness in your chest, and feelings of isolation and loneliness, can leave you with a feeling of not being in control. Sudden memories or events may lead to a periodic upsurge of grief – which is very normal, but quite unpleasant. People do get sick, however, and grief may be the catalyst for a visit to the doctor.

TIP: Please don't neglect yourself and attribute everything to grief. If you are feeling unwell, seek medical attention, but also let your doctor know that you have recently suffered a loss.

THOUGHTS DURING SHIVA

During shiva, you may find yourself reflecting on the days and months leading up to the death. While you may have felt that you did not have enough time with your loved one, this may be tempered by the degree of discomfort they were in, and their own readiness for departing from this world. You may ask yourself if you ever could have had enough time to be together, and in what way having time or lacking time may have changed anything. It is important to focus on the positive in terms of the time that you did have together, and what you were able to accomplish during this very difficult period. It is natural to focus on what you may have done differently, and the "what ifs" had you "only known," but this only leads to guilt, which takes you nowhere. You may feel better when you focus on all that you did do, and not what you didn't. We all regret things that in hindsight we wished we had been able to do differently. Please look to find a place of forgiveness for yourself and others whom you love. This is essential in order to move on in your grieving. This may not be easy, especially given that these are the early days after such a traumatic loss. As time goes on, and if you are struggling with this, it may be helpful to discuss it with a professional.

> *Death's unanswered questions*
> *After my loved one died, there were so many questions that seemed to go through my mind, with so little clarity with respect to answers. I often had a lot of self-blame. Did I do all that I could do? Was our relationship as good as it could have been? Was I there for them? Could I have done anything differently? Is this really happening to me? Was it okay if I wasn't there? Was it okay if I did not say my final goodbyes or I love you – could there ever be a final goodbye that I would be okay with? How can I make sense of it all? Am I allowed to be angry with God? Do I need to ask forgiveness? Sometimes I think I need answers, and other times I feel as if I need to allow myself not to think – to turn off all of my thoughts. It all feels as if it is too much. I feel so out of control. Living with such pain and with so many unanswered questions is so difficult. People tell me that I need to give it time. I simply cannot imagine that that will change anything. I don't really know how I feel. I want to wake up and know that this was all a bad dream.*

REFLECTIONS: MAKING SENSE OF SHIVA

Shiva is Judaism's remedy for carrying you out of the depth of sorrow and sadness back into the land of the living. Much that you do this week is so different from any behavior you would have described as "normal or typical" of who you are. You've just had a tremendous loss, and may feel incredibly alone.

Your house is full of people from all walks of life, at all hours, and they see you at your worst – bedroom slippers, ripped shirt, no makeup or perfume, and eyes that reveal more than you'd like. This is not a time of vanity, and in fact you will stay in the same outer clothes, rent top, barely having showered, and unshaven all week. People, some of whom you may not know at all or know well, simply walk in – with no warning. They don't even ring your bell. And you don't even get up from your seat to greet them or offer them as much as a glass of water. No, you stay seated in your very low (and usually uncomfortable) seat. How strange is that? These people may come from near or from far, be close friends of the family or you may barely know them. They may stay briefly or overstay their welcome. They may come over and talk to you or ask questions about your loved one; they may simply take a chair and sit down in silence. They may wait until you speak to them first, and if you are busy, or speaking to others, or are unable to speak – that, too, will be okay. They may come and go without a single word being exchanged between you. There may also be periods of awkward silence that neither you nor the visitor will fill in. You may be lost in your own thoughts. That is okay, and it is up to you to set the tone. Regardless, their eyes and face may suggest that they are very much there for you, and words themselves may seem irrelevant. Sometimes there are simply no words; nothing can be said or need be said. The role of the visitor is simply to be there and join you in your pain.

During this week, you generally don't leave your house, certainly not to go to work; you may go to the synagogue for prayer if there is no minyan in your home. This week resembles no other. Yet, your sense of loneliness and despair after your loss is somehow reduced as you derive comfort from people simply being there, being very much present for you. When visitors say, "Tell me about your loved one" and you have the opportunity to talk and share photos, moments, or stories that were meaningful and perhaps even funny, over and over to a variety of people during the week, it enables laughter, tears and true healing to take place. Hearing stories from visitors that you may have never heard before also provides comfort, in that they reveal an aspect of your loved one that you may have never known. Even someone stating that they are so sorry for your loss or that they have no words or don't know what to say, speaks volumes with respect to their being there for you and showing that they care. This experience may repeat itself over and over again throughout the week and, in a very strange way, your raw and unprocessed feelings somehow get transformed. The process of shiva truly works.

> *When my mother was ill, she said in passing, "You don't have to sit shiva for me when I die." In my mind, it was never a question, as of course I would sit shiva. She spoke often about the celebration of life, and wanted her death to not be steeped in sadness. She felt she had a life well lived in spite of its relatively short duration. I think she said this to me to unburden me of any sense of responsibility. My response was, "Of course I will sit shiva. Shiva is important, and its goal is to bring comfort to those still alive." When she heard this, she then agreed that it would be okay to sit shiva, under those circumstances.*

FAMILY DISAGREEMENTS DURING SHIVA

As much as shiva is a time to draw comfort by being together with other family members, it may also bring up present and past areas of conflict. Being in the shiva house together at a time when people are especially fragile can create friction, especially if there were strained relationships before the death. Disputes about caregiving, financial issues, how to deal with the deceased's belongings, what to write on the tombstone, and the contents of the will when it is probated may all cause arguments. Knowing in advance that these may be issues at the time of shiva may lead family members to decide to sit in different places in order to avoid conflict. Likewise, in families where there has been a remarriage, if there is tension between various family members, the decision may be made to sit separately. After shiva, family members may choose to meet with a mediator to help work through some of the issues that were not resolved – or were in fact made worse before or as a result of the death.

> *When my husband's grandfather died, his mother and her two sisters were standing together at the cemetery. A female member of the ḥevra kaddisha approached each one of the women to help them tear kriya, and gave them a piece of paper with a printed prayer.*
>
> *My mother-in-law asked the woman what was in the prayer and why it should be said. Her answer was that it was a prayer so they would "not fight with each other over the inheritance." My mother-in-law was annoyed. She was close with her sisters, and she was insulted by the insinuation that the death of their father would cause them to fight. She gave the paper back to the woman.*
>
> *During the week of shiva, my mother-in-law shared with me that many of the visitors had shared stories regarding the arguments they had with their siblings regarding the will and inheritance left by their parents. People told stories about siblings not being on speaking terms with each other. My mother-in-law admitted: "The lady at the cemetery was right. We should say a prayer before the burial that we will not fight over the inheritance."*

COMFORTING THE MOURNERS

The Jewish value of *niḥum aveilim*, comforting mourners, refers to the obligation to visit the house of mourning during the shiva period. The Talmud (Sota 14a) teaches that consoling mourners was originally an act of God. Citing Genesis 25:11, which states: "After the death of Abraham, God brought blessing to Isaac, his son," the Talmud states that just as Isaac was consoled by God's presence after his loss, so, too, are we commanded to bring comfort to loved ones with our presence.

> Many commentators cite Job 2:12–13 as the first instance of a condolence call, with respect to Job's three friends: "And they sat down with him upon the ground seven days and seven nights, and none spoke a word to him, for they saw that his grief was very great. After this, Job began to speak...."

It is customary for those coming to comfort the mourner to not initiate conversation but rather to wait and respond only when the mourner begins to speak.

VISITORS DURING SHIVA

It is sometimes difficult for visitors to know when to make a shiva visit, as no time may feel like the right time. While some consider it customary for only family and close friends to visit in the first few days of shiva (because the pain is considered so intense), many believe that comforting the mourner already began at the time of the funeral, and may therefore choose to visit earlier. This is especially true if the mourner does not have a big family or is new to the area and would otherwise not have many visitors. Also, if people are unable to visit at another time, they may prefer to visit early in the shiva than not come at all.

Those who are unable to visit you during shiva may send messages to offer their condolences. You may also receive phone calls, but find it difficult to be available to leave those visiting you to speak on the phone. You may have to decide whether to take the call or have someone take a message and ask them to call again at a later time.

Ideally, most people will make a shiva visit during the times typically suggested by the family and often announced at the time of the funeral. These often center around prayer times (Minḥa – late afternoon or early evening depending on the time of the year, and Maariv – after nightfall), with some people staying just for prayers or the learning in between prayer times. This allows mourners to have lunch and dinner, and maybe even get some rest. If families are receiving visitors in the morning, that too may be an ideal and quieter time to visit. Inevitably, the minute the house is quiet, and you finally sit down for lunch, or you are ready to go to bed and the lights are out, someone arrives.

It may feel hard to be hospitable when you are emotionally drained and physically exhausted. Therefore, while you may feel obligated to receive visitors, if you do not have the energy, someone can tell them that now is not a good time. The visitor can decide to return at another time or leave a message that they came by to visit. This is just another reminder that shiva is for you, and not your visitor.

> *I wonder if I am the only one who at times found shiva quite intrusive. My house was taken over, and it often felt that the minute the door was closed and there was finally silence in my home, yet another visitor would appear, and I had to be "on." I often found it burdensome, as I felt in some way I had to look after those who came to see me. Neither the shiva minyanim nor reciting Kaddish spoke to me or gave me any degree of solace. That said, I was very moved by my colleagues – both religious and secular – who made the effort to come visit me, especially in the middle of the workday. In Israel, leaving work to make a shiva visit is surprisingly acceptable. I very much appreciated their support, as it meant a great deal to me and made my return to work just a little bit easier.*

A note to the visitor

There are times of the day that are better than others for the mourners, as they are more convenient and appropriate when visiting a shiva house. Take note of what day shiva begins and what day it ends before planning your visit. Some mourners or their family members may request that no visitors come during mealtimes, or midafternoon to allow the mourners time to rest. They may also say they would not like visitors to come to the shiva house in the evening after a certain time. Respecting this request shows that you are putting their needs ahead of yours at this time.

If you are visiting mourners, try to find out if and when prayers are being held, so that you can time your visit accordingly. You may want to participate in the prayers, but if not, you may find that the mourner whom you have come to see is unavailable to be with you until the prayers have ended. Many people arrive at the shiva house just before prayers begin, stay for prayers, visit briefly, and then leave. Others arrive at various times throughout the day not at all connected to prayer times. Women may or may not choose to participate in the prayers.

If you knew the deceased, but not the mourners and they do not know you, it is appropriate to introduce yourself and explain your connection to their loved one.

> *Upon leaving the shiva home of a woman whose husband recently died, I saw his wonderful caregiver standing in the corner of another room. I went over to her and told her how beloved she was to the whole family and how sorry I was for her loss. She seemed so appreciative that others understood her pain and cared about her, too. She remained with the wife and looked after her until she passed away a few years later. She was indeed a member of the family.*

In some specific communities, when coming to visit, you may find men and women sitting in separate rooms. It is important that visitors respect the customs of the mourners.

While many people may visit during shiva, it is also important to be there to provide much needed support after the shiva is over. It is at this time that the house may feel very empty, and sadness may intensify. If you are close with the bereaved, you may want to offer your support. Perhaps you will offer to go on errands together, take a walk, or go out for a cup of coffee. You may also offer to do things for your grieving friend such as drive carpool, do the laundry, make meals, and help with childcare so that they can have time alone or be with various family members. If they have children the same age as yours, it might be nice to have the children get together, enabling your friend to have some time to run errands or to join you along with their child.

> TIP: Try and anticipate the needs of a mourner, before and after shiva. Call just to check in and offer to do very specific tasks. A mourner will likely have little energy to initiate a call or suggest what could be helpful. You may need to take the lead. Don't be insulted if someone does not want your help, but offer it again at a later time.

Should I make a shiva call when I don't know the family very well?

We often are conflicted regarding visitation if we don't know the mourners or the deceased well. The rule that "We don't regret the things we do, only the things we don't do" applies here. The mourners appreciate your coming, and you may learn something valuable during your visit. It's also important to consider whether a person is new in town, and may not know many community members. Their family may live far away from where they are sitting shiva. If this is the case, a visit becomes even more important, regardless of your closeness or familiarity.

> *I often question whether I should make a shiva call to someone I don't know well, but know that when I've visited someone, afterwards I am always so glad that I did. Sometimes, some of the best answers we get in life come from taking the time to ask ourselves, how would we feel if the shoe were on the other foot? I ask myself how I would feel if those mourning had come to*

visit me. Would it feel intrusive or uncomfortable, and would I wonder why they came? Absolutely not. I would be so appreciative that they came to see me – especially since they did not know me very well. That answer gave me the strength I needed in order to go outside my comfort zone. I am so glad that I went. Simply saying, "I never met your sister, what was she like?" really gave them comfort as they had another person with whom to share their memories.

I came with a friend to deliver food to a shiva house. We received their name and address from the synagogue ḥesed group. Imagine our surprise to find the mourner sitting at home all alone. His family were new immigrants, and in addition a family member had been hospitalized. They did not know many people in the community yet. Our intention was just to drop off food for Shabbat and go, but when we saw the situation, we sat down with the mourner to talk. He was so grateful not just for the food, but also for the company.

People generally do not know how to deal with someone who has become bereaved. I didn't before I was bereaved. I would make excuses not to go to shiva houses, thinking that I didn't want to envelop myself in such sadness, or that I would be a burden on people who just wanted to be left alone with some peace and quiet to grieve on their own. How naive I was. For people to tell us stories… or just share their own experience with a sudden death… were some of the most important experiences I took from that harrowing week. These were some of the building blocks I needed to get on with my life.

Don't underestimate the power of making yourself uncomfortable by going to a shiva house or speaking to someone who is grieving.

There are times when I burst out crying, thinking about my loss. That is normal. Everything we go through in grief is normal. The key is knowing that we will be OK. We won't be the same, but we will be OK.

Joel Braham, *Jerusalem Post,* July 28, 2022

Is it appropriate for children to visit a shiva house?

With respect to having children visit a shiva house, it is a very individual decision. Some people may feel that children belong and bring life to a shiva house, whereas others may feel that having a child present (be they the mourner's children, or not), is an unwanted distraction and an added responsibility at such a difficult time. People are often concerned about exposing their child to death (see chapter 13 on children and death), but actually, it is more about how your child will be received if they visit with you. In other words, will bringing your child be beneficial to the mourners? If the answer is yes, a very short visit with your child may be appropriate. For example, grandchildren may come to visit their grandparent who is sitting shiva. This can be a needed reminder for the mourner of the continuity of the generations.

My soul aches.
My heart is broken.
I forgot how to smile.
Or how to feel joy.
So much pain.
Look the children are here
Sweet faces and smiles.
Who spoke of sorrow?
There is none now.

Margie Zwiebel, May 11, 2023

Before the visit, certain factors should be taken into consideration: the age of the child, their maturity and their relationship to the mourners. If a short visit would be comforting to the mourners then it might be appropriate to bring them. If it would be more disruptive, then give serious consideration as to whether you should bring them. As with everything, this requires sensitivity, and each situation should be judged individually.

> *When I was sitting shiva for my father, it was August and the summer vacation. I remember people coming to visit with their children or grandchildren in tow because they didn't have someone to watch them. I thought it was very inappropriate. A shiva visit is not a social call. If you don't have an arrangement for your children, perhaps a condolence message is better.*

Many parents may be unsure about exposing their children to shiva but for a child facing a loss, it is important and very helpful to be supported by their friends. If among the mourners there are children, it may be comforting to have classmates and peers visit along with a teacher or parent. Children can be prepared ahead of time, being told what to expect and how to behave. As much as you may want to shelter your children, depending on the age of your child, learning the importance of comforting a mourner is an important educational message for both your child and the mourner.

> *My daughter's middle-school English teacher passed away after an illness. The students were very fond of her. Some parents felt uncomfortable, and thought it was not appropriate for young people to attend the shiva. I encouraged my daughter and some of her friends, even though they were young, thirteen to fifteen years old, to go visit her family in small groups during shiva. I went with them as well. The family was very touched, and they appreciated it very much. As soon as they saw young people enter, they realized they were*

students and asked them to sit and share stories of their teacher. It was a meaningful experience for all those involved.

My father died after a short illness when I was in high school. I remember seeing a bus pull up to my apartment building and was so grateful to my teacher who brought my classmates to the shiva. It was so nice to see my friends after being only in the company of adults. It made me feel important that my friends were thinking about me, as I had been out of school all week.

SHIVA ETIQUETTE

If you are visiting someone who has lost a loved one, there are a few dos and don'ts:

- Make your visit brief. A ten- to twenty-minute visit is more than enough time to offer condolences.
- Pay special attention to the visiting hours, and make sure that you don't go late in the evening or close to Shabbat, when the mourners have other needs beyond visitation.
- Don't feel the need to wait for other visitors to arrive before leaving. If you sat with the mourners and offered condolences, it is okay to leave.
- Turn off your cell phone before you enter so that you can be fully available to the person you are visiting.
- Regardless of whether you came from afar, you had challenging weather, you got lost, or you went through great hardship to come and visit, these details are all irrelevant and should not be shared with the mourner. It is up to the mourner whether they acknowledge these details – if they even are aware of them. Knowing you have been inconvenienced may cause pain to the mourner.

- Don't get into a conversation with other visitors who may be there at the same time, unless it is relevant to the deceased and includes the mourner. It can be distressing to the mourner and may leave them feeling ignored. Since the mourner is seated in a low chair, while the visitors are seated in regular chairs, a conversation that doesn't include the mourner leaves them left out and feeling quite irrelevant.
- Be aware that the bereaved person is in a lot of pain. Don't tell them how they should feel, or how you felt when you lost someone. Their grief is theirs.
- Don't tell them that you know exactly how they feel. You do not walk in their shoes and cannot truly know how they feel.
- Don't ask intrusive questions or make judgmental comments about the deceased's medical care or death.
- Be there with them in their grief. This is a moment where it is all about them and not at all about you – unless they ask you how you are.
- Don't give platitudes such as "everything happens for a reason" or "this is for the best." These may be helpful for you, but not for others.
- Feel free to just lean in and listen. There are times when there are simply no words. You can tell them that.
- Being there in their silence can be very comforting. Your goal is to care and be present in their grief. Don't interrupt them to tell *your* story.
- Be patient with their loss. Their grieving is not time-bound. They will possibly need you more after shiva, when the house quiets down, than during the week of shiva. It is then that a simple question, such as "What can I do to help?" can validate and acknowledge their needs.

The Talmud (Berakhot 6b) teaches – "Rav Pappa said: 'The merit of attending a house of mourning lies in maintaining silence.'" How beautiful is it that the words "silent" and "listen" contain the same letters. What is the message for us to take away? Sometimes words are empty, and the best way to comfort is without words – but simply with your presence.

Ariel Horowitz, the son of well-known Israeli songwriter Naomi Shemer, told this about his mother: "There was a mother who was sitting shiva following the passing of her son who fell while serving in the IDF. He was not the first son of hers to have given his life for his country. My mother took a sheet of paper and wrote at the top of the page, 'I have no words' and signed her name, Naomi Shemer."

Interview with Sivan Rahav-Meir,
Mizrachi Magazine, May 2023

❧

I remember someone getting a phone call from Israel when they were sitting shiva in North America. They took the call, which lasted under five minutes, feeling so good to be connected "back home," but returned to find that some of the visitors appeared upset and others seemingly felt abandoned. A shiva visit is for the mourner and not the visitor, and when that priority gets mixed up, and the visitor starts telling about their losses, asks intrusive questions, and makes insensitive comments, it may feel that it is all about them or their story, and that may feel very upsetting for the mourner. In these uncharted and at times uncomfortable situations, the mourner is the guide – whether they choose to cry, tell stories, sit in silence, or take a phone call, visitors are there to comfort and support the mourner....

Words left unsaid and a visit not made

Many people don't know what to say or do at a shiva house, and their behavior may surprise you. Shiva visits often take people outside of their comfort zone and can feel awkward, uncomfortable, and heavy with sadness. As such, many people visit both out of a need to comfort the bereaved as well as out of a sense of obligation, and may choose to come together with a friend. Most people are often very glad afterwards that they did visit – both for themselves as well as for the mourner. Some people, however, may think that no time feels like the right time, and they sadly neglect to visit at all. It may therefore surprise you when you realize people whom you thought would visit don't come to see you – and worse, you may never hear from them again after your loss. Hopefully that list is very small.

For those who did not get to see you during shiva or were not in touch with you afterwards, there is often a more distanced feeling when you next meet, suggestive of words left unsaid and a visit not made. This can feel uncomfortable if not addressed, but similarly uncomfortable even if it is spoken about. Some people have stated that they found themselves avoiding eye contact, pretending that they did not see the mourner or even crossing the street to avoid "bumping" into them, all the while not knowing what to say. It's hard to pretend that nothing is wrong as the mourner is exquisitely sensitive to these nuances. As difficult as it is, it is always better to acknowledge the loss and not make excuses.

It is okay if you were not able to visit during shiva. A message or any other communication is also fine, and may be very much appreciated. Be careful if you do explain your absence. Some reasons such as "I was sick" or "I was away" are more palatable to the mourner than "the week got away from me." By stating the latter, you are putting the focus on yourself and making the mourner feel that they were not a priority.

> *My friend overseas had a loss. I know that sometimes during shiva you are not able to speak on the phone so I decided I would*

wait until after shiva ended, when I thought that they would be more available, and I could express my condolences. I did not realize until I called that she was upset with me because she was certain that I would call during shiva. She was waiting for my call, but it never came. I thought I was being considerate, but that was not how she perceived it. She felt that I had forgotten about her. I was glad that we were able to talk it through.

People mean well

The role of the visitor is to be there with you and for you; not necessarily to offer words of consolation, but simply to support you in silence until you speak. Often their words or stories about the deceased will bring you comfort. Some people, though, may ask questions or say or do things which may feel hurtful or may be perceived as being simply thoughtless or uninformed. Assuming their intentions are good, and they mean well, your task, which may not be at all easy, is not to judge them. While you know this, they may not, and thus may choose to comfort you in a way which inadvertently does the opposite. They will say things that will feel as if they are trivializing your loss, rather than having an appreciation of the depth of your grief. No one walks in your shoes and knows exactly how you feel. You are very sensitively tuned into the nuances of sights and speech and behavior at this time. This makes it harder for you to take a step backward and allow yourself to hear without being hurt, especially when you are in such deep emotional pain. Part of your healing may be to acknowledge and accept your vulnerability as you work to let go of someone else's comments or actions.

People say stupid things without giving it a second thought. My mom had just died, and I remember hearing various people complain about their mothers to me. "Seriously, now you are showing your ingratitude to your mom? At least you have a mother," I thought. Perhaps I too was overly sensitive.

Sometimes visitors will engage in small talk or conversation unrelated to you and your mourning. They might start to converse with other visitors, or the tone may feel for you to be too lively or irreverent. Someone may have forgotten to put their cell phone on silent, and the ring may feel intrusive to you at this time and in this moment. It is possible that a visitor will actually be on their phone or answer a call. All of these can feel very disturbing. While a ten- to twenty-minute visit may feel long enough when you receive so many visits in a day, inevitably some people will also overstay their welcome. Even a visit by close friends can be tiring, and you may feel talked out and drained. You may appreciate a visit or spending time with others after the shiva is over, when other family members and friends have gone back to their routine, and you suddenly feel very much alone.

If you are sitting shiva with other family members, you may not know some of the visitors who have come to see the other mourners, and your relatives may not know the guests who have come to see you. It may be important to each of the mourners to feel included in the conversation, and one mourner could introduce the other mourners if the visitors are coming from far away or are not part of their community. If there are many mourners, each mourner may be seated in a different area and be available for those visitors who have specifically come to visit them. Visitors may wonder if they should go over to all of the mourners or may visit only the mourner whom they know. If you think that one of the other mourners may feel left out, you may want to draw that mourner into a conversation with your visitor as a way to include them. On the way out, it is appropriate for visitors to acknowledge the other mourners.

FOOD IN A SHIVA HOUSE

Those sitting shiva often appreciate an organized roster (through the synagogue or friends) of meals coming into the house. When possible, it is also helpful when someone, other than a mourner, can be in the kitchen to help deal with food preparation and with serving the meals, cleaning up afterwards, and keeping a running list of needed supplies. The mourner should not have to think about these if at all possible, but those bringing food should ask if there are any dietary requirements. Some people have a custom not to eat meat during the week of shiva, except for Shabbat, whereas others do, so you may want to check before bringing something.

Meals and snacks are designed to provide nourishment and energy to those sitting shiva for the entire seven days. Some mourners eat a lot during the week of shiva, and others eat only a little. People often bring starchy items and comfort food when many mourners crave healthy salads and light meals. Actually, anything brought by friends or community members should be appreciated. Often, however, in addition to signing up on a roster, others may bring light snacks or food when they visit. It is not uncommon for the shiva house to have too much food, and sadly people's caring gestures are not fully appreciated. As a result, food may end up being thrown out, which can in itself feel upsetting for the mourners. If someone is managing the kitchen, it's also common practice to keep a list of food coming in or messages received so that at a later time, the mourners can, if they choose, access this information, and thank the appropriate people. Some people have the custom of not taking food out of the shiva house during the week. It is acceptable to donate unopened food or drink after the shiva, so that it will not go to waste.

> *My husband's work sent the most amazing care parcel to us when my husband was sitting shiva. A truck pulled up with several boxes of practical supplies – paper towels, toilet paper, cups, disposables, crackers, cookies, coffee, tea, and more. We were overwhelmed, but felt so embraced that in addition to so many people coming to see him, his workplace was so thoughtful and seemed to know exactly what we would need.*

There are different customs (*minhagim*) regarding visitors eating in a shiva house. Some visitors will not have so much as a sip of water, whereas others will sit with the family and have a full meal. Sephardic communities view it as an honor for others to make a *berakha* (blessing) for the merit of the deceased and then eat something. They put out food for visitors and encourage people to eat. They might be insulted if a visitor does not take any food. On the other hand, most Ashkenazi communities refrain from putting out food for visitors beyond simple beverages, and maybe a few light snacks. As the mourner, you will dictate what is appropriate for you and your family.

There is a custom to not take things out of a shiva house for the week, so any food going into the house is best brought in disposable containers with the name clearly marked on anything that is to be returned. The former is preferable, so that after shiva, the mourner is not burdened with the added stress of having to find all those who generously brought food the week before in order to return their nice platter or serving dish. It may sound trivial, but it may feel overwhelming when they have so much to do.

The rabbis of the Talmud (Moed Katan 3:7) stated that meals for the mourners should not be brought in ostentatious platters and baskets; the purpose of the meals is to help the mourners, not to demonstrate the comforters' wealth.

TAKING LEAVE OF A SHIVA HOUSE

Upon leaving the shiva house, in lieu of a goodbye, visitors may come up to you and recite the traditional sentences of consolation: "*min hashamayim tenuḥamu* – May you be comforted from Heaven" in the Sephardic tradition, and "*Hamakom yenaḥem etkhem betokh sha'ar avlei tziyon veYerushalayim* – May the Almighty comfort you among the mourners of Zion and Jerusalem" in Ashkenazic tradition. Some say "*Lo tosifu lada'ava od* – You should know no more sorrow." These are all the same words of consolation that the mourner heard when leaving the cemetery. In some shiva homes, these words are actually written on a paper above where the mourner sits. One could also simply say, "I am sorry for your loss," "May you be comforted by good memories of your loved one," as well as "*Shelo tedu od tza'ar* – You should know no more sorrow," as this reflects your empathy for them at such a difficult time.

It is also okay to leave without saying anything, if you see the mourner is engaged in conversation with someone else, and you don't want to disturb them.

Why do we refer to God as *HaMakom* – "the Place" in a house of mourning? God is everywhere, but a person who has lost a loved one often feels that they have been abandoned, that there is no place for God where they are. We pray that they be blessed by an awareness of God's presence, even in the place of grief in which they now finds themselves – for in that place, too, is *HaMakom*, the place of God.

Why do we call upon God to comfort the mourner? After all, isn't it the person visiting the mourner who is supposed to be comforting them? We can try our best to offer comfort, but our capacity for empathy is limited by our own personal experience. Only one who truly understands the person's loss can really offer comfort. Only God, who knows the depth of a person's pain, is capable of comprehending their grief. Because as humans we cannot fully comfort mourners, we ask God also to console them.

Grief is shared

"May the Almighty comfort you among the mourners of Zion and Jerusalem." Why do we add the words, "among the mourners of Zion and Jerusalem?" There are two reasons. There is a natural tendency to focus solely on those presently grieving. With this condolence message, we remind the mourner that although this specific person or family is mourning a personal loss, the entire

Jewish people share in their sorrow. There is comfort in knowing that your grief is being shared by other people. You are not alone. The concept of mourning together with others is very powerful, and an integral part of Judaism.

Upon receiving these specific words of condolence, it also brings the mourners to the realization that death is a part of life. Although your grief is yours and it is very individual to you and your specific loss, you are reminded that there are other people grieving as well.

> In the Book of Ruth, the family experiences many tragedies. First the loss of the patriarch, Elimelekh, and then the death of two sons, Maḥlon and Khilion. When Naomi decides to return home to Bethlehem, Ruth shows her dedication to her mother-in-law, and refuses to leave her. It is noteworthy that although Ruth herself was grieving the loss of her husband, she was able to see that Naomi was also grieving the loss of her sons.

SHABBAT DURING THE WEEK OF SHIVA

Just as this week is not like any other, so, too, is the Shabbat of the shiva week. To prepare for Shabbat, the mourners interrupt shiva in order to shower and change out of their shiva clothes into fresh Shabbat clothes, put on leather shoes, and sit in a regular chair. Shabbat is a time to pause and suspend public mourning, and may be the first time you actually leave the house and attend synagogue services. Even though we customarily don't comfort mourners on Shabbat, it is reassuring to be surrounded by a supportive community in your time of grief. If the burial is close in proximity to Shabbat and still very raw, then making a switch for Shabbat might feel more challenging. If Shabbat comes close to the end of shiva, then the family may see Shabbat as a welcome break from the many visitors coming into the house.

There is a custom to comfort mourners who are sitting shiva during Friday night services in the synagogue. The mourners remain outside while the congregation reads or sings the psalms that welcome the Sabbath (*Kabbalat Shabbat*). This is a difficult time for the mourner, when not only are they not in the sanctuary, but also congregants may pass by the mourner and not know whether to acknowledge the loss or not. The mourners enter the synagogue after *Lekha Dodi,* a song welcoming the Shabbat "Queen," and the congregation greets them with the traditional sentence of consolation. ("May you be comforted..."). The mourner is then ushered to their seat. Depending on their custom, some mourners may not choose to sit in their regular place during the year of mourning. Furthermore, during the week of shiva, the mourner is not called up to the Torah, or given any other honors.

This may be your first Mourner's *Kaddish* in the synagogue if the minyan all week has been at the shiva house. This is the time when you will now be joining others during their year of mourning through the recitation of *Kaddish*.

Attending synagogue on Shabbat during the week of shiva may also mean that other synagogue attendees don't necessarily know how to approach you. Since it is a time of suspended mourning, they may choose not to say anything to you about what just happened, thereby seemingly not acknowledging the loss publicly. This may feel awkward, as if people don't care, especially if they don't say anything, but then, too, being wished "Shabbat Shalom" may also feel surreal. While some congregants may choose not to acknowledge the loss because it is Shabbat, it is still appropriate to acknowledge the mourner. They can look in your direction, nod their head, put their arm around you, and even say "I'm sorry for your loss." This is a time where nothing may feel "normal."

Shabbat during shiva is challenging. Although outward signs of mourning are generally suspended and you eat regular Shabbat meals with family, the quiet of Shabbat and the absence of visitors may make you focus even more on your loss. Shabbat is counted as one of the shiva days and when Shabbat is over, shiva resumes, if the seven days have not been completed.

SITTING SHIVA IN MORE THAN ONE PLACE OR FAR FROM HOME

It is possible that you will choose to sit shiva in more than one place. In the first days after the funeral, you may sit together with other family members at the home of the deceased, and then spend the remainder of shiva in your home community with your friends, enabling them to have an opportunity to visit. If you attend the funeral in a different country altogether, you may choose to return to your community as soon as possible and mark the loss there.

You may also first return to your home community only after shiva has ended. In this situation, you may want to organize a memorial evening at the time of the *sheloshim* or even before. This can provide an opportunity for you to share memories of your loved one with your family and give them an opportunity to share and be comforted by others who may now visit if they were not able to travel with you for shiva. In addition, this memorial event gives your community, who may not have had the opportunity before, to now provide support. Offering a time period of a few hours enables you to share memories of your loved one without the intensity of sitting shiva.

> *"How's Ima?" one of my children asked two weeks ago, after my wife returned from sitting shiva for her father in Chicago.*
>
> *"Sad," I replied, honestly.*
>
> *"How long do you think it will last?" my son replied. "It'll take what it takes," I said.*

Deaths in the family are tough to integrate: they throw things off kilter, they change patterns, they alter things, they upset the applecart.

My son understood full well that his mother was going to be sad at the death of her father. That he was nearly eighty-six years old when he passed away in a hospice; that he was afflicted with a debilitating case of Alzheimer's; that he lived thousands of miles away – none of that mattered.

When a parent dies, a void emerges. Regardless of the age, or the cause, or the distance removed – physically or otherwise – a void emerges. My son understood that intellectually. But he wanted his mother back just the way she was before her father died – cheerful, smiley, optimistic, energetic. He wanted things to go back to normal.

He wanted her to "snap out of it," something – obviously – that doesn't just happen; something that takes time. Which is the psychological and emotional brilliance of the Jewish mourning laws – they mandate taking time. All that sends a signal that going back to life as normal, getting back to life as usual, is a gradual process; there is no "snap back" clause. The Jewish laws of mourning mandate that the mourners be patient with themselves – which is neither a given, nor necessarily an easy thing to do.

The grandchildren, my kids, knew their grandfather because, until he fell ill, he made an effort to visit Israel, and because we made an effort – when they were small – to send them to visit him for vacations. We wanted them to develop a relationship, despite the distance. Yet, the amount of time they spent together was limited.

When he died, one of my children noted that he didn't feel the way he thought he should feel. But there were no right or wrong feelings at a time like this, I counseled. You feel what you feel; nobody's grading.

My children had a relationship with their grandfather, but not the same type of relationship they would have enjoyed had they lived closer. We knew about that loss, that sacrifice, when we moved to Israel, and we don't regret the move because of it. But that doesn't make it any less of a loss, or make the pangs of longing and occasional guilt any less intense for what might have been had we all lived closer together.

Herb Keinon, adapted from "The Faraway Passing of a Close Relative," *Jerusalem Post*, July 30, 2015

Having recently gone to see my father and say my goodbyes, I chose to stay in Israel with my family and not travel to the United States for the funeral and for the shiva. I won't say that there wasn't a brief moment in the few days before he passed that I didn't second-guess myself. Knowing that everyone but me was there by his side at the last moments, and that they were together for the funeral and I was here, was hard to swallow. And it kind of made me feel a bit lonesome in a weird way for the whole week. Mostly knowing that they were all there hearing and sharing stories about dad that I was missing. But then, on the flip side, I found something else: the idea of kehilla (community). In a way, whether they know it or not, all of these "comforters" are now a part of a new kehilla. A kehilla founded in the living room of one mourner.

Ilene Spark Greenberg

WHEN A HOLIDAY CHANGES SHIVA

The traditional Jewish mourning period is seven days – the word *shiva* means seven in Hebrew. The seven-day shiva period has a certain momentum or flow to it. When a death or burial occurs before, during, or after a holiday, it alters the nature of a typical seven-day shiva, creating its own challenges.

Holidays are difficult in many ways with respect to shiva and *sheloshim* because depending on which holiday, the time of the death, and time of burial, shiva may be shortened and concluded before the holiday or delayed until after the holiday. There are many laws around the holidays regarding shiva and *sheloshim* observance. These are complex and add yet another dimension to the deep loss that you may be feeling. When a Jewish holiday (Rosh HaShana, Yom Kippur, Sukkot, Pesaḥ, and Shavuot – but not Hanukka or Purim) occurs during the mourning period, the shiva is shortened, and ends as soon as the holiday begins. If, for example, both the death and burial occur *Erev* Pesaḥ or Sukkot, one may sit for a few hours and with this, a brief shiva will be concluded and the weeklong holiday will begin. There would also be a shortened *sheloshim*.

> *Our father passed away on the twelfth of Adar. The funeral was held at noon. We began to sit shiva on the night of the Fast of Esther; in less than twenty-four hours Purim was upon us. Every shiva also includes Shabbat, and in preparation we bathe, wear Shabbat clothes, and sing zemirot. Shabbat is like a flight in a spaceship from our world to another world, a visit to the future (Me'ein Olam Haba). On Shabbat one does not talk about trivialities, business, or even politics – at least that is what one is supposed to do. Shabbat puts aside mourning for twenty-four hours, but Purim during shiva is a different story.*
>
> *As Purim began, we removed our torn garments and without bathing, put on Purim clothes. The Megilla was read at the shiva house, and immediately after, visitors arrived to console us. While not sitting on the floor, we were still grieving. It was very confusing. The next morning again the Megilla was read and more visitors came. That afternoon was even more bizarre, as we the mourners sat together with our family for the Purim*

meal. As strange as it may sound, mourners are obligated to eat the Purim seuda because they are obligated in the joy of Purim. And yes, there was also wine at the meal, but less drinking than every year. And although musical instruments are forbidden, there were songs along with tears of mourning for the deceased, and non-mourning family members danced. I understood then that Purim is not just joy over the current situation; it connects the present to a bigger, eternal story. Purim required us to be happy in spite of the difficult situation. In some ways it is more challenging than mourning on Shabbat, because on Shabbat you are asked to put the mourning aside and fly on the wings of imagination to a perfect world where there is no death. In contrast, on Purim, joy is demanded in the midst of life and its pain; maybe that's why we need to have a little wine. To look for the secret that is hidden.

Adapted from R. Lior Engelman, "It's Purim – Forget Everything?" *B'Sheva,* March 21, 2024, p. 56
(Translated into English by Gina Junger)

My mother's friend lost her mother Erev Pesaḥ, and therefore only sat shiva for her for a few hours before the Ḥag came in. She told my mother, "Sitting shiva is hard, but not sitting shiva is even harder."

While there is then no official shiva during the holiday, you may find visitors dropping by to visit, to informally express their condolences and share memories of the deceased. This helps to create for the mourners and visitors a "shiva-like" space to share and to be comforted; otherwise, it may feel very disconcerting to both have barely had the opportunity to formally mourn and then move into celebration. While the mourner may not be "sitting" as such, there is often a space created for this grief to be acknowledged. This in itself suggests just how important and helpful the shiva rituals may be for both the mourners and those who want to visit or express their condolences.

If a death occurs on the holiday of Pesaḥ, Shavuot or Sukkot, then the burial may occur on Ḥol HaMoed, but shiva begins only afterwards. This may feel uncomfortable because there is now a disconnect between burial and shiva of several days, and one is faced with the difficulty of going through all of the *Ḥag* without an official shiva, and only commencing public mourning at the conclusion of the holiday. If the holiday falls during shiva, then shiva is cut short and ends with the beginning of the holiday.

> *How can we understand or make sense of shiva or sheloshim being either shortened or broken? The Torah commands us to rejoice on the festivals. The community mitzva of rejoicing thus takes precedence over the private mitzva of mourning, when individual grief and communal celebration collide. Rabbinic tradition states that celebration together with the community assumes greater significance. Even in our loss, celebrating as part of the community helps to embrace us and lets us know that we are not alone in our grief. In the same way that we don't erase Shabbat during shiva, or the holiday during our mourning, the affirmation of life overrides death, and moving forward is our way to move out of the paralysis of our loss. Judaism fully recognizes how difficult this is, but nonetheless attempts to make a place for it. In the modern State of Israel, we see this play out in real life as the harsh reality of memorializing our loved ones on Yom HaZikaron is followed by the celebration of Yom HaAtzma'ut.*

For the bereaved families, every day is Memorial Day… So we grit our teeth, gather our courage, and resolve to switch those gears, no matter how tough it may be… We compartmentalize, creating a sacred space for silence and sadness, but reserving another corner for laughter and lightheartedness.

Adapted from R. Stewart Weiss (father of Staff Sgt. Ari Weiss *z"l*), "Silence, Soldiers, and Switching Gears," *Mizrachi Magazine*, April 2020

A friend's parent died a few days after Rosh HaShana, and Yom Kippur broke the shiva. When I visited him, I said it must be very hard for him not to have a full seven days of shiva. His answer to me was that he thought his mother was being "considerate" of them, shortening their grieving time. She would have wanted us to "get on with life."

GETTING UP FROM SHIVA

After Shaḥarit services on the morning of the seventh day, with the exception of holidays, the mourners conclude shiva and "get up." Some people have the custom to visit the grave of the deceased when shiva concludes. In your plan to move forward, even if in this moment it means simply to put one foot in front of the other, your goal is not to ask yourself how you are – as that is just too much to ask – but rather, how am I *today,* right now, in this moment?

Your physical state mirrors your emotional state, and Judaism acknowledges that your grief, your internal thoughts and feelings following your loss, continue, but mourning, the outward or public expression of grieving, will diminish over time.

Faith does not render us invulnerable to tragedy, but it gives us the strength to mourn and then, despite everything, to carry on.
R. Jonathan Sacks, "Between Hope and Humanity," in Covenant and Conversation: Leviticus, p. 156

Parashat Aḥarei Mot (Lev. 16) opens with, "And the Lord spoke to Moses after the death of Aaron's two sons, when they drew near before the Lord, and they died." The Torah then offers a detailed description of the service of the High Priest on Yom Kippur. Chronologically, Aaron's sons died much earlier, in *Parashat Shemini* (Lev. 9). Why does the Torah remind us here of the death of Aaron's sons and speak about the Temple ritual now? The instruction from God reminds Aaron that despite his loss, life continues. And that there are people in this world who need his help. He still has an important task. Both God and Moses say to Aaron – you are still needed; you are not alone in your grief; life continues and so does your journey and your mission. Aaron's pain does not vanish, but he is able to continue.
Adapted from David Wolpe, "Message for the Grieving," *Jerusalem Post Magazine*, April 29, 2022, p. 42

Tisha B'Av: And Now…We "Get Up"

On Tisha B'Av in the afternoon, we get up from our "low seat." We arise from the mourner's position. "Getting up" on Tisha B'Av teaches us that there are two motifs to this day. The first motif is sorrow and sadness; we cry about and mourn the loss of the Temple and the tragedies of the Jewish people. But in the middle of the day, when we "get up," the motif of the day changes. We become filled with resolve that we will internalize the lessons of Tisha B'Av, that we will fix what needs to be fixed, and correct what needs to be corrected. From the afternoon of Tisha B'Av, our outlook changes from looking backwards to looking forward. This is the strength of the Jewish people remembering the difficult past, but always preparing for a better future.

Grieving may be one of the hardest things you will ever do. It feels all-consuming, taking up so much more physical and emotional energy than you could possibly imagine. It is exhausting, making it difficult at times to focus and concentrate, and you may just want it all to be over. We don't get over a death or recover in the way that we do an illness. Our task is to learn to live with our loss. You may wake up in the morning after another restless sleep, feel numb, and then pinch yourself and discover it has all been one long bad dream. With great sadness, you realize it hasn't been.

Within the depth of your sadness you carry tremendous love, and in your immense love, you hold such deep pain. They are intertwined. You know that your life is forever changed and may wish that if you could only have your loved one for just one minute more, you'd be so grateful. You may feel that the more you love someone, the more pain you have. Some days just getting out of bed is challenging, but it is important to be kind to yourself, set realistic expectations, and break the more difficult tasks into small manageable ones so that you don't get overwhelmed. You may need to rethink your priorities for a while. As you adjust to the new normal for you, you will be surprised to discover that your ability to be more present within yourself and get things accomplished will improve.

EXCESSIVE GRIEF

The Torah prohibits the practice of self-mutilation as a sign of mourning. It is very clear that we are not allowed to cut ourselves, even in grief over a loved one's death. The customs generally accepted by the mourners, like sitting on a low chair and not shaving or bathing for pleasure, are meant to cause the mourner discomfort, but not pain. A person who expressed the desire to continue sitting shiva for longer than seven days or continued to wear his or her torn garment would be strongly discouraged. Judaism sets aside a time for mourning and its more severe customs, and then "pushes" the person to get up and move to the next stage of grief.

Nahmanides on the verse in Deut. 14:1 explains: "You are children of Hashem, your God. Do not cut yourselves or shave the front of your heads for the dead, for you are a people holy to Hashem, your God." Even when coping with the death of a loved one, a Jew is commanded not to engage in excessive rituals of grief. Nahmanides suggests that Judaism's belief in the eternity of the soul enables us to understand why we don't need to grieve excessively. Even so, he adds, we are right to mourn within the parameters set by Jewish law since, even if death is only a parting, every parting is painful.

Maimonides rules that a person should not become excessively brokenhearted because of a person's death: "While it says, 'Do not weep for the dead nor bemoan him' (Jer. 22:10) this means, 'Do not weep *excessively*.' For death is the way of the world, and one who grieves excessively at the way of the world is a fool" (Maimonides, *Hilkhot Avel* 13:11). With rare exceptions, the outer limit of grief in Jewish law is a year, not more.

How do we grieve the loss of the Temple?
The passage in the Talmud (Bava Batra 60b) explains: "The Sages taught in a *baraita* (Tosefta, Sota 15:11): When the Temple was destroyed a second time, there was an increase in ascetics [people who avoided forms of indulgence, for religious reasons] among the Jews, they refused to eat meat and drink wine. Rabbi Yehoshua joined them. He said to them: 'My children, for what reason do you not eat meat,

> and do you not drink wine?' They said to him: 'Shall we eat meat, from which offerings are sacrificed upon the altar, now the altar has ceased to exist? Shall we drink wine, which is poured upon the altar, now the altar has ceased to exist?' Rabbi Yehoshua said to them: 'If so, we will not eat bread either, since the meal-offerings that were offered upon the altar have ceased.' They replied: 'It is possible to subsist with produce.' He said to them: We will not eat produce either, since the bringing of the first fruits has ceased.' They replied: 'It is possible to subsist with other produce.' He said to them: 'If so, we will not drink water, since the water libation has ceased.' They were silent.
>
> "Rabbi Yehoshua said to them: 'My children, come, and I will tell you: to not mourn at all is impossible, as the decree was decreed. But to mourn excessively is also impossible, as the Sages do not issue a decree upon the public unless a majority of the public is able to abide by it.' Rabbi Yehoshua continued, 'Rather, this is what the Sages said: "A person may plaster his house with plaster, but he must leave over a small amount in it without plaster to remember the destruction of the Temple from the verse, 'If I forget you, Jerusalem, let my right hand forget its cunning. Let my tongue cleave to the roof of my mouth, if I remember you not; if I set not Jerusalem above my highest joy' (Ps. 137:5–6)."

Typically, leaving behind the week of shiva and going on to the next stage of *sheloshim* begins with the reentry back into the world of the living. A short walk outside, perhaps around the block, may feel like seeing the world anew. In many ways, shiva was a protective cocoon. It may seem as if the world has stood still since your loved one died, often as if weeks and not just a single week, has passed. Time seems to have ground to a halt, removing you from everyday life. Yet, life has gone on. Things may feel strange and strained and everything seems so different – even if in many ways it is much the same. For many, it is jarring to walk outside and see that it is "business as usual." The birds are singing, people are going about their everyday activities, and you may feel that your life will never be the same.

> *Torah and tradition knew how to honor both the dead and the living, sustaining the delicate balance between grief and consolation, the loss of life that gives us pain, and the reaffirmation of life that gives us hope.*
>
> R. Jonathan Sacks, "The Limits of Grief," https://rabbisacks.org/covenant-conversation/reeh/the-limits-of-grief/

The house where the mourners stay for the week of shiva becomes a house of mourning, a serious, often sad, place. The act of physically stepping outside, taking a walk, and reentering the house, provides a distinction between what "was" during shiva and what "is" now.

There is a need to restore the home to a place of the living. Dishes are returned, chairs are picked up, the mirrors are uncovered and, if there is a sign on the door, it is taken down. Now, without the structure of shiva, there may be lots of paperwork and procedural dealings to look after, as well as getting back to work, moving towards reintegrating into society, and returning to a new life, albeit with restrictions of *sheloshim*. The end of shiva may bring with it a sense of tremendous relief, and yet you may feel anxious about getting back to some sense of normality.

> *When getting up from shiva, I couldn't wait to get my kitchen back and have some sort of order. There were dishes that were not familiar to me, and food that I had not prepared. As appreciative as I was for it all, it was a reminder of this difficult week, and in the same way that shiva had ended, I now needed to*

take control. Therefore, I knew those dishes had to go so that I could move forward. Because people didn't come to retrieve their dishes, I found myself in the driver's seat, letting my husband go to the door. I couldn't imagine having to discuss with each person how I was doing with each stop we made. After my experience, while I may think it looks less nice, it is actually thoughtful to bring someone food in a container that they don't have to return.

❧

These are just a few of the things that I learned from sitting shiva....

I can sit still. Sitting shiva is very literal. One is required to sit in one chair for hours at a time and focus on people and their words. I think I managed both pretty well. I imagine that every shiva house has a vibe. An energy of its own. Whether that energy comes from the person sitting or from the person who has died, I'm not sure. But what I do know is that the energy filling my house for the week allowed me to sit, to hear the words of others, and to laugh. I learned how to accept help graciously, how to receive hugs and words of comfort, how to maintain eye contact for the length of time it takes someone to get through hamakom yenaḥem, how to daven three times a day, and how to watch the world go by without actively participating, all from a very low chair.

At a shiva where I just enter and visit for a while, I have always felt a certain awkwardness, almost to the point of questioning whether my presence has any added value. This past week, I saw how every single person who walks into a shiva house provides comfort in one way or another. A smile, a nod, the hamakom yenaḥem, it all makes a difference. Every last one. I didn't know. Not really until now. That just by showing up for someone in their shiva house, you can change that moment for them. Maybe, at that very second, your entrance lifted them up out of a dark moment. Maybe your story gave them a new memory.

Ilene Spark Greenberg

The transition to an empty house is a difficult one, and Judaism's rituals help ease you back gradually. The time parameters of the death, followed by the funeral, through the seven days of shiva, the thirty days of *sheloshim,* the eleven months of the recitation of *Kaddish,* and the twelve months of mourning, slowly demarcate the year, and naturally take you through the grieving process and allow you to move forward. As you mark the passage of time, you move on – but do not ever forget.

VISITING AFTER SHIVA HAS ENDED

Sometimes, because people were not available to visit you during the week of shiva, or they didn't know about your loss, they may ask to come and see you after shiva has formally ended and you've entered *sheloshim*. You may want this – to see your friends and to chat with them – or it may feel like a painful extension of shiva – adding time to sit yet again, when you have finally gotten up and are moving forward and returning to work. You may decide to have them come and visit, or to meet them elsewhere in a less formal location such as going out for coffee. You can also suggest that now is not a good time for you. All are acceptable options.

My father passed away in August and many friends and community members were away on their summer holidays. I appreciated the messages of consolation they sent me. Some people reached out when they returned from their vacation, and wanted to come visit me. I was honest. I already got up from shiva and although they regretted missing it, I didn't want visitors anymore in my home. There were some people I met for coffee, but to most I answered, "Your message was enough; there is no need to visit personally." I know some people were offended by my response. In the end, if the shiva has passed and you missed it, that's it. Offer condolences and move on.

CONDOLENCES ARE ALWAYS ACCEPTED

After Shiva has ended , and time has passed, it is still appropriate to acknowledge a person's loss and offer condolences.

I barely knew the acquaintance of a close friend of mine. I'd often exchange a word or two in passing, but that was about it. When her dad died after a lengthy illness, I debated making a shiva call. In the end, I decided not to go. I knew her mostly to say "hi" to, and thought it not right to intrude on her privacy. I often wondered whether I made the right decision, and that in itself was my personal red flag – that I probably had not. A few weeks later, I literally ran into her in the mall. Both of us were in a hurry. Surprised to see her, in passing I said a quick, "Hello, how are you?" and off we went. Suddenly, after we parted, I remembered I had not said a word to her about her loss. How could she feel? I knew, not very well, and it was then that I felt terrible. Not only had I missed the opportunity to make a shiva call, but my "How are you?" was more of a passing greeting.

We sometimes do get second chances, and I finally got mine. We were both in shul one evening for Minḥa. She was there to say Kaddish as it was the end of her mourning period for her Dad, and I was there to say Kaddish for the yahrzeit (annual date) of my Mom's death many years before. I finally got to talk with her, and more importantly – to listen. I confessed to her how sorry I was that I had not outwardly said anything to her about her father. It was at this time, her final Kaddish, that she spoke about her Dad, sharing some memories. I learned from this that it is always appropriate to offer words of comfort, regardless of how much time has elapsed.

I had come full circle. As I reflect back on her caring and kindness, I realize that she made it easy for me to tell her how sorry I was for her loss. This encounter taught me a valuable lesson. In spite of my discomfort, I needed to go the extra distance. Sometimes by taking a detour on our own journey, we end up having a more meaningful trip. We don't know it at the time, and in fact because of our discomfort, we may go out of our way to avoid it, but at the end of the day, we feel we did the right thing. Once again, I realized that I am only sorry for the things I don't do in life, not the things I do. She reached out to me, and this time, I was able to reach back. I like to think that we both gained something in the process.

Adapted from B. L. Ludman, "Life-Death Passages. Reflections on Shiva," in *Life's Journey*, 263–265

REINTERMENT AND SITTING SHIVA AGAIN

Reinterment in Judaism is not encouraged, but under certain circumstances it is permitted. If someone, for example, wants to exhume a body that has been buried abroad and bring it to the Land of Israel, or if there is a concern that the graves might be desecrated, reburial may be permitted. As a result, mourners will then tear *kriya* and sit shiva a second time, although only for one day. During COVID-19, when many people were unable to bring their loved ones to Israel for burial, some opted to do so at a later time.

Chapter 5

The Transition from Shiva Through *Sheloshim*

Sheloshim is the bridge between the speechlessness of mourning and the babble of normal life.

R. Scott Perlo, "*Sheloshim*: The Bridge to a New Normal" *My Jewish Learning*, November 2, 2022

SHELOSHIM

The thirty-day period of mourning following burial is called *sheloshim*. It includes the seven days of shiva and the remaining twenty-three days. In Judaism, thirty days is considered a measurement of time. Jewish rituals designate *sheloshim* as the period of time to mourn and grieve for our loved ones. Thirty days resembles the moon's cycle, which waxes and wanes much like our changing emotions.

These days are less restrictive than shiva, and the mourner may return to work and engage in other routine activities. It is customary, however, not to shave or cut your hair, purchase new clothes, or attend parties, social gatherings, or other forms of entertainment during this time.

> When the Jewish people mourned the death of Aaron, they mourned for thirty days (Num. 20:28–29).
>
> So, too, was the length of time that the nation mourned for Moses (Deut. 34:8).

I used to be scared of so many things. Once my dad died, I didn't care anymore. I was suddenly no longer afraid to get up and speak in meetings at work. It felt like the worst thing in the world had happened, so I no longer had anything to lose. In a very bizarre way, it was quite empowering.

Sheloshim marked a transition for me that I was grateful for. I was ready to leave the intensity of shiva behind; although in some way it felt oddly protective, not having to leave the comfort of my home. I was tired of people coming into my house at all hours and needed to venture out, to get some air, even for a short time. I was glad that I was returning to work and a familiar routine, although I felt fragile and uncertain as to what to expect. My colleagues, for the most part, embraced me and were there for me while giving me the space that I needed. Slowly, I got back into my work, and appreciated having a world outside of my grief – while still being able to hold a place for my loss, when necessary. I realized that while I was carrying this loss, neither I nor others around me knew just how to address it. If I were a man, my not shaving for thirty days and letting my hair or beard grow may have made my loss more obvious to others. This may have afforded them the opening to inquire if all was okay, thus allowing the opportunity to

share what happened. As a woman, few people even knew what had happened in the past month: meaning, that while I valued my privacy, my loss was often not acknowledged at all, making it feel both strange and awkward.

❧

A community member shared with me that as a recent widow she would drive an hour away to do her shopping in a supermarket where she was sure she wouldn't bump into anyone she knew. Getting back to life and doing mundane chores like shopping was difficult enough, without having to deal with questions and comments from people she met like, "How are you coping?" or "You are so strong."

The contrast between the busyness of shiva and the empty house as the last visitors leave may or may not feel good. Those who are not your closest friends will have visited during shiva, and now, as you settle into your new reality, you may feel more alone than you had imagined. When shiva has ended and the door is metaphorically closed, you are left alone with your thoughts. You may suddenly realize that people all have their own lives and, when you least expect it, this thought may begin to fill you with sadness.

While ideally your close friends will continue to reach out to you after shiva concludes, you too may have to signal in some way that you value their presence as you navigate this strange and difficult time. Reaching out while you are in pain may be more challenging than you have the energy for, and you certainly don't want to be pitied. If you have a friend or family member who understands your needs, perhaps you can let them know what they can do for you and how they can be of help. Whether it is procuring copies of the formal death certificate (needed for almost all legal and financial transactions), banking, translating, and making sense of documents, purchasing groceries, or just being there for you during difficult times to be a listening ear or to provide distraction, you will appreciate them checking in.

> *I was not offended by the question "How are you?" I answered honestly, "It's difficult," or "It's an adjustment. Day by day." I could see why some people would find the question trite. Do you actually expect me to answer that I'm fine? But I preferred that to being ignored. What I didn't appreciate was the "head tilt." I need your support. Not your pity.*

NEW CLOTHES DURING THE YEAR OF MOURNING

The *Shulḥan Arukh* writes that mourners should not wear new clothing throughout the shiva and *sheloshim,* because new clothes are thought to bring joy. Some halakhic authorities permit wearing new clothing after the *sheloshim* if it is first worn by another person. This is seen as taking away the feeling of newness of the garment. Many people refrain from buying new clothes during the year of mourning unless it is considered necessary. Some find that not "shopping" during the year is a difficult but constant reminder of their state of mourning. For others, it is not a big sacrifice. As with many customs throughout the year, this is personal, and it affects people differently.

> *A colleague, a mora lehalakha (female halakhic advisor), suggested that the question posed to her, "Can I purchase a new dress for my son's bar mitzva during my year of mourning?" may have been more than simply a halakhic question. It may reflect the emotional element attached to the upcoming celebration. The woman probably had something appropriate in her closet. The real question behind purchasing a new garment might more likely reflect her ambivalence regarding the celebration of this*

special occasion, and the sadness over her loss and the person who will be missing at her simḥa.

GOING THROUGH YOUR LOVED ONE'S PERSONAL BELONGINGS

Going through your loved one's personal belongings and clothing can be physically and emotionally exhausting, and only you can decide when, how, and with whom you will attempt this task. You may want or have to deal with this immediately, or you may simply not be able to face anything for a while: either approach is okay. If the situation does require you to act immediately, this may be difficult when you need time to absorb this aspect of the loss. It is a very personal decision, so try not to feel pressured by others who may have a different timetable than you. This may be an opportunity to sit with your memories, and you may find yourself more or less tearful than you expected. When was the last time you saw your loved one in that sweater, or drinking from that cup? Whether you go through the belongings alone or with someone else, you may find that you are not as ready as you may have thought, so try and remember to be kind to yourself. You may also discover that your loved one held onto many more possessions than you may have known about, and the process of going through things that initially held little value for you may suddenly take on meaning – or may in contrast now feel very painful. Don't be surprised if you feel upset or resentful.

When my mom died, my dad reminded us during shiva that once shiva ended, we girls really had to come to the house and get rid of our mom's things, as he wanted to donate to charity whatever we did not want as quickly as possible. We started to go

> *through everything, but we could see that the process would be too long and arduous, as we were not ready to part with things. Finally, my sister and I decided to split everything quickly, take it to our homes and decide, in our own time, what we wanted to do with each item. We then made piles of what we did not want but thought the other might, and swapped. It was close to a year or more later that I discovered that I had taken things to hold onto that I needed at the time – for the memory, the scent of my mom, etc. and only then was I able to pass it on to charity. In some way I needed that time to sit with the memories, on my own and in my own time, shed a tear, and then let it go.*

When the loss involves a child, it can be extremely difficult to go through their possessions, and take apart the room or use it for someone else.

What, if ever, is the right time? Opening the closet and attempting to sort out clothes may feel like an impossible task. While some people may feel good donating clothes and other personal possessions to family members (and thus keeping the memory of their loved one alive), others may not yet be ready to part with these emotional treasures. You need to do it at your pace. It is a part of the grieving process, and with it will come many memories – and often tears.

COPING WITH NEW REALITIES

There will be many new changes, and with them, things you are dealing with for the first time. Keeping up to date with tasks you had depended on others to take care of along with procedural "stuff" to look after may feel empowering, but it may also generate renewed sadness. Whether it is learning how the different appliances and remote controls in the house work, paying the bills, or dealing with repairs, each task may feel like an unwelcome first that can be overwhelming. A seemingly simple undertaking such as taking your spouse's name off the account may leave you in tears.

It is so important to have someone who can be there for you. Each of your family members, friends, and colleagues can offer support on a different level. Some will hold you when you are sad, others will want to distract you, and still others will deal with speaking to the bank or to the insurance company. Let these people help you. You may be in a fog, finding this stressful, and will benefit from another set of eyes and ears.

With the onset of *sheloshim*, you have to make decisions that are right for you. You may ask such questions as, "Can you go out to eat, or to a community Kiddush? Do you feel left out of religious life, or derive comfort from participating? Do you feel alone or supported by the community? Should you go to someone's house for a Shabbat meal, regardless of how many guests are there? These are questions that you will need to answer for yourself, based partially on your comfort level – but even this may change over time. You may feel one way, while others may have done something very different. It is not helpful for others to judge your loss and how you express your grief. You may want to consult a rabbi if you have questions you don't know how to answer. You may discover that more is based on *minhag* (custom) than halakha (law).

THE END OF *SHELOSHIM*

As the thirty days pass, and you slowly process your loss, some things will start to feel more familiar and more comfortable. Judaism recognizes that grief is very real. As such, we don't move forward, forgetting about what has happened, but rather acknowledge the rawness of our feelings, making the space and time for our healing, little by little.

The daily routine may now be dominated by making time for and finding a minyan for the recital of *Kaddish*, and life may feel very much punctuated by this new routine. Sadness, too, may prevail when you least expect it; this feeling reminds you that while you may take comfort in the old familiarity, life is very different now. You may at times experience a sense of relief that your loved one is no longer suffering, yet possibly feel guilt or regret for your feelings or actions. Life may not have the intensity that it had during shiva, and while you may feel thankful that you can get back to your past "routine," this is a new and different routine.

> *I often find myself reflecting on my father's passing. It is during such moments that I experience a profound sense of love, pride, and appreciation for my Jewishness. Losing a parent can leave you feeling adrift and disconnected. Observing my non-Jewish friends who have experienced loss makes me feel incredibly sad, while also incredibly thankful for the grief structure that Judaism has provided me. Unlike my non-Jewish friends, I had a framework that enabled me to navigate the grieving process. Through shiva and sheloshim, I was given an opportunity to begin to process my loss. My daily repetitions of the Kaddish prayer were a salve that gave me focus and purpose. As to customs relating to the thirty days following my father's death, I did not shave or cut my hair. When you lose a parent, your life is divided into pre-loss and post-loss. This was represented in my unkempt appearance. I didn't look like myself because I no longer was myself, at least not the person I had been.*
>
> *What is particularly remarkable is how that comfort came to me, despite identifying as a secular Jew. It is in these practices that I discovered, on a deeper level, the profound beauty of Jewish practice and its significance in my life. By engaging with Jewish customs, I felt a connection to the unbroken thread of Jewishness that stretches throughout history. These practices go beyond mere traditions. If we allow them, they can offer us a compass for navigating the trials and tribulations of life.*
>
> Adapted from Ben Freeman, "Jewish Rituals Can Profoundly Enrich Our Lives," *Jerusalem Post*, July 3, 2023

WHAT DOES NORMAL GRIEF LOOK LIKE?

Grieving is difficult, often very difficult, and we grieve with our entire body – which seems surprising to the uninitiated. It impacts every aspect of our being, it is more exhausting than we could have ever imagined, and it lasts much longer than we think it should. You simply cannot be prepared for what lies ahead and really, how can you be? Your grief is your own, and the most important to you. Don't let anyone tell you otherwise. So, while you cannot compare your grief to another person's, they cannot compare theirs to yours. Each person's loss is different, and in many ways may feel the worst to them.

Each death, too, is a different experience. It may leave you feeling totally out of sorts and in both emotional and physical pain as you grapple with the various aspects of your loss – physical, cognitive, emotional, and behavioral. These all seem to work together to leave you feeling depleted. At the same time, you may feel pushed by others to just "get over it already." Because grief comes in all sizes and shapes, and since no two people grieve in the same way, the following sampling of symptoms will not necessarily represent how you may personally feel. We are sure that you could add others to this list.

SYMPTOMS OF GRIEF

Physical

- Sleep difficulties, fatigue
- Exhaustion
- Dizziness, weakness, chills
- Increased heart rate and blood pressure
- Nausea
- Chest pain and other physical distress
- Headaches, body aches, and other somatic complaints
- Muscle tremors
- Decreased or increased appetite

Cognitive

- Confusion and spaciness
- Intrusive thoughts and images, rumination
- Poor memory and concentration
- Difficulty making decisions
- Blaming others
- Disorganized thinking
- Focusing and attentional difficulties

Emotional

- Shock
- Disbelief
- Relief
- Sadness
- Despair
- Depression
- Anger
- Irritability
- Numbness, a sense of unreality
- Emptiness
- Crying
- Loss and disconnection from others
- Helplessness
- Loneliness
- Feeling overwhelmed and dysregulated
- Vulnerability
- Spiritual pain and malaise
- Guilt, self-blame
- Regret

- Fear or panic
- Anxiety
- Agitation
- Decreased sense of security and confidence
- Careless and reckless behavior
- Self-harming behavior
- Desire to be reunited with the deceased

Behavioral

- Withdrawal from social activity
- Strained relationships
- Avoidance of people or activities
- Lack of interest in activities that usually bring pleasure
- Work-related issues
- Increased drug or alcohol usage
- Change in activity level
- Decreased sexual interest
- Decreased self-esteem
- Euphoria
- Preoccupation with self, disinterest in others
- Increased responsibility
- Hypervigilance
- A sense of heaviness, sighing

For many months afterward, and at many times since, I was swallowed up in the deep fog of grief – what I think of as the void – an emptiness that fills your heart, your lungs, and constricts your ability to think or even to breathe.

Sheryl Sandberg, *The Boston Globe*, May 16, 2016

My wife died several months ago, and I thought that it would get easier, but it hasn't. Somehow, I feel more acutely aware of my loss. I am less numb. The days are difficult, and the nights are harder. I am still thinking of my wife all the time, but just maybe sometimes without the same intensity and pain. I walk around the house, and I keep thinking that she will return. She will pop up as if she has just come back from shopping, but took longer than expected. I look at the clock and I know that it is time to eat, and I often did the cooking before. Now everything looks bland, and I can't be bothered. In the grocery store, I actually thought I would eat the things I brought home. I don't enjoy shopping. I don't want to meet anyone, and I've already had my tears when I saw the special cheese my wife used to love to eat. But cook for one and sit alone at the table? No way. The community and my children have reached out to me; they want to ensure that I am never alone for Shabbat. While I appreciate it, sometimes it is very hard to put on a brave face and socialize. I'd rather grab some chocolate and sit in my chair. I have no patience to read, and I often fall asleep only to awaken to the sound of the television. The bed feels so large now and I'm not comfortable on my side or on my wife's side of the bed. I don't sleep well. I feel as if I am in control of so little. There is not much that I really want to do. Sometimes, the days feel endless.

THE STAGES OF GRIEF

Many death educators (Kubler-Ross, Kessler, Rando, Bowlby) have written about the various stages and phases of grief. People often like to think of stages, as it allows for a natural progression from the time of death until a later period, when one is doing "better" and perhaps has even "moved on." This pseudo fast-tracking allows for a sense of semi-predictability, which can at times feel comforting. However, one does not necessarily "move on," so much as "move through" one's grief, sometimes gently moving forward and at other times plowing through one's pain. The grief process will have many ups and downs and you will not always be able to anticipate what will upset you, and when. While grief is our instinctive and normal response to loss, we may put off or delay examining our grief because we may be too busy or too distracted by the vicissitudes of everyday life. We saw this, for example, during the COVID outbreak, when even our sense of self and who we were in a topsy-turvy world was threatened by the lack of normalcy.

During the initial stages of both the dying process and grief after a loss, there is often a sense of denial. This may be a time of shock and numbness, and you may experience a sense of disbelief and feeling that "it can't be happening to me" or "that this simply is not true." This stage is often marked by a sense of feeling overwhelmed and avoidance.

With time, you will be better able to consciously acknowledge the death of your loved one. You'll start to recognize and confront your loss and separation from them, and come to realize that in never seeing your loved one again, life will never be the same. You may go through a process of intense yearning for them, or be preoccupied with thoughts of your loved one. Simultaneously, you may also review and relive the intrusive memories that you had in your relationship with them.[2] Kubler-Ross and David Kessler refer to this as a time of anger (with the world, your loved one, family, the medical community, and others), bargaining, (If I…then…), despair, and even depression or sadness in your loss. In reacting to the separation and re-experiencing the loss as you begin to "get it," you come to acknowledge and accept that your loved one is truly dead. The nature of your relationship, as well

2. Bowlby, 1980.

as the various assumptions you may have had, all now need to be modified.[3]

Rando describes many processes that must be addressed in order to successfully move forward. To confront the reality of your loss and adapt to a life without your loved one, you will need to fully acknowledge the death and understand just what the loss entailed. You don't simply get over the loss of your loved one, but rather learn to live with the reality that this is forever. This is permanent, and your loved one is not coming back. Death is final and irreversible.

Judaism's rituals of having to identify your loved one and tear *kriya,* along with the shoveling of earth into the open grave and hearing the thud as it lands, as well as the week of shiva all help force you to deal with this stark reality. Our relentless search for soldiers missing in action or for remains after a plane crash reflects our need for closure in order to begin to grieve. Without a body, it is almost impossible to fully mourn. In the early stages, it is so easy to imagine that your loved one is simply "away on vacation." This gives us a reprieve from acknowledging the aspect of "forever" over "temporary."

Rando goes on to describe the need to experience the pain and react to the separation. Going through pain, or "opening the closet" as we discuss in great detail later – even slowly or for brief moments – will provide the path of healing. Learning to be in this new world without your loved one's physical and emotional presence can be very difficult, and may require a huge adjustment on your part. In this relationship with your loved one, you were connected in many areas and on many different levels. Now with your loved one no longer there in the same way, this circuitry between the two of you will need to be rewired, and you will need to form new bonds of attachment in what is now your new world. Your

3. Rando, 1991; 1996.

emotional energy will have to be directed from what *was* and be revised and redirected into what *is*. Through this grief work and with time, you will be able to do things that at one time you would have thought impossible. You will be able to speak of your loved one without pain, recognize both their positive and negative character traits, and experience your loss with less intensity. At this moment, all of this may feel difficult, if not impossible, to imagine.

While not forgetting about your old life, with this less pervasive sense of grief comes the ability to begin the journey of moving into the next phase. You will develop a new relationship with your loved one, which will continue forever, as you find an adaptive way to appropriately keep them "alive" in your heart. Rando[4] talks of using this freed-up energy that was once invested in your loved one and reinvesting it now in your new identity. This is a very important, healthy, and freeing shift in the grieving process. It is important to remember that this takes not only time, but also tremendous energy. While your religious beliefs may enable you to feel that you will be reunited at some point with your loved one in the World to Come, in this world, in the here and now, you will need to be present-focused.

As you confront your losses and adapt to a life without the physical presence of your loved one and the void left behind, you gradually move forward. With it comes a decline in your symptoms of acute grief, as you reach a stage of painful acceptance of your new reality and, with time, find meaning in your loss.[5] Your grief is not over, but it will start to feel more manageable as you begin to accept the inevitable reality of your situation. It is at this time that you will start to recognize glimmers of normality, learn how to enjoy life again, and look forward to the future.

4. 1988.
5. Kessler, 2019.

While each proponent of the stages of grief sees things slightly differently, they all generally recognize that the stages are not linear. There is overlap, a multitude of variables that impact the grieving process. The progression of healing and recovering meaning in your life takes tremendous time and energy. You might get stuck for a while in one stage and may even need some help to move on. You may also go back and forth, and at times wonder if you are regressing. Perhaps, too, you will experience periodic upsurges of grief, with increased symptoms at various times in the first year of mourning and wonder what is happening. We will discuss this in more detail later. Thankfully, you are resilient, and you will grow in ways that you never could have imagined. You will have good days and bad days, even good moments and bad moments, and that simply is how it will be for quite a while.

WHEN *SHELOSHIM* ENDS

> *I have lived thirty years in these thirty days. I am thirty years sadder. I feel like I am thirty years wiser.*
>
> Sheryl Sandberg, Facebook. June 2015, after the completion of the *sheloshim* for her husband

Judaism teaches us that when we have mourned for thirty days, our time of intense mourning comes to an end. Thirty days ends the mourning period for those who have lost a sibling, child, or spouse. For a parent, the mourning period continues for twelve months, with the reciting of *Kaddish* finishing a month earlier, at eleven months. Some people who have lost a sibling, child, or spouse, may choose to continue to say *Kaddish* for the full eleven months, without taking upon themselves the additional restrictions that come with the year of mourning.

In reality, although the official mourning period may conclude after thirty days, your mourning can continue for much longer. The fact that society no longer recognizes you as a mourner is significant, even though you may not be ready to move forward.

While a man may decide to grow a beard for the year, it is customary for both men and women to cut their hair after thirty days as a way to signal to the outside world the end of the *sheloshim* period.

In Israel, at the conclusion of the *sheloshim*, it is customary to erect the tombstone.

> *After the sheloshim for my father, I made an appointment at the hairdresser. I usually kept my hair short. As my father passed away right after Tisha B'Av, I had not had a haircut since before the Three Weeks, and my hair was quite long. I was walking to the salon, when I met a community member. This person had been away while I was sitting shiva and offered condolences. I told this person I was on my way to get a haircut to mark the end of the sheloshim. It was important for me to share this step. As I paid the hairdresser, I told her, with tears in my eyes, that I was moving out of sheloshim with a haircut. She understood as only a fellow Jew could, and wished me comfort and that I should come to her to fix my hair for future semaḥot.*

> *As the sheloshim comes to an end, perhaps when, or as, the numbness wears off just a bit, I start to ask myself questions. Perhaps it is because I can't make sense of the loss, but yet I think I need to, in order to move on. I ask myself – why did this death happen now, why at all, why just before a holiday or at such a terrible time, and how do I use this to help make sense, peace, or purpose out of the loss? Why don't I have more faith? Things happen, and we often do not understand the reason at the time – or ever. Maybe faith would help me cope better – I ask myself what, if anything, did I do or not do that helped contribute to his death? What did*

I miss? Perhaps I didn't miss anything. Sometimes life and death are out of my hands. I'm slowly starting to accept this.

SELF-CARE AND SELF-COMPASSION

It is so easy to forget about yourself and your own needs – both basic and otherwise – in the early days of mourning. While it may feel as though with your loved one no longer present, you have no need to look after yourself, ask yourself for a moment if that is what they and the rest of your family would want for you and for themselves. When you are dealing with a loss, you may live your life moment by moment, and then, with time, hopefully hour by hour, and day by day.

It is important to remind yourself that in this moment you can make the choice to be kind to yourself, not rush things, not pass judgment, or have any expectations. Now is the time to be your own best friend. Expect from yourself less than you would a friend, and give yourself permission to honor your grief with kindness and compassion. As you move into the world without your loved one, you will be forever changed. You will need to determine just how and in what ways you can make life meaningful for yourself.

Take note of the messages that you tell yourself, and ask yourself if they are helpful or critical. Are you patient and gentle or judgmental? Do you tell yourself that you "should" be over your grieving by now, or at least grieving differently? Do you give yourself permission to "take breaks" from your grief, and be wherever you are in that moment? It is not easy. Try to set up small islands of calm within the rocky seas, and ensure some quiet time away from the work of grieving. Meeting with a friend who makes you feel good, or spending time with your grandchild might be just the tonic you need.

While it may be difficult to have a routine with respect to anything right now, a sense of structure can be helpful to both you and your family; it allows for some semblance of predictability when all else seems fraught with uncertainty.

Here are some "grief aids" or self-compassion tools that are worth noting. If you have had other losses in the past, whatever tools you used to help you cope can guide you now as well.

Look after your health

It's not at all uncommon to feel unwell after a death. You may have put your own health and well-being aside to look after your loved one. Given that you grieve with your whole body and not just your head or your heart, parts of you may physically hurt. It is known, too, that immune functioning decreases in the months after a death. So as hard as it may be, it is important to look after yourself. It is important to drink and eat well. You may have no appetite, food may seem tasteless, it may be hard to cook for just yourself or minus one person, and you may feel as if it takes too much energy to prepare food or sit down to eat. This may be the time to call upon a friend to make you a hearty pot of soup, which can be frozen in small servings. Look for some flavored teas and other foods that may pique your appetite. Your body needs more strength than you might have imagined as you grieve. Eat and drink small amounts of nutritious snacks throughout the day if you find that you cannot face a full meal. Also, if you find that you are turning to food in an unhealthy way for comfort, try and sit down to eat a healthy prepared meal at least once a day. Remember that comfort food in the short term may not make you feel better in the long term.

Keep moving

Daily exercise is a key to helping you feel better and to lower your level of stress. Finding a buddy to exercise with and/or an activity that you like might make it more likely that you will get into a good exercise routine. No-one wants to disappoint a friend. Getting out and enjoying nature while sharing the walk with someone who makes you feel good may just change your day completely. You might be surprised that you feel more energetic and sleep better. However, be cautious about using exercise as an escape to the point where it is detrimental. If you overdo it, you might just discover that you are increasing your stress. Don't overschedule yourself as a way to avoid facing loss.

Sleep

You will need to find a balance between getting enough sleep and sleeping too much. Your nighttime sleep may be disrupted for a while, but try not to sleep during the day for too long. Notice your fatigue, and allow yourself to rest or take a brief nap. You may also find that you are having difficulties falling asleep or sleeping well throughout the night, especially if the other half of the bed is now empty. Often your sleep may not feel restorative, because you have a lot on your mind. Even if you get enough sleep, you may have increased physical pain or discomfort. Try to establish a bedtime routine, shut off all devices, and practice mindfulness relaxation and breathing techniques.

Beware of drugs, alcohol, and the impact of caffeine. Self-medication is never a good idea and especially now. If you are reliant on these, see the section on seeking professional help.

Be in this moment

In this moment, and only in this very moment, are you okay? How did you handle the past five minutes? What was helpful for you? Being mindful is a tool that can keep you focused on the here and now, instead of on the past or future. It can be very effective in keeping you from feeling overwhelmed. While of course you will have times when you feel like life is cascading down on you, focus on how you have just handled these last few minutes. Note that you may have handled them better than you thought. If you didn't handle them the way that you would have liked, realize that they are now over, and your task at hand is to focus on this new moment. There are many meditation techniques that are available and free of charge that can help you focus on mindfulness.

Keep a journal

Writing in a journal is not for everybody, but many who choose to keep a journal and document their feelings find that it does give them a place to put down their thoughts, as well as the many memories of their loved one. It also provides a place for you to write down the small things that you are able to accomplish each day, and notice the many blessings around you in spite of your grief. Reviewing it later can add clarity and meaning as well. Some, too, like to speak out loud as they are writing. They find that this gives them a sense of reassurance and relief, especially when there are raw feelings that cannot yet be shared with others. There are many online resources for grief journaling.

Relaxation

While what you are going through may be perfectly normal, be patient with yourself and slow down if you need to. There are many relaxation techniques that are easy to learn and are very effective. Many involve mindful breathing, which can be wonderful for restoring a sense of calm, keeping you focused, and helping improve your sleep.

Some people find a bath or a massage to be soothing, whereas others find cleaning, cooking, gardening, reading, painting or other forms of art calming. Some find that creative outlets such as journal writing, tai chi, or pottery may help them feel better.

Even a person who usually finds reading relaxing may find it hard to focus and concentrate and may prefer light reading, or simply flipping through magazines.

Music, too, can be a wonderful way to relax, though it may bring up some feelings that you may not be ready to handle. Over time, this might get easier, or you may choose to listen to different types of music during your year of mourning.

In feeling generally unsettled during this time, you may find it difficult to relax without guilt. There are always things to be done, and with lots on your mind, you might need to give yourself "permission" to take a break.

Spirituality

Anything that creates a healing environment at this time is very important. Prayer can be a way of helping you regulate your thoughts and feelings. Participation in communal prayer can be spiritually uplifting, and give you a sense of belonging. Making a point to start your day with gratitude may help bring you a sense of calm. You may discover that when you say the morning gratitude prayer *Modeh/ah Ani* and think of five things that happened in the past twenty-four hours that brought a smile to your face, your mood subtly changes. Whether it was something nice that you did for yourself, that happened to you, or that you saw, even the smallest glimmer of something you are grateful for or appreciate can serve as a reminder that there are good things in the world happening to you.

Social support

Social support is essential in helping you through your grief. It is easy to become isolated during your year of mourning. Checking in, even for brief periods with friends or family, while perhaps not comfortable, provides a reminder that life does continue.

Everyone has differing needs for support from others. Judaism's rituals envelop you and ensure that from the beginning of your grief you are not left alone, but rather are embraced by both individuals and the community at large. Others don't necessarily know what you need, so as difficult as it may be for you to reach out, it is important that you tell them. You might start with the simple sentence, "It would be really helpful for me if you could ..."

Also, recognize that you may have difficulty deciding in advance about socializing. While you may be looking forward to the prospect of being with others, as it gets closer, you may feel some trepidation. Only you can decide when to try and share what's going on and push forward, or if you need to bow out at this time. You can always tell your friends to please keep inviting you and to be patient because you hope that you will be able to say yes in the near future.

> TIP: For the non-mourners: Have patience with your family members and friends who are grieving. Don't avoid them, but also don't smother them. Shiva and *sheloshim* may conclude, but the pain lasts beyond the "technical" period of mourning.

Volunteering

While certainly at the beginning you may feel that it is all you can do to get through the day, as time goes on, offering even in a small way to help others can bring a sense of satisfaction as you become a little more outwardly focused. It may be a good way to get out and slowly reintegrate back into society. Donating time, food, or blood, while perhaps difficult at first, may have a tremendous impact on others and be helpful to you as well. It is important to keep active, but not to overschedule yourself as a way to avoid facing loss.

TRANSITIONING FROM *SHELOSHIM* TO THE YEAR OF MOURNING

Of the seven relationships that we mourn, parents are the only loved ones for whom the mourning period does not conclude after thirty days, but rather continues for a full year. The Talmud (Moed Katan 22b) explains that mourning rites for parents are longer, and therefore more restrictive than those for other relatives. The Talmud is not suggesting that the grief for one's parents is more intense than the grief for the loss of a child or spouse, but rather that our parents are in a separate category. Just as the Torah singles out parents for special respect in their lifetime (the mitzva of *kibbud horim*), we honor this bond after their death.

Why do we mourn our parents differently? The relationship between parent and child is typically the longest, and when a parent dies, we lose our basic foundation and historical continuity with the person who knew us from infancy onwards. The fracture of this generational bond may feel profound. Perhaps this twelve-month period of mourning provides an opportunity for introspection and reflection on the relationship, and the values and beliefs that were learned from it. After the year of mourning, there can be renewed appreciation for all that our parents have done for us that we ourselves may not have been aware of up until now. There is also the painful acknowledgement of finality and the inability to ask questions and seek their advice.

At this point in the grieving process, it is helpful to set short-term goals for yourself. This may, for example, involve returning to some regular routines that you may not have done during the *sheloshim* period. This may involve attending a *shiur*, accepting an invitation to a Shabbat dinner, rejoining an exercise class, or other leisure activities.

Chapter 6

Mourning Practices During the First Year

The first year will hold a great many challenges, whether you have completed the *sheloshim* and your mourning has officially ended, or you are in the twelve-month mourning period for your parent.

THE RHYTHM OF MOURNING

In his column, "The Rhythm of Mourning"[6] in response to the death of his father, Herb Keinon notes that when there is a death, the rhythm of life can be destroyed both suddenly and also over time. He notices that the Jewish rituals recognize this, and are structured to help the mourner to recover during the first year after a loss. This is a slow, gradual process. He speaks of the rhythm throughout the shiva, *sheloshim*, and end-of-first-year *yahrzeit* period, but also of the thrice-daily recitation of *Kaddish*, with its repetition both within each prayer service and during the day and throughout the week.

6. *The Jerusalem Post Magazine,* October 28, 2021, 34.

Perhaps initially we are meant to notice the profound absence of rhythm within our daily life as it once existed, and only during and by the official end of the mourning period to note that the rhythm itself can give us comfort. When your world is turned so totally upside down, the structure of the synagogue and the repetition of *Kaddish* can help you feel some order in the chaos.

Like a swimmer who jumps into the water to do laps, it takes time to catch your breath and only then establish a more comfortable pattern of breathing. As this starts to happen, you begin to bring a sense of calm and rhythmicity back into your swim. You may feel awkward at first, but with time you may feel more comfortable and are reminded of a similar experience when you last "jumped in."

THE MOURNER'S *KADDISH*

Kaddish – the mourner's prayer – is only recited with a minyan, and the community plays an important role when it answers "Amen." When the mourner hears the congregation answering Amen, it reinforces the words of the *Kaddish* prayer that praises God and provides an embrace from the community. The recitation of the Mourner's *Kaddish* may help heal some of the grief felt during the first year, as it provides a structure of daily prayer and a supportive minyan "community."

> "*Ha'oneh yeheh shemeh rabba mevorakh, muvtaḥ lo shehu ben ha'olam haba* – One who answers 'May His great name be blessed' – is guaranteed a place in the world to come."
>
> Talmud Bavli, Berakhot 57a

Kaddish is not a prayer for the dead, but rather a prayer that praises God, which is evident from the key words: "*Yeheh shemeh rabba mevorakh* – May His great name be blessed."

Some have described the thrice daily recitation of *Kaddish* as having a calming effect, by emphasizing over and over again the peace that God makes in the heavens, and the peace that He brings to people on earth: "*Oseh shalom bimromav hu yaaseh shalom aleinu ve'al kol Yisrael* – He who makes peace in His high places, may He make peace for us and all Israel."

Within *Kaddish*, words such as *ḥayim* (חיים, "life") and *shalom* (שלום, "peace") are repeated, and leave an impact on the mourner, perhaps even subliminally. This hopefully enables the mourner over the course of the eleven months to move from turmoil to peace, from despair to hope, from isolation to a sense of belonging within the community.

The recitation of *Kaddish* alongside other mourners in the community creates a fellowship of the bereaved in a time of sadness and loneliness. Consolation (*neḥama*) can be found when standing in the company of other mourners. Some even refer to those who are saying *Kaddish* with them at the same time as "my *Kaddish* buddies." It reminds the mourner that others are experiencing similar pain, and that death touches everyone. *Kaddish* gives you a place in the prayer service to acknowledge your loss. With its own rhythm and tempo, despite the difficult language (Aramaic), it carries us through a difficult time.

Rabbi Simcha Bunim of Przysucha (hasidic master, Poland, nineteenth century) explains that the Mourner's *Kaddish* also serves to comfort God. "In God's world, if a single Jew is missing, then there is already a lack in the greatness and the holiness of God. Therefore, we pray that His Name may be 'magnified and sanctified,' that is, that His Name be made complete for what it has lost with the death of the deceased."

The poet laureate S. Y. Agnon, expanded on Rabbi Simcha Bunim's analogy. "When a human king orders his armies into battle, he does not know the individual men. If there is a loss, he regrets the death, but he doesn't mourn any individual. Not so with the King of Kings. He is Master of the World, yet He cares for each individual life. When God's soldiers die, He mourns each person. When a person dies, God's own Name is diminished, His own sanctity lessened. His Kingdom experiences a terrible vacancy. God suffers, as it were, just as the human mourner suffers. When we recite *Kaddish,* we offer God consolation for His loss. We say *Yitgadal:* Your name has been diminished; may it be magnified. *Yitkadash:* Your sanctity has been lessened; may it be increased. *Yamlikh malkhutei:* Your kingdom has suffered a sudden loss; may it reign eternally."

This different interpretation of the *Kaddish,* which sees it as the mourner's attempt also to offer consolation to God, recognizing that God suffers in the loss of every one of His creations made in His image, can be a source of comfort to the bereaved.

Many people who are not affiliated with a synagogue or Jewish community will still feel it important or expected of them to recite the Mourner's *Kaddish.* They may find that a community is comforting and helpful during the year of mourning. It may even be the community of the deceased parent. On numerous occasions, after the year of *avelut* (mourning) concludes, some people, now feeling very connected to the minyan, continue to come to the synagogue. They may also want to express gratitude towards those who made up the daily minyan when they were saying *Kaddish* by being present for them.

The source for the recitation of *Kaddish* by children in merit of their parents appears in many different sources: Talmud, Midrash, and Zohar. This story told about Rabbi Akiva implies that the recitation of *Kaddish* is seen as a merit for the deceased.

Rabbi Akiva was in a cemetery when he saw a man rushing about carrying wood. Rabbi Akiva asked, "What is

> this harsh labor of yours?" The man replied, "I am dead. Every day, they send me to chop wood upon which they burn me every night." Rabbi Akiva asked, "And when you were in this world, what was your work?" "I was a tax collector," the man answered. "I would favor the wealthy and persecute the poor." Rabbi Akiva asked, "Is there any way you could be redeemed from your punishment?" "Yes," the man replied. "They said that if I had a son and if that son would stand among the congregation and say *Kaddish* and the congregation would answer, 'Amen! *Yeheh shemeh rabba mevorakh!*' then they could relieve me of my punishment."
>
> Rabbi Akiva resolved to search for the man's child. After finding him, Rabbi Akiva taught him how to read Torah and to say the *Shema*, the Silent Prayer, and Grace After Meals. Then he stood him before the congregation, and he said *Barkhu* and they answered him. He said *Kaddish* and they answered him, "Amen! *Yeheh shemeh rabba mevorakh*!" The father came to Rabbi Akiva in a dream. "Let your heart rest assured that you saved me from the judgment of *Gehenom* [Hell]."

From this story, we see that through meritorious deeds a child can bring virtue to their parents even after their death. When a child says *Kaddish*, it elevates the soul of their deceased parents.

The rabbis did not place the obligation to recite *Kaddish* on women, as it is a time-bound mitzva from which women are generally exempt. However, many women have chosen to take the recitation of *Kaddish* upon themselves, and by doing so also bring merit to their loved ones.

> *I recited Kaddish for my father at the funeral and during the shiva. Reciting Kaddish with my siblings was actually very powerful. I felt their grief, but also their support. We would get through this together. I decided to continue to say Kaddish in a minyan three*

times a day if possible. The daily obligation was stressful, especially in the winter, but the structure of the daily prayers and Kaddish gave me comfort. There were people who questioned my decision, asking: "Why are you saying Kaddish when you have brothers?" My husband and children were very supportive of my daily Kaddish, even when the timing affected our family routine. Most of the male congregants were respectful and supportive, as they saw me coming to the davening on a daily basis. I did have some unpleasant situations, where there was no women's section, and there were some insensitive comments, but overall, my Kaddish was a journey. As with any journey, there are some bumpy roads and some that are smooth. I came to appreciate the men who make up the daily minyan, as their commitment to communal prayer allowed me to say Kaddish. I didn't need Kaddish to remember my father. I thought of him and missed him every day. But the three daily prayers gave me a place for my grief. I met other women during that year, who like me were struggling with their own personal losses. I was so very grateful to the women around me in the women's section on Shabbat who answered Amen to my Kaddish, as throughout the week I was often standing alone. Eleven months of Kaddish was challenging, but I did it as my way to give honor to my father.

My father supported my path in women's Jewish learning, but saying Kaddish in his memory was not about "feminism." Rather, it was about love, honor, and respect. When the eleven months were over, there was a certain sense of relief and, dare I say, accomplishment. But there was also a feeling of "now what?"

When the children are unable to do so, grandchildren can also recite *Kaddish*. The Sages also permitted the hiring of someone else to say *Kaddish*. If someone died without children, it was established that relatives or others could say *Kaddish* on their behalf, so that the name of the deceased would not be forgotten.

My Journey Through the First Year of Kaddish

I have recited Kaddish in a minyan every day since my father was buried. That is one of the things we can do as mourners to honor the dead. It is very difficult to go from being someone who never prayed once a day in a minyan to becoming a person who prays once a day in a minyan.

I go to an Orthodox synagogue which is right near my house, but when I find myself away from my neighborhood, I plan ahead and find a minyan where I can recite this prayer.

Here is why I have made the decision to recite Kaddish every day in a minyan.

Routine: The routine of daily prayer encourages you to sit with your pain and grief on a daily basis. I can't ignore my grief, because it's sitting with me in my pew every single day. It's also the reason we say Kaddish in a minyan rather than alone. Community surrounds you and helps you define yourself. They are not mourning. I am. They are here with me, and I am obligated to acknowledge my grief so as to remind everyone to please be gentle with me; I am a mourner. Because I am virtually performing the same prayers and going through the same motions daily, I have a fairly accurate gauge of how my grief shifts and ebbs and flows in this routine of prayer and meditation. On one day, it's a remote wish for God to comfort me because I feel no comfort at all, but as time unfolds, I embrace the notion of God comforting me. I can see my heart opening a bit more every day because I exercise it every day.

Meditation: My time in shul is quiet time. In the Orthodox synagogues where I have gone, I am literally the only female there. It's private and quiet in the women's section. Sometimes I listen, and sometimes I chant, and sometimes I shokel – rocking back and forth gently to the rhythm of the ancient words. This is time to think, and to move, and to also just be still – a rare commodity in most lives, but in particular mine. It's a gift.

Discipline Among Chaos: Grief is chaotic. It mushes up your brain and makes it hard to think straight, and see straight, and talk right. The fact that I can show up somewhere every day in the midst of the chaos of grief gives me hope that order will return. I can have discipline even though I am grief-stricken, out of sorts, feeling crazed.

Learning Something New: I have never been to a morning service except for Shabbat, so I am learning how the structure of prayer in Judaism happens through this process. I am watching men pray while wearing tefillin (phylacteries), something I had only ever seen my grandfather do every morning by himself when he would come and stay with us when I was a child. In the middle of loss, I am gaining something: knowledge.

Life doesn't go on, but it does: Losing my dad felt incompatible with life going on. Not so much because I felt I could not live without him, but because it felt impossible to live without him being alive too. I had to go back to work, care for my kids, feed myself, make decisions, email, schedule, and do. I had to be a productive member of society again, separate from my new identity as a mourner. Life goes on; it has to. But saying Kaddish every day has allowed me to step out of the "life goes on" part of my day to enter a sanctuary (literally!) where I again am a mourner, and I feel again that life can't go on because it's OK to feel that way. It's healthy to hold that tension in your brain. Grief is dissecting life going on from life not going on again and again.

I will continue to recite Kaddish every day. For the routine, the meditation, the discipline, the learning, and the tension it brings.

Adapted from Mayim Bialik, "The First 30 Days of Mourning My Father," *Kveller*, May 14, 2015

> *The ritual of reciting the Mourner's Kaddish in the presence of a minyan has taught me the value of taking time to slow the busy-ness of my life, to decide who and what is truly important, to still my mind, and to connect with that which is larger than myself.*
>
> Sarah Birnbach, "The Powerful Healing from the Mourner's *Kaddish*," *Jerusalem Post*, November 17, 2022

FINDING A MINYAN

For those who are saying *Kaddish*, there is often the tension of finding a daily minyan. The prayer times change for the afternoon and evening prayers (Minḥa and Maariv) depending on the season. Some people are fortunate to have a synagogue nearby, but it becomes challenging when you are at work or far from home. Technology comes in handy, as there are now apps such as "Find a minyan near me" (although they are not always accurate and cannot be relied upon). We have heard many fascinating stories firsthand of people who needed a minyan to say *Kaddish* and found a quorum in the strangest and most unexpected places. We also heard touching stories of how people went to great lengths to facilitate a minyan for a mourner, understanding how important it was for them to recite *Kaddish* for their loved one in a minyan.

> *Just as the strength of any chain is as strong as its individual links, so too does the minyan depend on its individual members. When one link is missing, the bond of communal prayer is broken. Each of us struggles to find a place in the world where we are needed and valued.*
>
> *Judaism has enshrined that reality at the very heart of our prayer ritual. We cannot pray as a community without reaffirming that we need each other, and that every single one of us is infinitely valuable. Judaism's requirement for a minyan for prayer reminds us of this truth.*

Sarah Birnbach, "The Powerful Healing from the Mourner's *Kaddish*," *Jerusalem Post*, November 17, 2022

It was early one morning, prior to the corona crisis. The driver of the bus seemed to be doing a count of how many people were boarding. Frequently, drivers have to check that there aren't too many people standing in the aisles. It turned out, however, that this driver was checking if ten men had boarded the bus so far. Once he determined that he had a minyan (the quorum necessary for public prayer), he asked the passengers if they minded a slight delay so that he could say the final Kaddish from Shaḥarit, the morning service.

He explained that he was in the midst of the eleven-month period, when Kaddish is recited after the loss of a parent.

It is done several times during the morning service.

"I had to rush out of synagogue to start working early this morning; so if you really don't mind, I just want to say the last Kaddish that I missed. I can send a note to your boss if you need one explaining why you were late." The passengers all agreed. No one asked for a note to bring to their boss. The driver shut off the engine.

He seemed quite emotional. Those of us who have had the experience of needing to find a minyan three times a day for all those months of reciting Kaddish are aware of just how challenging, though also rewarding, it can be.

By the way, the men were not asked to cover their heads. In fact, the driver did not even confirm that they were Jewish. But Kaddish was recited, men and women answered at the appropriate places, and the commute continued.

David Jablinowitz, "Bus Stories: Life-Cycle Events," *Jerusalem Post*, March 10, 2021

LEADING THE PRAYERS DURING THE YEAR OF MOURNING

In many synagogues, before the *tefilla* (prayer service), the *gabbai* (beadle) customarily asks if anybody "has a *ḥiyuv*" (formal obligation to lead the prayers). The people who are considered to "have a *ḥiyuv*" are *avelim* (mourners) and those observing *yahrzeit* for a parent. If there is anybody with a *ḥiyuv*, he is asked to lead the prayers from the *amud* (podium) and to be the prayer leader. To lead the prayers during the week (not on Shabbat or holidays) as a mourner is a custom, and is considered a way of honoring one's parent. It is not necessary to accept it, especially if you don't feel fluent in Hebrew or comfortable leading the prayers. People have been known to say half-jokingly, "my parent's death made me an *avel* [mourner], but not a *ḥazan* [cantor]."

> *I always enjoyed being the shaliaḥ tzibur [prayer leader], especially on Friday nights for Kabbalat Shabbat services. I'm not a ḥazan, but I've been told I have a pleasant voice. That has changed now that I'm asked to lead the tefilla during my year of mourning. I make an effort to arrive on time to say Kaddish, but the addition of being the ḥazan, three times a day, puts a strain on me. There is an advantage, that as the ḥazan I can dictate the pace of the tefilla, but sometimes I am relieved to find that a community member has yahrzeit and I get a break.*

COMING TO THE END OF THE YEAR

The end of Kaddish at eleven months

It is customary to recite *Kaddish* for a parent for eleven months. Even during a Hebrew leap year, which lasts thirteen months, *Kaddish* is recited for only eleven months. The talmudic Sages teach that even the most wicked person is only punished in the afterlife for a maximum of twelve months. As we presume that our parents do not fall into that category, the practice in most communities is to recite the *Kaddish* for eleven months.

Shul attendance and *Kaddish* have in many ways helped to keep you connected to the community over the last year. *Kaddish,* as we have noted previously, is one of the prayers that you do not say on your own, but rather with a minyan. Having the other attendees, who are in many ways there for you at that moment, say "Amen" to your *Kaddish* is very life affirming. It helps keep you connected when all else may feel uncertain. Day after day, the repetition of *Kaddish* enables you to be with others, and have the members of the minyan absorb some of the pain of your loss.

After eleven full months, you will say your last *Kaddish* for your parent. If you have been going to the synagogue daily and it is now time for your recitation of *Kaddish* to end, perhaps you have already been anticipating this moment. After eleven months, you may be more than ready to give up that stress of having to find a daily minyan at whatever time you need to, and to ensure that there are ten men present.

Yet, possibly you may feel somewhat apprehensive and anxious that this protective isolation from the world of outside social responsibilities will soon be lifted. You may feel conflicted and not quite ready to stop. There is something to be said for the comfort that routine brings. You may be quite surprised to discover that you miss the daily *Kaddish,* and are thinking more of your loved one, especially now as you get closer to the end of your mourning period.

> *The twelve-month journey of mourning one's parents begins, with a single prayer: Yitgadal, veyitkadash, shemeh rabba.*
>
> *Then another, and another, and another, and another.*
>
> *Five times in the morning, once in the afternoon and once in the evening: Yitgadal, veyitkadash, shemeh rabba.*
>
> *My eleven-month Kaddish journey for my father ended last week – the mourner does not recite this prayer during the*

last month of the twelve-month mourning period – and I'm conflicted.

On the one hand, I am relieved. Greatly relieved.

I can't tell you how many times I played with the statistics in my mind about how many days were left, what percentage of the eleven months I had finished, and what percentage still remained. But mostly I did mental calculations about how many more services I would have to lead. Because in addition to reciting the Mourner's Kaddish, it is customary for the mourner – if able – to lead every morning, afternoon, and evening prayer service.

Though not necessarily willing – I have never enjoyed standing at the front of the shul – I am able, and because I was able, I felt obligated. So I did, day in and day out.

As my father would say, "That's a lot of davening, son."

Indeed, it was.

My life revolved around this for eleven months. In the thirty-eight years since I had to say Kaddish for my mother, I'd forgotten how all-absorbing this was.

If I had out-of-town meetings in the morning, I would search a minyan app the night before, looking for synagogues near my meeting place where I could pray.

If I had an afternoon meeting, I would make sure to go to the first minyan past noon. If I was out at night, I would make sure to get back at least by eleven o'clock to make the last minyan in my neighborhood.

So, with the eleven months now over, and not having to jump through those kinds of hoops day after day, there understandably is a sense of relief. It's not that until this year I was a stranger to a minyan. I wasn't, but if I missed it, I missed it.

This past year, however, I felt that if I would miss saying Kaddish, I would somehow be letting my father down. I dreaded catching corona, less because I didn't want the cough, fever, and fatigue, and more because I was just afraid it would keep me from saying Kaddish.

Funny, the most difficult thing about getting to a minyan three times a day was not even getting to a minyan three times a day. It was having to be among the first ones there – because Kaddish in the morning service is one of the first prayers said – and having to be the last one to leave, since Kaddish is at the end of all three prayer services. That was something I was not accustomed to.

Then there's the relief of not having to lead the prayers. Here, however, I learned something humbling: people are not as aggravating as I talked myself into believing.

I braced myself, during the first few days in my role as reluctant cantor, for what I thought would be a barrage of criticism. I expected to be corrected constantly about my pronunciation. I also expected that some people would complain because I was going too fast, while others would complain that I was going too slow. I'd get nervous before each pre-prayer approach to the bima.

But after 964 services – I missed eight times while in transit and in pandemic lockdown – I was only corrected three times… and it was done graciously.

So, if I feel relieved that my eleven months of saying Kaddish has come to an end, what's the flip side?

The flip side is that now I feel an emptiness, though not necessarily for the reasons I was warned.

Some people told me that an emptiness emerges when reciting Kaddish ends because it was a period when they felt a special connection to their loved ones, when they thought about them. When reciting Kaddish stopped, so did that feeling of being connected.

For me, the emptiness is of a different sort.

I don't need to recite Kaddish to feel my dad. I think about him, what he would say, and how he would react, when

I wake up in the morning, when I set out on the road, and when I lie down to sleep at night. I hear his voice constantly, and it has nothing to do with reciting Kaddish.

No, the emptiness I feel is of a different sort. It's an emptiness born of no longer having any more obligations to my dad, of a realization that that period of my life – of having obligations and duties to my parents – is over. Forever.

Obligations are often tiresome and a burden, but they also give purpose and meaning and satisfaction when fulfilled.

The emptiness I feel now is that there is nothing more I can, should, or must do for my parents, because there is simply nothing left for me to do for them. Nothing.

Yes, it's a relief to no longer have to say Kaddish. But it also makes my dad's death seem so starkly final.

Adapted from Herb Keinon, "Musings on the End of Saying *Kaddish*," *Jerusalem Post*, July 30, 2022

The opportunity to carry on one's obligation of honoring parents is ever present, even long after their passing. Every time I make a donation in my father's memory to a cause he would have supported, I feel I am honoring him. The same goes for every time I give a Dvar Torah in his name, or I keep his yahrzeit or those of his parents. These types of opportunities provide comfort that I'm sure Herb is looking for.

Letter to the editor by David Gilad in response to Herb Keinon, "Musings on the End of Saying *Kaddish*," *Jerusalem Post*, July 30, 2022

PRAYER FOR THE END OF *KADDISH*

The last *Kaddish* for a parent can be very emotional. With no formal ritual to mark the end of these eleven months, people have attempted to write their own prayers to help provide closure for this very significant milestone.

The original prayer below was composed by Rabbi Benjamin Lau to mark the end of a mourner's journey. It was originally posted in Hebrew on Facebook on the fifteenth of Ḥeshvan, 5776 (2015) marking the end of his *Kaddish* for his father. It was published in English on the fifteenth of Kislev 5776, the first *yahrzeit* of his father, Naphtali Lau Lavie, of blessed memory. It was translated into English by Shira Pasternak Be'eri.

A Contemporary Prayer for the End of Kaddish
(For a Father)
To be recited after the last Kaddish at the end of eleven months of mourning

Our Father in Heaven,

I have been privileged to complete the recitation of *Kaddish* to elevate the soul of my father and teacher, from the time when he was taken to the Heavens until now.

I tried to honor my father during the course of this year with all my heart and all my might.

And now I stand before You filled with emotion, and say:

I did all that You commanded me to do.
At this time, as I stand before You
during the afternoon prayer,
I raise my voice in supplication before the throne of Your glory,
and ask that all of my prayers will go up to You
and be acceptable to You.
And grant my father
his place in a world that is all good,

among all the created beings
who shined favorably upon You in Your world.
Therefore, God of mercy,
shelter him in the shadow of Your wings forever,
and bind his soul in the bond of everlasting life.
God is his inheritance.
May he rest in peace, and let us say: Amen.[7]

A friend was questioning if it was appropriate for her to mark the last Kaddish for her beloved parent, even though she had not been reciting Kaddish. Her brothers, who had been saying Kaddish for the duration of the eleven months, were making a Kiddush in her parent's memory. Being in a different country, she still wanted to participate in this significant milestone with her brothers. On the same day that her brothers were making the Kiddush, she decided to make a "Seudat Amen," inviting her close friends and sharing words of Torah and beautiful memories of her loved one. By doing this, she felt that she had connected with her siblings and was honoring her parent's memory in a very significant way. While it was unusual to have a ceremony focused on the eleven-month period, it was also very meaningful for those who participated.

At the end of a full twelve months after your loved one's death, the first *yahrzeit* will be observed, and you will be back in the synagogue once again saying *Kaddish*. In some strange way, you may feel different, even though only one month has elapsed. Is it that in some way you may have begun to move on in this short period of time? The answer is quite possibly yes.

7. Hebrew text for the above and prayer for the loss of a mother in English and Hebrew may be found in the Appendix, p. 361.

Visiting the gravesite

As a way to remember and honor your loved one, you may visit the grave as early as the end of shiva, but more frequently the first visit to the cemetery takes place when marking the end of the *sheloshim* period. At this time, the mourning period officially ends for all but a parent, which continues for twelve months according to the Hebrew calendar. (Unlike the end of *sheloshim,* which is anchored to the time of burial, the twelve months are determined from the actual date of death, and therefore must be calculated according to the Jewish calendar.)

Whereas in Israel, an *azkara,* or memorial ceremony, is often held at the end of *sheloshim,* outside of Israel, an unveiling of the tombstone is typically held closer to the end of the twelve months of mourning, which is usually the first *yahrzeit.* (In a Jewish leap year, which adds a whole extra month to the calendar year, the mourning period lasts twelve months as well, but the *yahrzeit* will be a month later, on the exact Hebrew date of their death.)

Judaism does not encourage excessive visitation to the gravesite, especially in the first year when your grief may be very raw. Rather, the focus is on life, living, and trying to move forward. Visiting the cemetery may keep the mourner stuck in the loss of their relationship with the deceased. So, while one may visit on special occasions such as a birthday, just prior to Rosh HaShana, to mark the *sheloshim,* and on the *yahrzeit,* one does not go to the cemetery on Shabbat, as well as most holidays. After the first year, while some people may find it comforting to visit the gravesite during the year, others don't feel the need to go often. There are those who would like to visit more frequently, but because of the distance are simply unable to. The choice as to how often to go to the cemetery is very much an individual decision – it depends on what feels right for *you.* It is customary when visiting the gravesite to place a stone – an unperishable reminder – on the grave to mark your visit.

THE ERECTION OF THE TOMBSTONE/UNVEILING

> "And Rachel died and was buried on the way to Efrat, which is Bethlehem. And Jacob erected a tombstone on Rachel's grave."
>
> Gen. 35:19–20

While some suggest that erecting the tombstone (unveiling) be done as soon as possible after shiva, and often to mark the *sheloshim*, outside of Israel many wait to do this until closer to the first *yahrzeit* (at twelve months after the death) as a way of marking or remembering the date of their loved one's passing.

The custom of erecting a tombstone originated during the times of the Temple in Jerusalem. Jewish priests (*kohanim*) became ritually impure if they came in contact with a dead body. As a result, Jews began marking graves with piles of stones in order to indicate to passing *kohanim* that there were graves in the area, and they should avoid being in the vicinity. The second reason for demarcating the grave was to show precisely where the person was buried, so that others could find it in order to visit. Finally, the tombstone was seen as a symbol of honor for the deceased.

The wording on the tombstone

In Hebrew we call the grave a *kever* (קבר), and the tombstone itself a *matzeva* (מצבה, "monument"). In Israel, the wording of the tombstone, as well as the particulars of the stone, are often discussed and decided upon during a quiet moment throughout the week of shiva or shortly thereafter, and then the stone itself is cut. In Israel, while you may feel pressured to complete the wording and find a stone-setter within thirty days, this helps keep you present- and future-focused, which in itself may in some small way feel comforting. Outside of Israel, you may want to start this process around nine or ten months after the loss, as it often takes longer than you may think to get the stone ready.

The wording on the *matzeva* is very personal, and usually chosen by the family. Usually a biblical verse (*pasuk*) or quotation that symbolizes the person's life is chosen, in addition to the deceased's Hebrew name and Hebrew/English year of birth and death. Often the relationships to other family members are written, for example: father/mother/husband/wife. Certain symbols may be added as well, such as two hands spread like the Priestly Blessings if the deceased was a *kohen*. The symbol of a pitcher signifies a Levite – as members of the tribe of Levi were responsible for cleaning the hands of the Temple priest. A candle or candelabra often is used on the tombstone of a woman. At the top of most Jewish tombstones is the abbreviation *peh nun* (פ"נ) which stands for *po nikbar/a* or *po nitman/enet*, meaning "here lies." The letters *zayin lamed* (ז"ל) stand for *zikhrono/a livrakha* – May his/her memory be for a blessing. (When referring to the deceased, many people will add this after the person's name. For example, "My grandfather, *zikhrono livrakha*, said *tehillim* every day.")

Many tombstones are inscribed with the Hebrew letters ת.נ.צ.ב.ה. These letters are an acronym for the Hebrew words "תהא נפשו/ה צרורה בצרור החיים – May his/her soul be bound up in the bond of eternal life (*tzror haḥayim*)." This paraphrases the words that Avigail told King David (I Sam. 25:29): "But my lord's soul shall be bound in the bond of life with the Lord your God."

Tzror in Hebrew also means a stone. In ancient times, shepherds needed a system to keep track of their flocks. They would carry a sling filled with pebbles that corresponded to the number in their flock. In Psalm 23:1 God is described as a shepherd who watches over us, his flock. When we place stones on the grave and inscribe this motto above on the tombstone, we are asking God to keep the departed soul in His sling. Among all the souls whom God watches over, we wish to add the name of our departed.[8]

8. David Wolpe, 1995.

> *My father was buried in the United States, and my mother and my family were now living in Israel. Knowing that I would not travel to visit my father's grave, my mother instructed me to put my father's birth and death dates on her tombstone as well. When she died, I did as she suggested. Now on both my parents' yahrzeits I go to my mother's grave. I know my father is not buried there, but having his name on the tombstone and having a place to visit gives me great comfort.*
>
> Miriam Fenster

THE MEMORIAL SERVICE/*AZKARA*

For many, especially in Israel, erecting the tombstone, which may include the unveiling of the stone itself, and an *azkara* (memorial prayers) are held at the end of *sheloshim*. The custom outside of Israel is to do the unveiling at the time of the first *yahrzeit*. The *azkara* usually includes the reading of psalms and the prayer *E-l Maleh Raḥamim* and Mourner's *Kaddish*. Family members may speak about the deceased, sharing memories and words of Torah.

Whenever the trip to the cemetery is made, it may be your first time visiting your loved one since their death. This is often a time of renewed sadness and possibly increased anxiety, as wounds are temporarily reopened. That said, the unveiling of the tombstone, the *azkara*, and first *yahrzeit* in many ways all help to bring closure, and often with it you may experience a sense of relief. This is an appropriate time to eulogize again, share memories, or even write down some thoughts and feelings you may have.

NAVIGATING THE YEAR OF *AVELUT*

The year after a loss is often a painful one, in which you transition from having your loved one physically with you to holding their memory in your heart.

In the first year after my loved one's death, when I had the urge to speak to them and consult on something I needed help with, I found my mind trying to deceive me of my new reality. My loved one wasn't really dead – my mind kept telling me they were on vacation or a business trip, and surely would be back soon. Similarly, whenever I thought of something I wanted to share, my urge to pick up the phone and just call was so strong. When reality hit, I felt so sad.

No matter how prepared you think you are, or how well you feel you are coping, life will have mini surprises for you around each corner: whether it is the smell of someone's aftershave or perfume, a reminder of your loved one's favorite food, or catching a glimpse of someone who walks in the same manner or has the hairstyle of your loved one. Little things may suddenly seem bigger than we anticipated, and while we need to go easy on ourselves, that may be difficult. We are often left wondering if we did enough for them in their lifetime, and if we could have done more. Loss is huge and we, too, are human. Nice things happen also, and some of the things that may initially bring pain can ultimately be very comforting. Someone who looks or acts like your loved one may, over the ensuing years, help keep your loved one alive in your thoughts and in your heart.

Four months after my mother passed away, I was trying to purchase a Mother's Day card for my very beloved mother-in-law. Scanning every card in the store, I was feeling very teary-eyed, as every card reminded me of my mother. I finally left the store with the first card I had seen, and probably not the best one. I am also reminded of attending a play in the months following my mom's death. In the opening scene, which had little to do with the rest of the play, someone died, and I was no longer watching the play but was caught up instead in aspects of the death and comparing it to my loss.

DECISION-MAKING

While you may feel overwhelmed with all of the decisions – both big and small – that need to be made, you only need to tackle the ones that need to be dealt with *now*. You can prioritize the most important one or two decisions, and put the rest "in the drawer" to deal with a later time.

For those that need to be dealt with right away, you may have no choice but to attend to them. They may be difficult. For example, you may have to clear out your loved one's belongings from a rented apartment. This does not mean that you need to throw everything out, but rather, taking it one step at a time, first empty the contents of the apartment. For this huge project, who can you enlist to assist you?

> TIP: When in pain, we often make decisions that we later regret. It may feel that we must sell the house, go on that trip, or throw out things that are a painful reminder of our loss. We think that doing these things will lessen our pain, only to discover that we take our grief with us. While there will be times that you will need to make decisions, try to postpone the more important ones until your grief is less raw and make sure you discuss them with someone whose opinion you value.

> *We are not always masters of our emotions. After the death of my father, I felt an existential black hole, an emptiness at the core of being. It deadened my sensations, leaving me unable to sleep or focus, as if life was happening at a great distance, and as if I were a spectator watching a film out of focus with the sound turned off. The mood eventually passed, but while it lasted, I made some of the worst mistakes of my life.*
>
> Adapted from R. Jonathan Sacks, "Healing the Trauma of Loss," in *Studies in Spirituality*, p. 206

Some family members and friends have gone out of their way to protect me during my grieving, shielding me from decision-making. It has not worked. I feel alienated from them, and not consulted when I should be. I know they mean well, and I know they may be afraid of my tears, but leaving me out of important decisions has only made me feel more upset. I do have thoughts and feelings, and it is important that I be able to voice them. I question whether I want to go to certain events or not attend them at all. I hate it when I'm seated with other singles. I feel as if they don't know where to put me, especially now that I'm without a partner. On top of it all, I often have to hear them say to me that it must be hard for me to come to their event. This feels so insensitive. I feel like I am to be pitied, which feels terrible. "It's so good to see you," would feel so much better.

REFRAMING A TRAUMATIC EVENT

After the death of a loved one, we are often left with certain unpleasant pictures in our mind. This may relate to how they looked when they were unwell, in the hospital, or just before or at the time of death. It will not happen right away, but with time, during the grieving process, those images will fade or can be reframed. Similarly, we may remember our loved one with only their positive or negative attributes; also with time, this too will change, and you will be able to see a more "whole" version of your loved one, with both their strengths and their failings.

My mom was taken by ambulance to the hospital, and I followed by car. I still remember the image of her being put into the back of the ambulance and the doors being closed. I discovered on arrival that the medics forgot to reconnect her oxygen for the fifteen-minute ambulance ride, resulting in her having greater difficulty breathing. This was traumatic for her and for me. After my mother died, it took me a while to get the image of the back of the ambulance out of my mind. Initially, I didn't want to think about it, and reminded myself I didn't have to think about that now. With time, I slowly forced myself to look at the back doors of the ambulance in the ambulance bay near the hospital in which I worked; ultimately, I could separate my anger, sense of loss, and helplessness from her discomfort and the horrific ambulance ride. One day, I realized that the good memories had returned, and the more difficult ones had faded. They were a small and traumatic part of her illness towards the end, and I was able to see them as just that. Those incidents had a beginning, middle, and end, and they were over, so no longer had to remain a visual reminder for me. The memories of her smile, her caring, how beautiful she was, and so much more, took precedence once again as they should.

The first year after your loved one dies continues to be very much a year of transitions and firsts. While in theory you may be able to reintegrate into society at the designated time, you may feel very raw and not necessarily be ready to face the world as if nothing has happened.

As my friend, I need you to be there for me. Please don't suggest that so much time has gone by and ask me if I am over "it" yet, or hint that I need to "move on." Rather, take a seat beside me and remind me that you are there for me – always. Ask me what I need to do today, or what would be helpful. I may or may not know. I have been focusing on just getting up and starting my day – again. But I do know that I will need you to come back and be there for me over and over again for a very long time. I need your love and warmth now more than ever.

HOLIDAYS AND SIGNIFICANT EVENTS DURING THE FIRST YEAR

As the year progresses, it will be marked by various holidays and significant events, such as the birthday of your loved one, an anniversary, a *yahrzeit,* or other family milestones. When a death occurs close in time to these events, it is not at all uncommon for the two to become linked, and to be a reminder forever of your loved one: their illness, their death, the empty seat around the family table, or their absence in the synagogue. Holidays also always bring up memories of past celebrations that are now taking place without your loved one, and future events where your loved one will be forever missed. You will most likely experience an upsurge in grief at this time, which may last for a short period of time but, in anticipation of these events, more likely several days. You may feel that you are backsliding when these waves of grief seem to wash over you, but in reality, you are just more painfully aware of the loss of your loved one. It will get better again, and you will breathe a sigh of relief when these events are over, and life seems to settle back down once more.

Considering the Jewish calendar has so many holidays, it seems as if a death is often defined as falling around or in between them. The holidays are a stark reminder of your loved one's absence, and pose a challenge on so many levels. Remember, that with regard to holiday preparations, which are often overwhelming and anxiety-producing, with almost every decision, you can choose what you would and would not like to do. You may want to delegate some of the planning or cooking, or it might be very important to you that you be involved in every small detail. While holidays can be exciting, they are also exhausting, and probably will be more so this year than in the past. There is often a desire to simply get past them. You may worry about how you will cope, but in the end, you must do what is right for you. Often the dread and anticipation are worse than the actual event. This may have been a time when you naturally spent time together as a family, and your memories of past holidays serve as a reminder of what you have now lost. Whether you spend it alone or with others, the holiday will not, and cannot, feel the same. The emptiness and loss and upsurge in grief you may feel are very normal. It is hard to feel joyful at this time, whether you're at home in your familiar surroundings or you have agreed to go elsewhere and be surrounded by others. Neither place may feel particularly safe or comfortable.

In spite of the sadness you may feel, if your family has created its own set of rituals and traditions, you may be able to find those that give you meaning and joy. This year may be a time when you need to focus on reevaluating your priorities. Your goal for now is one of survival, of getting through and past this holiday. You need to do what is right for you. You may feel differently by the next holiday, so be present-focused as much as possible. You may not even know what you will be able to handle comfortably or what you will want others to take over for you this year.

When you think of the holidays, be it the special foods, the table set beautifully, the tranquility of the flickering candles, Kiddush, and davening, you may be transported back to those memories of a time not so long ago when your loved one was with you. Each holiday has its own reminders. Now, whether you are missing Seder Night with Dad as the regular leader, Mom's wonderful Hanukka latkes recipes, or the young child who always found the *afikoman,* you'll need to ask yourself how, with this holiday feeling so different, can you still make it feel special. You may discover that you have no energy to ponder these questions, and that, too, is okay. Is there someone – a family member or close friend – who would be willing to take on that task this year? Would it be okay to go elsewhere this year? Each decision may feel weighty, and you have to do what is right for you. Change in itself may feel scary, but it can make things easier. Again, you may really not know until the time just how you will feel about anything; the things that you think may concern you won't; and those things that you least expect may affect you more than you might have imagined.

> *Who will put up the sukka this year? As Sukkot approaches, I find myself feeling anxious that I will have to put up the sukka all by myself. I will definitely have to ask for help. Is this the year that we don't build a sukka? Just thinking about it makes me feel so sad. Should I put up the decorations they liked so much or leave them off? I'm not sure which would make me feel worse.*

It is important to find a way to include family members. You may need to involve your children and hear their opinion in order to ascertain what is meaningful for them and what they would like to do this year. Some families choose to see this as a time of reaching out and volunteering as a way to memorialize their loved one. They may actually choose to invite others to their table or work in a holiday soup kitchen. Can you ask yourself, with your knowledge today, what you would like to do differently? How could you imbue your life with greater meaning in honor of your loved one during the holidays?

Synagogue attendance may also feel different, and it may be difficult to predict whether it will feel right for you or not. Sometimes the synagogue environment can feel familiar and comforting, or it may fill you with fear, anxiety, sadness, or dread. Does the shofar or *Unetaneh Tokef* prayer on Rosh HaShana now take on a different meaning? Thinking about it ahead of time can help you prepare for the actual moment with greater clarity and calm.

> *Every year, we waited excitedly for my Bubbie's matza balls. They were simply the best. Never too hard or too soft, they were just the right texture and spiced perfectly. She always made the chicken soup, and her special big pot was a reminder, too, that it was Pesaḥ. I'm not sure how we will get through the Seder*

> *this year. She won't be sitting in her seat at the table, and she won't be regaling us with stories as to what her Seder was like as a child. Our Seder will never be the same. How can it be? Just thinking about it this year fills me with sadness.*

In your first year after a loss, you are not exempt from observing the mitzvot of the holidays. Even when it is challenging and you don't feel ready or even capable of celebrating, you are still required to do so. As the holidays approach, just as in your daily life, you may feel as if you are simply going through the motions, so it is not surprising that you find yourself feeling quite unsettled. This is all part of the grief process. There is no right or wrong way. It just is, and that, in itself, may feel difficult.

You may be faced with the challenge of separating the "how you are feeling" with the "what you are doing" with respect to holiday observance. On Purim, for instance, you are still required to hear the Megilla and participate in a more subdued *seuda* (feast). As a mourner, you are still required to give *mishloaḥ manot,* but you don't personally receive any in return. This may feel contradictory: you are grieving, and it would be nice to receive. Yet the focus is outward – on giving or doing for others. You are being asked to perform the mitzva of giving at a time when you may be feeling at your lowest, but this may actually be a form of healing.

NEARING THE END OF THE FIRST YEAR

While grieving for the loss of the person themselves, we too have lost our former role as wife, husband, parent, sibling, or child. Now we are forced to adapt to different roles, all while taking on new and unfamiliar responsibilities. When the world we assume to be one way is shattered by our new reality, we are thrown into a state of disbelief and upheaval. As we go through a year of firsts, we are thrown off balance and out of control. As we learn with time to make sense of things, or feel less helpless and more competent, the haze begins to clear, and we see glimmers of hope. We all want to hurry through the first year as it feels so uncomfortable, but it can't be rushed. Perhaps we are meant to feel uncomfortable, and sitting with these feelings is what we need to be doing at this time. As we slowly integrate the loss, we do move forward, taking the memories of our loved one with us.

> *As I look back on that first year, I have a hard time recognizing the specifics of the world around me. A year of foggy realities and overwhelming emotions left me grasping for what I believed was real in a world that suddenly didn't make sense.*
>
> *During that first year, I didn't realize the extent to which I was impaired. Looking back, now I realize that my body was in a complete state of shock and my logic of truth seemed to be completely immersed in protecting my newfound fragile heart.*
>
> *Grief is a beautiful and ugly process, with everything in-between. The person you are becoming through internalizing the unparalleled awareness of the temporariness of this life can be hard to keep up with. It is natural to feel overwhelmed with this knowledge; to feel that no one really understands the depths of your pain.*
>
> Melissa Wilder Joyce, "My Journey Through the First Year of Grief," *strongertogether@huffingtonpost.com*

> *One day, as I was driving to work down the huge hill to the highway situated next to the harbor's edge, I suddenly noticed the beautiful green, red, orange, and yellow fall foliage. Until that moment, I realized that I had been going through the motions, but my life was being lived in black and white. When the color returned, it was with such a startle that I realized just how numb and distracted I must have been. I had always loved the*

changing colors of the leaves, but lately had been oblivious to it. I had turned the corner figuratively and literally. Meaning was starting to return to my life.

A Torah Perspective on Finding Comfort After Loss

In *Parashat Ḥayei Sara,* we read about the death of Sarah, and Abraham's mourning for his beloved wife. It is very strange that the Torah does not mention Isaac's response to his mother's death, or even his presence at her burial. It is only after his marriage to Rebecca that we get a glimpse of Isaac's fragile state: "Isaac brought her into the tent of Sarah, his mother, and he took Rebecca, and she became his wife, and he loved her, and Isaac was consoled over his mother." From this verse, we understand that Isaac had been grieving for his mother for three years, and his marriage to Rebecca helped him overcome his loss.

This is not the only time in Tanakh where we see that overcoming loss is aided by forming new ties and affirming life. At the end of *Parashat Bereshit,* (4:25–26), after their son Cain murders his brother Abel, Adam and Eve have a third child and call him Seth. The Torah does not describe their grief over the tragedy that had occurred, but this child's name reflects their decision to move forward. She calls her new son Seth (שת), *"Ki shat Elokim zera aḥer taḥat Hevel ki harago Kayin–* For God has appointed me another seed instead of Abel, whom Cain slew."

In *Megillat Ruth,* Naomi eventually finds comfort after the loss of her husband and sons with the child born to her loving daughter-in-law Ruth and Ruth's new husband Boaz. Naomi is called the child's "nurse" or "foster mother." The women in the neighborhood actually say, "Naomi has had a son." This child provides consolation to Naomi for the losses she has suffered. For there to be consolation, we must have love and support, but we must also focus on and embrace life, and move towards new stages and beginnings.

This is what Isaac found in Rebecca. Rebecca did not replace Sarah, his beloved mother. Rebecca was Rebecca, but Isaac saw in her the same values and strengths that his mother and father held dear, especially the traits of kindness and hospitality. It is with her that Isaac could be consoled for his loss and build his "own tent."

My parents met when my father was saying Kaddish for his mother and my mother was the librarian at the shul library. My father often told us that like Isaac's marriage to Rebecca, he, too, felt comforted for the loss of his mother when he met my mother.

Chapter 7

The End of the First Year

During your first year of mourning, you may be focusing on an *azkara* or some other ceremony to mark the end of this first year. Now as you prepare to go back into the community and your daily life with no restrictions – the ability to purchase new clothing, go out in a larger social gathering for the first time, and more – you may find yourself more than ready, but you may also find yourself missing the comfort and protection this past year of mourning has, in some way, provided.

REMEMBERING YOUR LOVED ONE

> *As the years pass, we are granted a moment to engage with our grief through the observance of yahrzeit, the anniversary of the death of a parent or close relative. Every year, I light a yahrzeit candle. In that moment, I am transcending time, allowing myself to fully feel and experience the grief that becomes tempered with the passage of time and the demands of life.*

> *Having this dedicated moment to shed tears and mourn makes the rest of the year manageable. It allows me to move forward and get on with my life, without feeling guilty. Although I often think of my father, these practices allow me to continue to process his loss in a structured, meaningful way without being constrained by it. Yahrzeit acts as a pressure valve, allowing these feelings to flow through me and into the world.*
>
> Adapted from Ben Freeman, "Jewish Rituals Can Profoundly Enrich Our Lives," *Jerusalem Post*, July 3, 2023

YAHRZEIT/AZKARA

There is no right or wrong way to memorialize your loved one – just your own, and very personal, way. It should be something that feels comfortable for you, and reminds you of your loved one. Judaism memorializes through the yearly *yahrzeit* or *azkara* ceremony held on the anniversary of your loved one's death. The first *yahrzeit* is observed on the anniversary of the day of the burial, whereas in subsequent years the *yahrzeit* is observed on the anniversary of the death. As the *yahrzeit* commences, the custom is to light a twenty-four-hour candle at home in your loved one's memory, and perhaps during the day to visit the gravesite. Some people choose to spend the *yahrzeit* in a serious, somber mood, not doing anything entertaining. Others may decide to spend the day doing various activities that their loved ones would have liked, such as a hike, a sing-along or other gathering, scrapbooking, making a memorial quilt, or adopting a *ḥesed* project, such as picking or packing food for the needy. There are opportunities to do something alone or with those who want to join you in memorializing the loss and help you to celebrate life over death. Not all family members will choose to memorialize your loved one in the same way.

Memorializing a loved one can also be done through making a donation to charity, or dedicating something specific (a synagogue, hospital, university, a favorite charity, etc.), creating a special project or activity (such as planting a tree, a garden, or instituting a memorial run), or writing and dedicating a *sefer Torah*. Your loved one can also be memorialized by collecting stories, pictures, letters, and other memorabilia. The list of special projects you can do is limited only by your imagination. Modern technology and COVID-19 also caused an increase in online or "Zoom"-style memorials. This allows people from far away to join together and share memories both during an *azkara* as well as at other times.

You may also decide at some point that you would like to dedicate time to learning Torah in memory of your loved one. This can be your own project, or you may want to involve others.

Judaism encourages you to make meaning out of your loss, and to continue to give to others in the name of your loved one. Many programs that help lone soldiers, sick children and adults, terror victims, and various other educational and social initiatives were founded by people who had their own personal losses.

> *Reflections on a First Yahrzeit*
> *I write this article as I prepare to mark my "little" sister's first yahrzeit. I took Chana for granted. She was the youngest of us three siblings; and I suppose I never stopped seeing her as the baby of the family. Imagine my astonishment when, after her untimely passing at the age of sixty-two, I had the opportunity to see Chana through the eyes of others. Countless students, parents, and colleagues came to pay tribute to a master teacher; the educator who was able to reach students no one else could reach. Friend after friend spoke of their own true friend who cared deeply, whose selfless loyalty never wavered, even when others gave up. Community members told of continued acts of ḥesed, performed without publicity or fanfare. All this, while Chana*

and her husband, Avraham, raised nine wonderful children; all married in her lifetime, now raising families of their own. I recognize the general rule that, sadly, we often don't realize what we have until it's gone. In Chana's case, however, I am convinced that another phenomenon was in play. I spoke of it at her levaya, and I share it with you as a Tu BiShvat message this year.

Many years ago, I heard a particularly penetrating observation in the name of Rabbi Joseph Soloveitchik. The Rav noted the distinction between the way the Torah portrays builders and planters. Builders, the Rav maintained, are generally painted in the Torah in a negative light, while planters are portrayed positively. The Torah describes Cain as a "boneh ir," the builder of a city. In contrast, concerning Abraham the text relates: "He planted a tree in Be'er Sheva and he proclaimed there in the Name of Hashem, God of Existence." A builder strives to make his own mark on the world. A planter remains uniquely attuned to the natural rhythms of a surrounding world. A builder is driven to realize his own vision. A planter works with shared visions. A builder wants to change reality. A planter wants to enhance reality. A builder's achievements are temporal. A planter's seeds carry the potential for self-replenishment. My sister Chana was, above all, a planter… More important to her than making her own mark was enabling others to make theirs. Planters are less noticeable than builders. They make less noise. They fly under the radar. That's why, I believe, I didn't fully see my sister during her lifetime. She was too busy making a difference to make a commotion... And now, a year later, Chana's presence challenges me to pay more attention to the planters in my life. She tenderly urges me to be more like them. Chana reminds me how much healthier we are when we recognize our shared place with others, instead of seeing ourselves as the "center of the universe." How much smarter we are when we find ways to "plant" seeds of knowledge in the minds of those around us. How much richer we are when we focus on giving to others, rather than receiving from them. Last Tu BiShvat I sat shiva for my "little" sister. This Tu BiShvat I reflect upon the lessons of a true "planter." Let us appreciate the planters among us and strive to be more like them.

Adapted from R. Shmuel Goldin, "Learning from a Planter," https://tinyurl.com/3av8suw8

❧

My Dad died in November 2005 (Ḥeshvan) and my Mom in January of 1992 (Shevat). I think of these months as bookends in time even after so many years have gone by since their deaths. I find myself feeling strangely unsettled as the winter approaches and start to feel relief as Tu BiShvat arrives and I take note with some sense of accomplishment that I was able to catch all three minyanim on their yahrzeits. It has never been easy. Children's competing schedules, work responsibilities, surgeries, and appointments all contribute to making it tricky to get out of the house. I don't actually "have" to go, and don't really "want" to go at all – but I cannot imagine not going. I am grateful that as a woman in my shenat avelut [year of mourning], I chose to recite Kaddish every Shabbat but not daily, as I cannot begin to imagine the pressure of finding and attending minyan one to three times a day. I breathe a sigh of relief. I don't derive any sense of satisfaction in saying Kaddish and yet, in thirty-one years, in two countries, with family obligations, COVID restrictions, and other life events, I have never missed the Maariv, Shaḥarit and Minḥa trio of yahrzeit Kaddishes.

I have talked and taught about their deaths, and have given honor in their lives and in their deaths – so I often wonder why I feel I need to rush out of my house or my office at six a.m., in the cold of winter, making alternative plans for my family, to be at a minyan mostly of men where I have always been welcome, but feel remarkedly unsettled. It is not that on that day as I light my yahrzeit candle, I think of my parents more or even differently. In their physical absence they are very much present in my life, my actions, and my thoughts. I could never forget them. As time passes, I see more and more of them in my own actions and words. So, while it does not feel at all good or comforting to go to shul, it also would not feel at all good not to go to shul. I visualize myself as if in two worlds, and I have decided that it is meant for me to be uncomfortable, that I am not supposed to feel comfortable, and that perhaps sitting with this feeling of being on the edge is exactly where I am meant to be sitting. And that in itself is okay. I am grateful that it is for just over twenty-four hours, and I can allow myself to feel settled once again.

Two people meet at the podium, they both have yahrzeit and both want to be the ḥazan. The rabbi turns to one of them and says, "Surely it would be right for you to step down and let the other man pray. I'm sure your father would have naḥat ruaḥ – comfort from that." Answers the man, "Respected Rabbi, you obviously didn't know my father very well. He would have wanted me to fight for the right to daven today."

R. Lior Angelman, *B'Sheva,* June 8, 2023

YAHRZEIT IN ADAR

When a person passes away in Adar, when is the *yahrzeit* observed in a Jewish leap year (which has two months of Adar)? This issue may create anxiety because one wants to know what the most appropriate time is to memorialize one's loved one. Most halakhic authorities agree that if a person dies in Adar I of a leap year, then one observes the *yahrzeit* in Adar in a regular year and in Adar I in a leap year. Similarly, if a person dies in Adar II, one observes the *yahrzeit* in Adar during a non-leap year. However, what does one then observe in a leap year? There are three options: Adar I, Adar II, or both. There are halakhic opinions that support each of the three answers. There is also a difference between Sephardim and Ashkenazim. It is appropriate to ask your rabbi, but since there is no clear consensus as to whether an Adar *yahrzeit* should be observed in Adar I or Adar II, there is also a place for the family to choose. For example, if the person died after Purim, it may feel strange for the family to observe the *yahrzeit* in Adar I, since Purim is always observed in Adar II.

> *My mom passed away in Adar Bet (II). When I asked my rabbi when to commemorate her yahrzeit during a leap year, he said that I should keep both dates, meaning I would have to recite Kaddish twice, one month after the other. This was emotionally very difficult for me.*

YIZKOR

Yizkor is a memorial prayer recited in the synagogue four times a year. It is said following the Torah reading before Musaf on the last (seventh) day of Pesaḥ (on the eighth day outside of Israel), on Shavuot (the second day outside of Israel), on Shemini Atzeret/ Simḥat Torah (Shemini Atzeret outside of Israel) and on Yom Kippur. Some people have the custom to light a twenty-four-hour *Yizkor* candle before the holiday. The word *yizkor* means "remember." We remember our loved ones who have passed away, and we ask God to remember their souls on these special days. Historically, *Yizkor* was first introduced into the service during the massacres of the Crusaders, and it was recited only on Yom Kippur. It was a way of seeking atonement for the living as well as for the dead. It was then added to the liturgy on other festivals along with the pledge of giving charity.

Often, *Yizkor* starts with communal prayers for the memory of the victims of the Holocaust and for those who died in defense of the State of Israel. Personal prayers for loved ones then follow. The *Yizkor* prayer ends with a pledge to give charity following the holiday in honor of the deceased. This enables us to perpetuate their memory through giving to others. It may seem very strange to recite a sad memorial prayer on the Jewish holidays which are "happy" times – Yom Tov literally means "good day." Rabbi Daniel Beller (who served as the rabbi of the Shivtei Yisrael community in Raanana from 1997–2016) explained in a short *derasha* given just before the recitation of *Yizkor*, that *Yizkor* on Yom Tov is not meant for us to focus on sadness and loss, but rather on appreciation of our loved ones for how they enriched our lives. It is customary in some communities that a mourner during the first year remains in the synagogue, but does not recite the *Yizkor*, because in the first year the person is naturally grieving without "having to" remember – and therefore saying *Yizkor* would be redundant. In addition, it is thought that in the first year a mourner may be still too distressed, and *Yizkor* will cause them too much sadness and tears during what is actually a holiday, when sadness is not encouraged.

To recite *Yizkor* or not in the first year is left up to the mourner. It is customary for those whose parents are alive to leave the synagogue during the *Yizkor* service. However, there is no halakhic obligation to do so and, regardless of whether you choose to stay in or not, it is appropriate to wait until after the prayers for victims of the Holocaust and for Israel's fallen soldiers have been said before leaving. You should then wait quietly outside for those saying *Yizkor* for family members to finish. *Yizkor* service attracts Jews of all levels of affiliation, including those who wouldn't normally attend synagogue the rest of the year. The tradition of saying *Yizkor* is a strong one.

Although halakhically you don't need a minyan to say *Yizkor* (something people experienced during COVID-19, when there were fewer or no synagogue gatherings), many people come to the synagogue on the festivals specifically to memorialize their loved ones. The memory of our loved ones should motivate us to do good deeds and to strive for a path in life that would be a source of pride for those who are no longer with us.

> "In Judaism, we remember not just for the past but also, and especially, for the sake of the future… Judaism gave two majestic ideas their greatest religious expression: memory and hope. Memory is our living connection to those who came before us. Hope is what we hand on to the generations yet to come. Those who remember live on in us: in words, gestures, a smile here, an act of kindness there, that we would not have done had that person not left their mark on our lives. That is what *Yizkor* is: memory as a religious act of thanksgiving for a life that was, and that still sends its echoes and reverberations into the life that is. For when Jews remember, they do so for the future, the place where, if we are faithful to it, the past never dies."
>
> R. Jonathan Sacks, *The Koren Yom Kippur Maḥzor*, p. 758

SEPHARDIC TRADITIONS

Sephardim recite a memorial prayer that is specific to an individual, called *Hashkava*. It is traditional to have this prayer recited on the Shabbat closest to the person's anniversary of passing. On holidays, they do not recite the Ashkenazi *Yizkor* prayer, but instead offer *Hashkava* prayers, as on Shabbat. During High Holiday services, it is traditional to recite these prayers for all loved ones who have passed, regardless of the anniversary of their passing.

> *A friend of mine was staying with her children over a holiday. Nearby, there were Sephardic and Ashkenazi synagogues adjacent to each other. This is quite common in Israel. She said she went to the Sephardic synagogue to pray as she enjoyed the prayers recited aloud, but went next door to the Ashkenazi synagogue to say Yizkor. She explained that for her, Yizkor was always associated with the prayers on the holidays, and it would have been missing for her had she not heard this prayer from the ḥazan.*

> *I remember as a child leaving shul for Yizkor. Everyone would file out, even though the rabbi said we need not leave. There seemed to be a mysterious quality as the tone seemed to change for those who stayed, and I always wondered what happened inside. I remember walking back in to the sound of sniffling and seeing people with tissues in hand. Then, suddenly I had access to the inside. My first Yizkor after my mom died, I remember staying behind with all of the "older people" as my friends all filed out. Suddenly I had joined a club where I felt I was much too young to be a member. To this day, as I watch younger people who have a yahrzeit, my heart goes out to those who lost someone when they themselves were so young.*

> *We were taught from the time we could follow the prayers in shul that if your parents were Barukh Hashem alive, you went out of the shul during Yizkor. I don't know if this was out of respect for those mourning loved ones or because people were*

superstitious that you might lose a parent if you stayed inside. When I was younger, I did as I had been taught and during the holidays filed out with the others during Yizkor. But as I got older, made aliya, and had children of my own, I began to question whether the departure from the shul was correct. If I stayed in for the communal Yizkor in remembrance of the victims of the Holocaust and Israel's fallen soldiers, why should I then leave the shul? Although my parents were alive, I had grandparents whom I had grown up with and other relatives who had passed away, and it would be appropriate to think of them at that time. Besides, as the years passed, I noticed that outside the atmosphere was one of gaiety. The people outside were happy, they felt that they had been granted a reprieve from the long davening. It bothered me that there didn't seem to be any recognition or empathy regarding the people who were saying Yizkor inside. The people leaving their seats seemed to me to be a disturbance. Before the next holiday, I explained to my parents how I felt and asked them if they would understand my decision not to leave the shul during Yizkor. They understood. As my children have grown, I have asked them to stay in during Yizkor. Our shul has a wonderful prayer to be said by a person whose parents are both alive. The prayer gives thanks that our parents are alive and asks God to give them strength to continue to fulfill the mitzva of "honoring our parents."

❧

Judaism takes "vows" very seriously. When we promise something, our word is binding. For this reason, we are careful to use expressions like bli neder and to do Hatarat Nedarim before Yom Kippur. When I started to say Yizkor, I was surprised that the memorial prayer ends with a "vow" to give tzedaka in memory of the deceased. I asked myself, "Do people remember to do that after the holiday?" I posed the question to some friends, and one gave me a suggestion that I have adopted. "Whenever I put money in the pushke (tzedaka box)" she said, "I say 'le'ilui nishmat' – that the souls of my loved ones should have an aliya." This ensures that the vow I made at Yizkor is kept throughout the year.

THE NAMING OF A NEW BABY

The naming of a new baby after a deceased loved one is a longstanding Ashkenazi custom. It often provides people with the hope that the child will grow up with the qualities and good traits of the loved one no longer with them. It is especially meaningful to explain to the community why the parents chose the name and hopefully, with time, the young boy or girl will grow up hearing stories of their namesake. Some parents may choose to find a more modern interpretation of the name, or use the name of the deceased as a second name. This is a very meaningful way to memorialize someone, but it is the personal decision of the parents.

My daughter, who is named for my mother, carries not only her name, but also her smile, her twinkling eyes, and her kind heart. My great regret is that my mother never met my daughter, and my daughter never met my mom. They would have truly loved each other.

My son had a baby boy. At the brit when the name was announced, I was so shocked. His second name was that of my late father. My son had a wonderful connection with his grandfather, but he passed away so many years ago. I was overcome with emotion when I held my new grandson in my arms and

> *called him by his full name. My father's name and good qualities would live on in the next generation.*

The relationship with your loved one does not end just because they died. It changes because they are no longer physically present, but they are still present for you in that their memories are very much alive. We often think, "my loved one would have told me this," or "they would have done it this way," or "if they were alive, they would enjoy this so much." With the passage of time, you may be more appreciative of your loved one, and grateful that, in spite of their loss, you did have them in your life, in some way and for some time. Their influence on you is seen in both the little things and the greater moments throughout your life. Your loss is bittersweet, and you may often experience mixed emotions. The longer they are not around, the more they have missed out on – births, weddings, and other family events. Yet your loved one left behind their own legacy, and who they were adds to the meaning of your life and to those events. You cannot help but carry them in a special place in your heart, and this is a gift that remains forever. You'll find yourself laughing as you think of something they did, you'll hear your words reflecting their thoughts, and you'll see their behavior in your loved ones. Each of these will bring you joy. You may worry that you will forget the sound of their voice, what they looked like, or their own special scent, but it all comes back to you. We don't forget our loved ones or the connections that we had with them. The pain fades, but the love remains.

> *Over the years, as I have moved on, I have kept my memory of my mom alive in things that I have done or thought about, often wondering how she would have dealt with a parenting situation. I knew she clearly would not be able to tell me, but somehow, given her wonderful values, thinking it through in this way gave me more clarity and appreciation for how she mothered us. In*

wearing a piece of her clothing or jewelry, I often feel as if a part of her was with me at an event and that in itself was comforting.

❧

The thing about losing someone is that it doesn't happen just once. It happens every time you do something great you wish they could see, every time you're stuck and you need advice. Every time you fail. It erodes your sense of normal, and what grows back is decidedly not normal, and yet you still have to figure out how to trudge forward. Talking about my father was hard, but not talking was worse. So often I'm trapped between the pain of remembering and the fear of forgetting.

Rachel Lynn Solomon, *The Ex Talk*, p. 121

COMING TO TERMS WITH THE LOSS: TRANSITIONING PAST THE FIRST YEAR

In the first year after losing your loved one, you may have felt as if you were on a roller coaster of emotions. You might have found yourself vacillating from being numb to being in horrific pain with seemingly little warning. So much depends on who it was who died, when and how they died, and your relationship with them. Sadly, we all will lose people whom we love very dearly, and as long as we love, it is inevitable that we will have to mourn their loss in our lifetime. This cannot help but cause us pain.

Your first year may not have felt like a smooth sail, but there were probably times when you realize in looking back that you were not just treading water, but actually managing to swim. There were small windows of happiness along with the pain, and if you are now able to receive and appreciate them, they can bring you momentary joy. While your loved one is no longer physically present, you may feel that they are with you in a different way. You will relive and review the good and less good aspects of your relationship, as well as the dreams, hopes, and expectations that were met, surpassed, and sadly never realized. You will do this over and over again as you work to detach from your loved one, accept the finality of the death, and readjust to your "new" life.

Treading water can be exhausting. Part of the difficulty in the first year is that you never knew when, why, or how the water would become turbulent. Uncertainty, as we have learned during our experience with pandemics and other traumatic events, can feel uncomfortable and be destabilizing. You may have arrived at holidays or life-cycle events, with past experience providing little preparation for mastering your "new" reality alone and without the physical presence of your loved one.

> *I know, dear friend, that you mean well, but don't take away my voice and tell me what I'm feeling. I was at a simḥa and the music was so loud that I developed a headache. I went outside for some fresh air and three people came over to ask me if I was okay and tell me, "This must be so difficult for you." It was not that attending was easy for me, but not everything needs to be seen through the prism of grief. I simply went outside because I had a headache.*

> *I realized that when I had breast cancer, it was important for me that this did not define me. I was a woman, a mother, a wife, a friend, a professional, and so much more. This, too, applied to me in my grief. I would not let it define me or who I am. Grief does not have to define you, unless you choose it to.*

YOUR TIMELINE IN GRIEF: REALISTIC EXPECTATIONS

It is important to ask what your expectations are for yourself in your grieving process. Are these at all realistic, and would they match the expectations you might, for example, have for your best friend? (Often the expectations that you may have for yourself are far more stringent than those you might place on those you care about.) Finally, what do others expect of you, and how do they view things? This can't help but impact how you view where you are at any given time. Do you feel that you have to be at a certain place in your grief, and if you are not there, that something is wrong? Only you can decide what is and what is not realistic for you at various times throughout this period.

With the year of mourning having ended, in theory you are supposed to be ready to "move on." What does this actually mean? How do you even *define* moving on for yourself, and how do others define it for you? The past year has been a year of so many "firsts," and in theory, nothing should feel new or at all insurmountable as you have already "been there" – and made it through the most difficult time you could ever have imagined. Right? Wrong.

> *My Dad died a good death. What does that mean? I was with him when he died. I gave him the permission he needed, I closed his eyes and removed his oxygen after he took his last breath. I kissed him goodbye, I pulled the sheet up over his face, and I even shoveled dirt onto his casket. I sent him on his way to his eternal resting place. That in itself should give me comfort. Yet I miss him. I miss not getting his daily emails that just let me know all is okay. I miss not hearing his voice at the other end of the telephone. I miss his famous "Poppy's cookies" that he loved*

to make. While he lived a good life and died a good death, finality is nonetheless a very difficult concept to grasp.

Grief is not linear. It's important to remember that no matter how well you think you are handling things, you can never be fully prepared. There will always be something you don't expect that will catch you off guard, leaving you upset. Again, what you think may upset you often doesn't, and what you are not really thinking about may devastate you. Our senses and attention to nuance are working overtime.

Compounding how you may feel, is that some family members and friends may expect you now to have fully moved on, to be past your grief, and for the most part, to be perfectly fine. The reality is that often this is not the case at all. Grief is not timebound. Even the early stages of grief may last well over a year. There are no magical dates and times when you suddenly are done grieving and go back to the way you once were. You never fully return to how you were because you simply cannot turn back time. Now a significant person is missing from your life. There has been a tear in your heart, and while you may "sew it up," the scar remains. That said, at some point, and often when you may least expect it, you will emerge from the depths of your loss and start to see the world differently. If you saw it in shades of gray before, you now may start to see color or life in some small way anew. While you may take two steps forward and one backwards, the overall trajectory is one of moving in the right direction.

We don't quit loving our loved one once they have died. We used to love them in their presence. Now we need to learn to love them in their absence.

David Kessler, "Interventions for Dealing with Unattended Grief," webinar, December 22, 2021

DOES LIFE EVER RETURN TO NORMAL?

While the loss of your loved one is truly forever, the first year (and for some, the second), may feel more difficult and intense than later years. While initially you may not have any idea as to how you will manage to carry this burden and its accompanying pain, with time as you begin the work of processing it, little by little, it will become easier. Grief is a natural healing process after a loss. The journey of healing in itself becomes your life, and it will move you forward. As you read this now, it may be difficult to believe, but for those of us who have walked a similar path, we hope that sharing how we felt may enable you in some small way to derive comfort.

As we have mentioned earlier, the cycle of Jewish rituals and expectations closely dovetails with your psychological state as well as your own emotional healing as you transition from loss through the first week, the first month, and now as you move forward through the first year and beyond. This transition is not an easy one, and of course you may not really be done with your mourning or feel that you are ready to move on. Your life as you once knew it is very different from your life today. Judaism's customs give you a gentle nudge and say, clearly and simply, we understand this and what you might be feeling, but nonetheless now the time has come to reintegrate back into society.

Even so, at times when you may feel that you are okay in accepting an invitation, you then discover that there are too many people, too much laughter, and that the place you are in at this moment is not a good place for you. You could not have known that until you were there. With time, however, you will once again find things that bring you joy. Nevertheless, even happiness, while good, may bring with it some discomfort initially – and that, too, is okay.

There are several ways to measure just how you are doing. While your grief may last a long time, it will at some point start to feel less intense, occur less frequently, and be of shorter duration. You will find moments where you feel calmer and happier, and you must give yourself time and not judge yourself. This is also a time to practice self-care. You will find that you have grown in ways you could not have previously imagined. Given the choice, you might do anything to have your loved one back, but your personal growth is in many ways attributable to them.

With the passage of time, you will hopefully rediscover joy and laughter in the small things. At this moment, you may think that you are not capable of this. When you discover that you are, as you see beauty and experience pleasure, it may feel both confusing as well as comforting. While it may feel strange or disloyal to smile or laugh again, as we move forward in our grief, we create a space around our loss that allows good to enter as well.

How you choose to perceive your loss will, in many ways, determine how you respond. Your grief will require you to examine past, present, and future losses with respect to both this death and other seemingly unrelated losses. As we know, death is cumulative. Yet this grief work – and it is truly hard work – will enable you to heal. As you begin to recover from your loss, you will also begin to make sense of the reality that the world of "what once was," and the world of what you thought would be, is not the world of what is now. This is not at all easy and very painful at times, but you will start to feel more in control. Your experiences, beliefs, and expectations will help guide you. Be kind to yourself. While you may feel that right now your loss defines who you are, you will not always feel this way.

The Talmud (Yevamot 62b) teaches that Rabbi Akiva had twelve thousand pairs of students and all of them died within a short period because they did not treat each other with respect. The world remained desolate of Torah until Rabbi Akiva taught Rabbi Meir, Rabbi Yehuda, Rabbi Yosei, Rabbi

Shimon, and Rabbi Elazar ben Shammua. The human tragedy was devastating, the loss to the Torah world unimaginable. And yet, from tragedy springs hope. After this incident, not only did Rabbi Akiva not give up teaching Torah, but some of our greatest rabbis are listed among his new disciples. Rabbi Akiva picked himself up and started again. No doubt Rabbi Akiva never recovered from the pain of the loss. Yet he didn't let this tragedy stand in the way of his life's mission.

Now that my shenat avelut had ended for my dad, I could officially go to events again. I had a year of being unable to participate in social events and I'm embarrassed to say it, but at times it was convenient and even felt more comfortable to pull the "avelut card." During this past year, I went to one event, and was given a "task" to do, allowing me as an avela to participate. I did my job diligently. This was a close friend and a relatively short celebration, and I knew it would be important to her to have me be present. While several months into the year, I still did not belong there, and it felt terribly wrong. There is a reason why we need the full year, and having been at this public celebration possibly made it even worse for me. I was a round peg trying to fit into a square hole and it did not work.

The first event, as it so happened, after my first yahrzeit for my dad was our daughter's bat mitzva. It went better than I had expected. Perhaps it was because I had no choice but to be "on," and after a year of not attending together with my daughter other bat mitzva celebrations, this was her time and I wanted it to be special. I so would have wanted my dad there, but I felt he was watching it all and would have been so proud. My daughter and I bought clothes for ourselves and it felt a bit odd,

but good to be wearing something new and special. After that, I told myself that if I could put together my daughter's bat mitzva and participate fully, I could socialize again. It felt surprisingly okay and finally, at times, actually good. I was ready to move on. Judaism got the timing just right.

It may not feel at all easy, and at times not even right, but as we are taught:

"Everything has its season,
and there is time for everything under heaven.
A time to be born … and a time to die...
A time to weep...and a time to laugh...
A time to mourn … and a time to dance...
A time to rend...and a time to mend … ."
(Eccl. 3:1–8)

ADAPTATION TO THE NEW NORMAL

As we have learned through experience with COVID-19 and the most recent war in Israel, as well as their concomitant losses, we are always "adapting" as we move in the direction of acceptance of our "new" normal. Each day will have its okay moments, some difficult periods, and even moments where you catch yourself smiling and perhaps even laughing – only to then feel "disloyal" to your loved one. As you attempt to make sense of your loss and find meaning in the death, you will move on. With time, there will be fewer difficult experiences, and these will even start to become more predictable.

You "move on" in ways you never thought you would ever feel at all comfortable with, as things become more familiar, and you begin to do them without thinking. Letting go of aspects of your loved one that were once special is not easy; your task is now to bring these special things into your new life in a way that imbues them with meaning. Grief is a process of constant adaptation. How you interpret your loss will determine how you ultimately handle its significance and allow yourself to make meaning of it in your world. This is a work in progress.

REMARRIAGE

When grieving the loss of a partner, we tend to rely on our children and others for emotional and practical support. It is not easy to be on your own. Judaism acknowledges that solitude and loneliness can be very painful. As such, it encourages those who are alone to seek out a meaningful relationship and if possible, to remarry.

As life goes on after the loss of your partner, you may begin to ask yourself if you need more. People might ask you if you would consider dating. Do you want to actively enter the dating scene again, speak to a *shadḥanit* (matchmaker), or go on a dating app? Are you ready to put yourself out there? Are you interested in meeting someone else or do you feel that no one can replace your partner? The answers may depend on your first marriage, the age of your children, and your own personal needs and lifestyle. You deserve to be happy, and if you had a good first marriage, you may or may not yearn for another loving relationship. With time, you may seek out a new partner, but may or may not want to remarry. Dating and remarriage versus child-rearing on your own may play a factor in any future relationship, as your first allegiance may be to your children. Your in-laws from your first marriage, if they are still alive, will be grieving the loss of their child, and may have difficulty providing additional support – even if they love you and want the best for you. They may also have issues with changing the family dynamics, which may make starting the dating process more difficult. Added to all of this is the ability and desire to be intimate with someone else while still searching to find the right place psychologically and emotionally for your previous relationship.

There may come a time after the death of your partner, perhaps when you least expect it, that you find yourself attracted in some way to someone else. Perhaps it is the adult conversation, or maybe the comforting presence of someone who is there for you. You may not be aware of it at first because of your deep love towards your former spouse as well as your parenting responsibilities. You may slowly wonder what is going on, and feel a sense of teenage joy and interest in the outside world that you have not experienced in a very long time. Perhaps you feel guilty for these feelings, or are scared by what they may even mean. Could it be that you are falling in love and feel anxious or have mixed feelings about what seems to be happening? That is okay: your feelings are very normal. You may ask yourself if you are entitled to be happy again or if you are expected to spend the rest of your life alone. You may question whether you can really love more than one person, but if this relationship is a good one, it may be easier to talk about your previous marriage. Being happy today does not diminish your loss; but neither does it bring your loved one back.

If you have grown children, you may discover that they are busy with their own children and partners at night, and your evenings can feel very long and lonely. It is hard to always be asking your children to be there with and for you – to fix things, run errands for you, or to spend Shabbatot together. Finding a new partner does not diminish the love that you felt for your spouse; it may actually give you a greater appreciation for what you once had. If you had a good marriage, you will still be in love with and miss your spouse. You had a shared and special history together. You may have had children and a long marriage, fond memories of starting out together, building a family, and growing together as a couple. This does not prevent you from having a different love for someone else. It is important to acknowledge that being with someone else is not a betrayal of your former partner.

A new relationship may leave you wondering whether you are just seeking companionship, or if you would want to share a home and be in a marriage again. It can feel exciting and confusing at the same time. Each relationship will feel different in almost every way; the goal is to move forward in the new relationship while carrying past memories of your loved one with you in a healthy way. In a good relationship now, hopefully you will be able to have open and honest conversations about your past marriage, both the good and the bad. While you may have idealized the positive aspects of the first relationship, both the former and new relationship will have differences and similarities.

In some situations, people remarry quickly – even as soon as after the *sheloshim* – especially if their partner had been sick for a long time, had dementia, or they had been anticipating the loss in any other number of ways. Some of their grief work may have been done before the actual death itself. Only you can determine what is best for you and your children. There may be no correct answer to what feels right for you, but others will surely weigh in with their opinions. No matter how lonely you are or how long you are alone, it will not bring your loved one back. While men frequently remarry earlier than women do, this is not always the case.

How do your children feel? Have they been the main people in your life for a long time? With a change of family dynamics, if you were to remarry, will your children protest someone else "intruding" into their relationship with you? Young children who are used to having a primary parent looking after them may feel they are being replaced by a new person, and may compete for attention or make it very difficult for everyone. Older children, no longer living at home, may have an easier time if their parent chooses to remarry, but even this is not always the case. At any age, no one can "replace" their beloved parent. While it may be more difficult to share their one parent with someone else or have less time with them, there may still be a sense of comfort knowing that their parent is no longer alone, and their responsibilities are reduced.

Blending a new family takes time and patience, but it is an achievable and exciting goal to seek. Your children also may have worries about you and your relationship with someone else. What will the financial ramifications of such a union be? It is very important to be able to have open discussions about financial arrangements with your partner and possibly even your children. It is also a good idea to speak with a lawyer and explore the possibility of a prenuptial agreement to protect you, your children, and your partner.

OPENING THE CLOSET DOOR AND EXAMINING YOUR GRIEF

For people who have experienced trauma or suffered a loss, the image of a closet stuffed full of "things" can help give them a sense as to what they might be feeling. A therapist's job is to help you sit or "just be" with your feelings in front of the "closet." If you open the closet door too quickly, everything will come tumbling out in no particular order and with no control on your part. If you choose not to open the closet door, you may feel safe. Nothing will fall out. However, everything remains hidden away and is not as accessible to you. If, however you choose very, very slowly to open the door in a controlled way, you may be able to pull out one thing, and then another, with no mess at all. If there is a light in the closet, you can choose when to turn on or off the light, and how much or how little you see when you pull something out. How much light do you want to let in? Will this increase or decrease your pain? Only you can determine when and how you are prepared to open or close the door or turn on the light. You can also choose to close the door if things start to fall, or when you've looked at enough things for today and need a break.

When you do take a piece out, one at a time, at *your* pace, you can savor the good memory, spend time with it, or process a difficult memory and surprisingly go through the closet faster than you might have thought. The closet may also contain lots of items that have been in there from previous losses or other traumas. While you may not have needed to visit those things in the past, addressing them now or in the future may cause you pain or give you answers, provide comfort, or simply help you to tidy up or organize each shelf as you make sense out of cumulative loss.

We may think we can avoid grief, but if you love someone, your grief is often in proportion to the love that you lost. You may want to isolate yourself, run from it, go on vacation, or move to a new house or a new location, thinking that a different city or country will take away your pain. You may then be surprised when the grief seems to follow you. You discover that it is not in your home but within *you*, as you are not settled. If you allow yourself to open the closet to your pain and your grief, and take out one small piece at a time, and reach out to others in the process, you may discover that attending to your loss may actually lessen your pain. Although sitting with your loss is painful, you slowly begin to imagine a future and find meaning in your life. As you slowly move forward, honoring the memory of your loved one, you come to realize that your deep love helps to lessen your pain. You remind yourself again that while you may want to feel all better already, there is no timeline to your grief, and you will revisit it many times.

Our love never dies, but some days the pain is so great that we will keep the closet door closed. At other times, we will desperately want to open it and look for something. The "closet" analogy is one that can be used to explore the therapeutic process in general, and understand how good therapy can work to "clear up" issues that come up during the grieving period. You don't want to avoid facing your grief, but you also don't want to be obsessed with the loss to the exclusion of focusing on anything else.

You will have a variety of feelings and they will change over time. If they overwhelm you or feel constant or unrelenting, make sure to seek professional help. You always need to be able to close the closet door. You are the boss.

What we resist may persist.

David Kessler, "What No One Tells You About Grief Healing," https://www.youtube.com/watch?v=M51dSkAVnb4

TIPS for Coping at Difficult Times

Talk to others. Share your story if it gives you comfort. Ask a close friend if they are able to listen for a few minutes to a small part of what you wish to share with them.

Check your language, and ask yourself if the words you use are accurate and helpful. Statements such as, "I will never get over this" and "I will not survive unless" may be softened by "I will need help" and "It will take me some time." This reframes things a little, and gives you hope that you will eventually heal. Watch out for words such as "never" or "always"; see, instead, if "sometimes" or "at times" could work. Words such as "should" and "must" are punitive and harsh on yourself, especially now.

Try and notice life even in the smallest form: a beautiful sky, a baby looking at their hands, or a young child watching a trail of ants.

Do something nice for yourself. It can be small – maybe putting on lipstick or cologne, coloring a picture, or buying a small treat. These small "pick me ups" actually make a difference. One step at a time.

It is important to look after your body. It is working overtime. Drink lots of water, eat well (even if it is frequent, small amounts), exercise (alone or with a friend), or get outside and just walk in nature. It has been said that immune functioning weakens in those grieving for the first six months. From clinical experience, we have seen that people can feel unwell, have multiple aches and pains, are exhausted, have low resistance, and pick up every illness.

Practice good sleep hygiene. It may be hard to sleep through the night now. That's okay. Try and go to bed around the same time every night and get up around the same time. Routine is important with respect to sleep and other daily activities.

Be mindful: notice with curiosity whenever you can. Bring in a bit of the outside world – just a bit. Listen to, or better still read, a "feel good" news story, or ask someone who is typically upbeat what is new. Just one person once a day. Make it meaningful and manageable.

Distract yourself – even if it is just for a few minutes. You cannot grieve 24/7.

Send a thought to your loved one. Right now, you are thinking of them in your pain and in their absence. David Kessler reminds us that it is okay to say out loud "I love you," as well as acknowledge your sadness, anger, and pain. Don't forget though to say that you sincerely hope that the tear in your heart will begin to heal when it is ready.

Notice that there are others there for you who will give you support. You don't have to do this by yourself.

Don't abuse alcohol and drugs to numb your pain or as a form of escape. This includes over-the-counter medications, which can also be addictive.

State at least five things that happened yesterday that you were grateful for. Pat yourself on the back, and give yourself encouragement when you accomplish even seemingly small tasks. Counting your blessings – even the smallest ones – with a focus on the positive, can reduce depressive thoughts.

THE USE OF MEDICATION DURING THE GRIEVING PROCESS

Grief is a normal process that has to be worked through. It is inherently complicated, and as such sadly often gets pathologized because of the pain and unpleasant symptoms. As a result, it's not uncommon for the medical community to suggest the use of medication to enable one to "get over it" and have it go away quickly.

Medication may have a place in the days following a loss, and may play a role if you have recently been diagnosed as being clinically depressed or are dealing with a severe sleep or eating issue. Medications for sleep and anxiety, such as benzodiazepines and other anti-anxiety medications or sleeping pills offer a short-term solution. They are not recommended routinely, as grieving is a more long-term process and medications have the shortcoming of being potentially addictive, with tolerance developing over time. It takes tremendous energy to grieve, and we do so on both a physical and psychological level. That said, it is important not to mute this process, and if that is the purpose of medication, to protect you from experiencing a painful loss, then, in general, it is not recommended. While it is preferable to work with someone who is able to feel, and whose affect is not blunted by medication, there are times when it is necessary to take medication and it will actually help in doing the difficult therapeutic work ahead. Sometimes, if you are on medication and decide to stop (which should be tapered very gradually), your friends may erroneously assume that you are "all better" and are no longer in need of their support in helping you deal with your loss. It is important to let them know that this may not be the case.

GRIEF VS. CLINICAL DEPRESSION

There are many similarities and differences between grief (typical and prolonged) and clinical depression. Both can result in tremendous sadness and feelings of isolation and hopelessness. However, while grief focuses on the intense sadness and other aspects of adapting to the loss of a loved one, depression tends to be more pervasive, more inward focused, and involves a general loss of interest and pleasure. Anxiety may be seen in both, but in grief, the anxiety tends to be related specifically to the loss, whereas with clinical depression, the anxiety is more generalized. In either situation, if you are feeling unwell, it is important to speak with your physician.

PROLONGED GRIEF DISORDER (PGD) / COMPLICATED GRIEF DISORDER

A return to "normal" functioning after a loss can take a very long time. Grief is our way of adapting to a loss while forming a continuing bond with our deceased loved one. We know that the more we love someone, the more we will grieve their loss. In some cultures, grief is seen as a normal response well into the seventh year. It is interesting that in the western world, a "Prolonged Grief Disorder" (PGD) diagnosis is made after just a year.

PGD is a relatively new term (coined by the American Psychiatric Association in 2022) to describe what until recently was referred to as "complicated grief." According to the DSM V manual (the Diagnostic and Statistical Manual of Mental Illnesses), "PGD requires the occurrence of a persistent and pervasive grief response characterized by persistent longing or yearning and/or preoccupation with the deceased, accompanied by at least three of eight additional symptoms that include disbelief, intense emotional pain, feelings of identity confusion, avoidance of reminders of the loss, feelings of numbness, intense loneliness, meaninglessness, or difficulty engaging in ongoing life." There may be a sense of being "stuck" in an endless cycle of mourning. This is seen to impact relationships, job performance, and other activities of daily living. Grief is considered complicated when it lasts too long and takes over a person's life. While considered normal to have intense symptoms of shock, sadness, and more during the acute phase of grief, the difficulty comes when these symptoms don't recede. This may result in difficulty coping, yearning continuously for one's loved one, and lack of acceptance of the loss for years.

The difficulty in the definition of PGD as described above is that grief is rarely simple, it cannot be bound by a time period, and the symptoms are seen in most losses involving someone who is dearly loved. Grief is likely to be more complicated when death is sudden, violent, traumatic, or involves a child. In other words, these can be seen as "normal" signs of grief. How does one measure intensity? Of course, there will be tremendous pain, sadness, and longing, relationships will be impacted greatly, and reintegration and re-involvement in society will be fraught with difficulty and ambivalence, a longing for the deceased, and a host of other emotions. In this sense isn't all grief complicated, complex, and multifaceted?

Complicated grief is defined within the parameters of what a culture defines as typical, but again where loss is concerned, society has difficulty not putting a specific time frame on how long it is "acceptable" to grieve, thereby withdrawing support after a short period of time and pathologizing a normal process. Grief is not an illness, such as a cold or influenza, that ends within certain time parameters. There is no one way to grieve, or an "acceptable" time frame for it. It cannot be rushed. It simply is, and one learns to live with it or adapt, rather than "get over it." Who determines what is normal – and how? One sees given values ranging from six weeks to a year, when often the early stages of grieving can last well into the second year. Finally, since everyone at some time or another will experience the loss of a loved one, is the term "disorder" really appropriate? While we would never want someone who has indeed been suffering intensely to be deprived of therapeutic services, it behooves us all to question the value any labeling may have.

Again, Judaism's beautiful mourning rituals assume that grief will go on forever. As such, *Yizkor* and *yahrzeit* are marked past the first year to remind us that grief, while less intense over time, does persist when we lose a loved one. Perhaps it is the extreme of emotion or intensity that is reflected in the definition, and our goal is to ensure that anyone who needs assistance gets it.

Helping Isaac Move Forward

While the Torah records the eulogizing and weeping of Abraham, we have no text regarding Isaac's grief. Surely, he was grieving the loss of his mother and yet the Torah is silent on this matter. Though Isaac was approaching forty, he had made no apparent effort to find a wife. Left to his own devices, he might never have married. Abraham, having just lost his own life partner, understood that his son needed a supportive wife at his side. Isaac had suffered a tremendous loss with his mother's passing, and it seems he was unable to be comforted for some time. Perhaps he was in a state of emotional turmoil having been traumatized by the *Akeda* (binding on the altar). This trauma may have caused Isaac to "freeze." As a result, he was unable to even seek his own wife. Despite Abraham's own loss, he realized that Isaac was "stuck," and could not move forward without his help. Abraham enlisted the help of his servant and the search for a wife began. This model teaches us that even after loss we eventually have to be able to look towards the future. With the assistance of his father and his marriage to Rebecca, Isaac began the healing process and found the capacity to love again.

Please make sure that if you are having physical symptoms, you get yourself checked out by a physician. You may need help in discerning what issues need to be treated with medication, and what is a normal, though uncomfortable, part of the grieving process. As we have discussed earlier, because you grieve with your entire body and not just your heart, you may be surprised to discover that at times you feel quite unwell in ways that you might not have expected. You may have somatic complaints, such as headaches or stomachaches, breathlessness or nausea, pain in very specific parts of your body, decreased appetite, tremendous fatigue, or insomnia. (See symptoms of grief table p. 146–148). Don't be surprised if your resistance is low and you seem to be sick more often. There is a scientific basis to the belief that one is more prone to illness when one is grieving. People feel less well, have more aches and pains, lethargy, decreased energy, and other symptoms as general resistance to illness is lowered. Grieving takes tremendous energy, and you may have emotional, behavioral, and cognitive symptoms, such as difficulty in focusing or concentrating, as well as memory issues. While all of these are common in grieving, they do not feel at all good, and you may wonder if you are losing your mind. You are not. These symptoms are as a result of your body and mind working hard to cope, and are all very normal reactions to a very difficult situation.

ACKNOWLEDGING NEGATIVE EMOTIONS TOWARDS THE DECEASED

Initially, you may be able to see only the positives in your loved one, putting them on a pedestal and elevating them in your mind. You may not be able to say anything bad about them, or recall their negative qualities without harboring tremendous guilt or regret. In any good relationship, there are bound to be areas of disagreement; no one person is likely to be "all good." Yet sharing any negative feelings may feel as if you are being disloyal to them and "speaking ill of the dead."

It is not uncommon to have anger towards your loved one for "abandoning" you, for leaving you "behind." This is especially true if they died suddenly, and you were not given any opportunity to achieve closure. You may also have some ambivalent feelings towards them in general. After all, there may have been difficult times, your loved one may not have always been easy to be with, the relationship may have been strained, and let's face it, most of us don't love everything about everyone. You may not initially focus on the negative after a loss, wanting or only being able to see the positive in your new situation. With time, this may change, especially if there was conflict in your relationship with them.

You may very well have had both positive and negative feelings toward your loved one, and as such may mourn what you wish you had in your relationship, what was not, and what now will never be. You may also feel numb – and embarrassed by this lack of feelings. You may experience a sense of relief, especially if your loved one caused you a lot of pain, or the death was prolonged, or they suffered from dementia or changed in a way that left you feeling that you no longer knew them. You may also feel regret, remorse, or guilt, especially if you had unfinished business, with much left unsaid for many reasons. You may think, "If only I…" but even if you did, your loved one still would have died. Sometimes, too, you may feel angry at having been left alone, for being burdened and feeling "Why me?" This may come with ambivalence, guilt, or shame, and your anger may be displaced onto others: towards God, the medical community, or even turned inwards. Again, this might be something that you choose to address when you are ready.

Even in a healthy, loving relationship, there are bound to be regrets and distressing feelings, which, while painful, are very normal. You can choose to try and work these through in order to resolve them, learn to let them go, and move on. Acceptance of these feelings allows room for further exploration, helps you to change unhelpful language, and enables you to move forward.

Letting go and forgiveness, both for yourself and towards others, is an important choice that you make in your healing process. One way to do this is to talk things through with a therapist, who can help reframe things for you and show you how to see a situation differently. By letting go of your guilt and reframing it as regret, you allow in self-forgiveness and compassion, which is so important. Often at these times, you may have unrealistically high or even irrational expectations. Sometimes you may actually find it helpful to write a letter that will never be mailed. What, for example, would you like to tell your loved one, and what do you wish you had done differently? What do you wish they could tell you? Could they recognize and acknowledge that you and they were human, and were not always patient, kind, and caring? Would your loved one forgive you for what you didn't do, and can you forgive them and yourself, let go of your pain, and move on?

What if your loved one was abusive, hostile, took out their anger on you, or was estranged from the family? You may feel tremendous relief that they are now gone, and your feelings are legitimate, but they may evoke self-criticism. In this situation, it is even more important to seek outside help to enable you to move forward.

"Of the dead nothing but good is to be said" is an expression that indicates that it is socially inappropriate for the living to speak ill of the dead because they cannot defend themselves. In Hebrew, one might say "*Aḥarei Mot Kedoshim Emor*," which may be translated as: "After the death, say they were holy." This expression is formed by names of three consecutive Torah portions in *Sefer Vayikra* (Leviticus): *Aḥarei Mot*, *Kedoshim*, and *Emor*, and has been taken to mean that one should not speak ill of the dead.

Actually, "*Aḥarei Mot Kedoshim Emor*" does not mean that at all. To speak of the holiness of the dead is to recognize the person in the fullness of their humanity, to remember all that was good and perhaps not so good, the successes and stumbles. The phrase is a caution not to whitewash or spin things in order to attribute perfection to less than perfect people. After death, there is both a greater vulnerability of the powerless, and a greater power of the living to damage and hurt the deceased. *Aḥarei Mot Kedoshim Emor* – after a death, when there is nothing the dead can do or say to help themselves, it is important that we promote healing rather than rend the fabric of our relationships even further.

Adapted from "After Death, Speak Holiness," *rabbisylviarothschild.com*, April 14, 2013

We had just moved back to my hometown after being out of the country for ten years. Soon after our return, my mom asked me to attend a mother-daughter dinner and fashion show with her at her synagogue. I was nine months pregnant and declined. The next year I was back at work, and having a one-year-old, I declined again. The third year she didn't ask me – and by the fourth year, she was dead. I didn't realize what I had missed until a few years later, when I was invited to the show by a cousin and attended. It was then that it hit me. My mom, my best cheerleader, was so proud of me and just wanted to show me off. I felt awful. I finally understood it – but it was too late. The guilt was painfully enormous. I had been too busy mothering to be there for my own mother. Over the years, I was able to reframe my guilt into regret. It was not easy. I truly regretted my actions. I had no idea how much it would have meant to her. If I could tell her just one thing, it would be that had I known now what I discovered too late, I would have happily gone. I realized I was meant to learn a valuable lesson about priorities. If something is important to those you love, find a way to make it happen. You only regret what you don't do, not what you do.

TIP

From a therapeutic perspective, while you may not have any control over the "package" you are given in life and the events that go with it, you can choose what you would like to do with this package. This choice, which is truly enormous, may allow you to both turn on and off your pain, taking a break from it when you need to. It also lets you lower the volume and better regulate how you cope.

Grief is in many ways a lifelong process, and that in itself can initially feel both very scary and far too burdensome. In many ways, you may want to think you are moving onwards or forward – and you are. Grief evolves over time and will eventually become less intense. There will be upsurges, but the overall trajectory is towards healing and, in the process, you might just discover strengths you may not have known that you had.

SEEKING THERAPY

When to seek out professional care is very much an individual decision. You may find yourself wanting to speak with someone for yourself or other family members early on after a loss, or you may choose to wait for several months or longer before speaking to anyone, if at all. Much depends on you and your own personal grief. While you may be experiencing tremendous pain in your grief, especially in the early stages, grief is a natural process, and one does not always require therapy or other treatment.

Psychotherapy may be indicated if:

- your reactions to grief don't feel right for you
- you feel that your grief is more difficult than it should be
- you avoid thinking about or push away your loss continuously
- you don't feel anything
- you haven't been able to open up or talk about things
- you have had to put your grieving on hold as you are busy taking care of others
- you are overly preoccupied with your loss and your grief feels excessive
- you feel stuck and your distress is not lessening
- you have tremendous anger
- you feel overwhelmed
- you are purposely isolating
- you are avoiding reminders of your loved one
- you are obsessing over them

- you are having difficulty accepting the death
- something feels wrong
- you are having suicidal thoughts
- you are self-medicating with alcohol or drugs

Most importantly, if you think you may need or would like to talk with someone, please seek professional care.

INDIVIDUAL THERAPY

Having the opportunity to sit down with a non-judgmental, experienced professional who understands you differently than your friends or family, who helps you navigate the grieving process and find a place for it, can be tremendously comforting. Sometimes just booking an appointment may already provide some relief, as you know that you have taken a step to share your burden with someone else. Walking through the door is a huge accomplishment, so make sure to take a moment and pat yourself on the back. Acknowledging what you have done is important.

> *I frequently tell my clients that I am there to walk the walk with them – to walk alongside them and be there for them in their grief. Unfortunately, I cannot take away or fix their pain, and most sadly, cannot bring their loved one back. I can, however, be there to acknowledge their loss, help make their worst moments a little easier, and guide them in the natural healing process as they work through their own grief. While not an easy process, it is often a very natural one, and requires minimal interference or intervention. We often want to believe that self-medication with drugs, alcohol, scrolling the internet, or excessive work and other distractions will be helpful, but working through grief at your pace is the best way to heal.*

Sometimes the role of the professional may be to help you resolve areas of conflict that are getting in the way of your grieving process. You may find yourself going over the details or the same story over and over, and feel you can no longer talk to friends or family about how you feel as you think they are tired of listening (especially if they feel they can't do anything), they have moved on, or they say things that to you feel hurtful. You may also find yourself questioning your own mortality, *raison d'etre,* and lifestyle choices. This is especially true if you identify strongly with the deceased, if the death was unexpected, or if your loved one was young or seemingly healthy.

Grieving is a very painful but normal process, and often you will heal yourself in the best ways suitable for you with little or no outside professional intervention. You may discover, too, that this bereavement brings up previous losses that were both resolved and unresolved, as grieving – as we have stated previously – is in many ways cumulative with respect to previous events. Some people initially "talk" more openly about their feelings, whereas others are focused more on "doing." They may be managing details and projects related to the loss, but talk less about their loved one.

This extra support at such a difficult time might be just what you need to help you discover that areas that were previously closed are now open for you in a healthier way. This can give you tremendous insight and comfort as you begin to work on the various issues that may emerge after a loss. Make sure that the person you choose to talk to is someone with whom you feel comfortable, so that you can have a good and honest therapeutic relationship. You need to feel free to ask questions, and if they say something you don't understand, know that they are open to explaining what they said. It is a partnership. Your therapist needs to get to know you, understand how you think, and most likely look at past loss and trauma in your life in order to examine the impact it is having on your current situation. This may take a greater investment of time and energy than you anticipated, but be very well worth the peace of mind that ensues. Remember, too, that much of your grief work actually takes place outside of your session with your therapist – in encounters with the rest of your world.

Finding someone compatible could mean that you need to speak with a few people before you find the person who is right for you. That is okay. Make sure that this person is licensed in this field, and that they have both expertise and experience in your particular loss. You owe it to yourself to give yourself the very best. Don't be afraid to ask.

> *Grief is the price we pay for loving. The more warmth and love and closeness we have felt, the more we will feel a hole in our hearts.*
>
> Janina Fisher, "What Does It Mean to Grieve?"
> Webinar, May 17, 2022

> *What we run from pursues us, and what we face transforms us.*
>
> David Kessler, "The 6th Stage of Grief,"
> Webinar, May 8, 2022

GROUP THERAPY

Another form of support can be by participation in a bereavement group either in person or online. This usually does not take the place of individual therapy, at least initially, but can be a useful adjunct to it. Some groups do not take in new members until three to six months after the loss because they feel that around then the numbness somewhat subsides and an attendee is in a more receptive place to take full advantage of the group experience. The support group may be facilitated by a mental health professional or by someone who has experienced a previous loss themselves. Some groups have a finite beginning and end date, with all members starting and finishing together. These often run for about six to twelve sessions. Other groups run for years with open enrollment, allowing new members to continually join or leave when they feel ready. The focus of the group may vary in specificity. It may deal with general bereavement, or focus on the loss of a spouse or a child, or specify the cause of the loss, such as a death from cancer. If the bereavement group has members with losses too dissimilar to yours, you may have a more difficult time benefiting from the group. The compatibility between you and the other group members will play a large role in your comfort level. There are now also many online bereavement chat groups and forums that may be helpful, again depending on both the group members and the similarity of other people's losses to your own.

Women are more likely than men to want to talk about their grief with others, and seek out social support groups. The group experience can certainly help you feel that you are not alone in your grief, and enable you to have a place to talk with others who have been through similar situations, gain important information, and hear coping strategies that have been helpful to others.

> *Often Marge, the facilitator of a bereavement group, starts out with a global question: "Where were you when 9/11 happened?" It gets people talking about a communal tragedy, and that sometimes makes it easier to talk about a personal one. Even so, there are always people who don't speak. Sometimes months go by before I even know what a new participant's voice sounds like.*
>
> Jodi Picoult, *The Storyteller,* p. 8

AREAS OFTEN ADDRESSED IN THERAPY

There are several components to psychotherapy, some of which may be utilized in individual therapy, some in group therapy, and many in both. One important component is psychoeducation.

Psychoeducation involves helping to teach the mourner what to expect, explaining the process of grief and mourning – focusing on the ups and downs, understanding normal grief, providing a roadmap for the healing process, teaching self-care, and exploring such feelings as guilt, regret, and anger.

Therapy may also involve helping normalize symptoms for the mourner. For many, the *situation* they find themselves in is very abnormal, but the *symptoms* themselves are very normal. Helping to reframe this can be a valuable tool for healing, and enable one to slowly begin to "open the closet door" and examine the various triggers that cause you pain. This is especially the case when one is trying to deal with and make sense out of multiple losses over time. Cumulative grief can in itself be quite complex.

With time, you may be ready to look at the various triggers that prevent you from moving forward. What past triggers now cause you sadness and pain? For example, if, in your youth, you were always told, "Children should be seen and not heard," perhaps you felt that you did not have a voice? If so, now, as an adult, do you feel that there are things – both good and bad – that were left unsaid by you and others?

You may also try to notice what is going on in your body. The words may get in the way of what you are actually feeling. Allow yourself to notice these physical cues, such as tightness in your chest or throat.

Spending time in nature can often be a wonderful resource and provide a path to healing. Focusing on your senses allows you to bring life and color back into a world that may have become monochromatic and empty. Teaching sleep and relaxation techniques, as well as methods for reducing anxiety along with realistic goal-setting can be helpful and are easy to institute.

Helping deal with the pain of grief can also be addressed through a social support network, which can be there for you. Your community can help you heal.

Finally, learning how to make meaning again as one moves forward can be both life-affirming and game-changing. These are just some of the topics that may be discussed in therapy. There are many others that you may want to explore.

ISSUES THAT MAKE GRIEF MORE COMPLEX

Working with clients, clinical psychologists assess the frequency, duration, and intensity of symptoms over time. With bereavement, there may be an increase or decrease of symptoms very much dependent on other factors. As we have discussed, an upsurge in grief related to holidays, anniversaries of the death, and other occasions is commonplace. This may result in an overwhelming increase in sadness, more difficulty in coping, and a greater longing for a loved one as the past years are recalled.

Sometimes grief is more than just grief, and not at all straightforward. People are complex individuals, and it is important to take this into account and be attentive to other issues that may precede or compound a loss. While it may be easy to blame everything on a loss, it is important to look at the whole person and assess their needs. There may be, for example, a background of previous trauma, depression, anxiety, helplessness and hopelessness, ambivalence, guilt, self-harming and abusive behaviors, stress, isolation, withdrawal, disorganization, lack of self-care, eating and sleep issues, or even spiritual issues, each of which may need to be assessed and addressed. Grief is not a "one size fits all" situation. Given a thorough understanding of the person who is grieving, friends, family, the community, and professionals can be both supportive and therapeutic.

DELAYED GRIEF

Sometimes you simply do not have time or are unable to grieve in the way in which you would like. With the sudden death of a spouse or a child, you may be overwhelmed by the enormity of the loss and all that now must be taken care of.

> *When my mom passed away, I didn't have time to "properly" grieve. I was so busy taking care of my father and making sure that he was okay. Only during the second year, when things started to settle, did I allow myself to grieve her loss.*

You may not be able to explore your grief until later, when hopefully you will have more time and the situation will better enable the process to move forward. COVID-19 led to delayed grieving for many who were not able to say their goodbyes to their loved ones, and were denied the rituals so important in making the loss feel real. The recent war in Israel left many people physically displaced from their homes and concerned for their families' daily needs, necessitating that their grief be put on hold.

CHOOSING NOT TO WORK ON YOUR GRIEF

There is an expression, "time heals all wounds." We partially believe this to be true, but only if you choose to work on your own grief. Processing what has happened is therapeutic when done in the right way and at the right pace; with the passage of time, you can then gain understanding and perspective that you may not have had earlier on in your loss. Using the closet door analogy discussed earlier, if you "slowly open the closet door," you can indeed work on and with your grief in a way that moves you forward. However, if you keep the door shut tightly, weeks, months and years can pass by, and you may be no further ahead in how you view and come to terms with your loss. The raw pain may be there as if it was the day your loved one died. Often then, those who could have given you support earlier on when your loss was fresh have now moved on, under the assumption that you were not going to do the grief work – or that you have completed it. It may be more difficult for you if you choose not to do the grief work needed to "clean out the closet" and make order at a time when others are more receptive to your emotional situation.

> *How does a thanatologist – someone who is trained in death education and counseling – deal with the death of a loved one? Slowly and painfully. My dad died after a courageous battle with cancer at the age of eighty-three. I asked myself if eighty-three was better than sixty-three, the age at which my mom died. When my mom died, I had hoped that I would be spared the grieving process – after all, I had worked with others, and thought I knew what to expect. Not only was my grieving at least as long and complicated as that of my patients, but often, as I look back, I think it was longer. It sure felt like it. After all, thirty-one years later, not a day goes by when my mom is not in my thoughts in some way. But I knew she would be, and I don't think I would want it any different. No one is spared grieving. We each have to decide whether we want to do the grief work that may accompany our loss.*

POST-TRAUMATIC GROWTH

After a loss, you will have changed. You cannot help being a different person than when you first lost your loved one. You will examine who you are in a different way. Your self-identity will change, along with your dreams. Your role within the family and in your community will also be different. You will find the tools to cope not just with the actual death of your loved one, but also with all of the secondary losses that inadvertently come along with it. While initially after a loss you allow for some stability while not making big life changes or decisions, with time you will confront these issues. Whether it is a move to a new home or a return to work after a hiatus, you will discover new strengths and what is important in a way you may not have thought about before. While initially you may not know just what it is that you need, with time, you will learn, and may need to let others know what might be helpful. Asking for help is a sign of strength, not weakness. Don't put a timeline on your grief, even if others feel that there should be one.

When you can grow from a challenging traumatic event or a loss, we refer to this as post-traumatic growth. Your job in the healing process is to find a way to make meaning out of your loss in a way that helps you move forward. This may come from developing a greater appreciation for all that you have been blessed with, an increased sense of gratitude in your relationships with others, seeing life itself differently and with new possibilities and opportunities, volunteering and giving back to others, or perhaps even developing an increased capacity for creativity. There is life after loss, and there can be joy and hope as well.

> *I miss my mother tremendously and talk of her often. There is so much in hindsight I wish I could have asked my mom about raising children and life in general. I do have wonderful memories though, and I hold on to them. I am grateful that I no longer feel the daily pain of her loss; the passage of time has enabled so many good things to come from something so bad. Professionally, her death has increased my sensitivity and empathy towards others, and I have grown stronger personally in my own beliefs. I also try not to take life for granted, but rather live each day as if it could be my last, making sure to tell those whom I care deeply about just how important they are in my life. I count my blessings for the small things in life. I have learned that there are many.*

Typically, with more growth you achieve greater personal resilience. As a result of this event, you may experience a change in your belief system, your philosophical outlook, and your spiritual world. Needless to say, if you could choose not to experience this adverse event and have your loved one back in your life, you would be happy to forgo any growth as a result. Unfortunately, life did not give you this choice.

> Seen through the eye of faith, today's curse may be the beginning of tomorrow's blessing.
>
> R. Jonathan Sacks, *Judaism's Life-Changing Ideas*, p. 43

> *In 2016, Rona Ramon was honored in Israel's Independence Day celebrations as one of the country's "civilian heroes." Simply managing to continue living after such a devastating double loss of her husband Ilan and son Asaf was a huge accomplishment, but that is not why Rona was honored. She was honored because she transformed her grief into something positive and empowering via the Ramon Foundation, dedicated to instilling in children the traits held by both Ilan and Asaf: academic excellence, social leadership, and groundbreaking daring. The legacies of Ilan Ramon and his son Asaf still live on. Years after their deaths, other children are learning to reach for the sky and beyond.*
>
> Forest Rain Marcia, "The Legacy of Ilan Ramon,"
> Israelforever.org, 2023

Chapter 8

The Second Year of Grief and Beyond

It is particularly hard, if not impossible, to look ahead and imagine what might be. Although slowly the fog does lift, and you realize that you have navigated the first year through endless challenges, you understand, too, that the more you love, the more you grieve. You potentially grieve forever (which may come as a terrible shock, because you may want to be done with your grief and move beyond it). Your expectations of feeling better are not necessarily met, as you realize that you will never forget what you had. Your feelings for your loved one don't fade with time. Therefore, it makes more sense that neither will your grief. However, in many ways the nature of your grief changes, as does the pain, and as you grow through your grief, you begin to create a new life for yourself as you heal. Ultimately, you will grieve with more love than pain – and this is very important.

It is normal to feel a sense of guilt when you discover that you just smiled or laughed or momentarily enjoyed yourself. There may be a sense that you need to deny yourself pleasure, or else your priorities are "wrong." The reality is that no matter how sad or happy you feel, it will not impact your loved one's status. If you asked yourself if they would want you to continue on and even find happiness in your life, the answer would most assuredly be "of course." That said, it is hard not to judge yourself for a myriad of feelings – both good and bad.

WILL I FORGET MY LOVED ONE?

People of all ages worry that they won't remember the sound of their loved one's voice, or even their smell. Yet the sensory connections are very powerful, and while for minutes you may have trouble recalling their actual tone, if you think of something specific, you will usually find it coming back. In this digital age, most people have some visual and audio reminder of their loved one. In addition, if you have held onto a book, a piece of clothing, or jewelry from your loved one, you might find yourself smiling as you connect the beloved object that is now in your possession with them, and this in itself feels good.

> *I can still hear my dad's recording on their answering machine, and it brings a smile to my face as I think of him. My mom loved her silk scarves, which she kept in her top mahogany dresser drawer. The smell of the drawer as well as her perfume comes back to me whenever I wear one of her scarves. It is perhaps a bittersweet moment, but I'll take it.*

We are often asked after a death if we believe that someone who has had a loss will see their loved one again, or feel their presence in some way. Often, they express a strong desire for this – to have a sign, any sign, that their loved one is okay. Many will report this sign if their loved one came to them in a dream and seemed happy, or if they saw a bird, animal, or something else that signified that their loved one had communicated with them. Rather than being distressing, these "signs" often give a sense of comfort in knowing that their loved one is alright. Of course, not everyone sees their loved one in a dream or attributes something as a sign from them. And this too is okay.

GRIEF REVISITED

Grief is a normal, painful, emotional, and internal process of reacting to and coping with the perceived loss of your loved one. It's not a single one-time event, but rather your ongoing, unique, subjective perception and experiential response involving the psychological (thoughts and feelings), physical (somatic and health issues), and social (behavior towards others) rupture of a relationship. This process may start with the initial diagnosis or not until the actual death itself. Grieving is the way in which we mend our broken hearts.

While there are often many stages or phases to the grieving process, grief does not follow a linear course. The acute phase of grief is often highlighted by tremendous sadness, longing for the lost person, numbness, anxiety, anger, difficulty focusing and concentrating, and more – all normal reactions to losing someone you love. This early grief is thought to last on and off for a few years after your loss. If your loved one died suddenly, leaving you with no opportunity to say a final goodbye and let them know how much you loved them and what they meant to you, or to tie up any loose ends and unanswered questions, it makes this stage all the more difficult. Life seems so unpredictable, and your sense of security and confidence may feel shaken to the core. This cannot help but impact greatly on other areas of your life.

Your grief will include non-death losses, such as a loss of a job or a move, and also symbolic losses, such as loss of identity or social status. It is important to recognize that grief is cumulative. When dealing with one loss, your previous losses can have an impact on what you are currently experiencing. Your grief will change over time, and will be dependent on a multitude of factors. Needless to say, everyone grieves differently, and your grief may look very different from that of your family and friends. Your loss is your own, and for you feels the worst. It does not, however, take away from someone else's loss; each person has their own burden to carry. There is no one right way to grieve, only what is right for you. Grief in many ways is a lifelong experience, and not simply something that gets packaged neatly and is then left behind. While there will be many highs and lows over time, thankfully grief does diminish and become more manageable, with more good moments and more good days than bad. You, too, will change with time. All of this may feel hard to believe in the early days of grief.

UPSURGE OF GRIEF

It is quite normal to periodically experience an upsurge of grief, especially in the first few years. It can be big or small, and is often as a result of something such as a holiday, a birthday, a memorial or the date of a loss, or even meeting someone who didn't know about the death. All of these examples serve as a trigger that reminds you of what once was and what is now lost to you – of a past relationship cut off. It may come with waves of guilt, regret, anger, and pain that are filled with sadness, as well as mood swings. You may vacillate between wanting to avoid the pain and not face what happened, and finding yourself preoccupied with the loss, leaving you with a sense of turmoil and unresolved feelings and somatic complaints.

Adjusting and readjusting to a world without your loved one – and forming a new and different relationship with them, while still holding onto many aspects of the past, takes time. It is hard to have self-compassion and allow yourself to feel whatever you feel and proceed slowly, in this as yet uncharted territory. Being kind to yourself and learning to be your own best friend is a healthy way to cope and move forward. This is typically a normal, but difficult, process. Give yourself the time that you need. There are no "shoulds, "ought tos," or "need tos."

DIFFERENT WAYS WE EXPRESS GRIEF

There are many factors that impact how someone will grieve. How one grieves will be affected by cultural background, religious beliefs, personality, past experiences, age and stage in life, and many other variables. Although these are certainly generalizations, men and women may express grief differently. Women tend to be more likely to cry and share, whereas men are more likely to withdraw and be more irritable. Understanding how you, your partner, or a family member is grieving is important in providing and receiving support during this difficult time.

In *Parashat Ḥukat* (Num. 20), we read of the death of Miriam. "And Miriam died there and was buried there." It is strange, as the Torah describes Aaron's death in great detail, while here there is just a simple factual description. The Midrash links Miriam's death and the nation's complaints regarding the lack of water at Mei Meriva: "And the nation settled in Kadesh, and Miriam died there, and there was no water." As long as Miriam was alive, the well accompanied the nation throughout their travels. When she died, the well disappeared.

The Ralbag suggests that perhaps it was not only the absence of water that caused a crisis among the nation, but also Miriam's death itself. The Torah text is equating grief with thirst, and comfort with water. The Jewish people expressed their grief for the deaths of Aaron and Miriam differently.

EMBRACING BROKENNESS

The Hebrew word *shever* means break. One of our shofar blasts is the *shevarim* sound. At the beginning of the Passover Seder, we break the middle matza in two, and set one part aside. When the bride and groom stand under the *ḥuppa,* we break a glass in memory of Jerusalem and the destroyed Temple. These represent broken events in both our personal and national lives.

Holy objects in Judaism are usually buried when they are no longer being used. The rabbis of the Talmud (Bava Batra 14b) ask, "What happened to the first tablets which were smashed by Moses?" The Talmud answers: *"Luḥot veshavrei luḥot munaḥim ba'aron* – The broken tablets were placed in the Holy Ark along with the second, whole set." Why are these broken pieces special? If they represent the Jewish people's sin of the golden calf, wouldn't we want to forget about them? Get rid of them? The two sets of tablets in the Ark show us that brokenness and wholeness exist side by side. *Reshit Ḥokhma,* the sixteenth-century kabbalistic work, teaches that the Ark is a symbol of the human heart.

After experiencing loss, there will be times of sadness but also times of joy. They are in the same box, in the same heart. The bereaved, and especially those who have suffered painful loss, often live their life with two compartments within one heart – the whole and the broken, side by side. Loss forever remains a part of us. We move forward, but we are never the same again. Life continues, but we are changed. The image of the broken tablets offers a picture of our lives and the lives of those around us. We carry our "broken tablets" with us always.

I keep thinking I will just call Mom. I find myself metaphorically reaching for the phone. I have things to tell her, so much to share

> *about the children's antics, questions to ask of her. How did she handle things? Then the reality hits me again that I cannot call, that possibility does not exist, and it feels like a slap. I can no longer pretend that my mom is away on vacation. I just want to see her, talk to her, smell her perfume, hug her, one more time.*

Accept yourself right now and in this very moment. Yes, it may feel uncomfortable, but this is probably where you need to be. You will put one foot in front of the other and know that some days are better than others. Be kind to yourself as you open the proverbial closet door. You may be ready to open it just a little more than previously, and touch your pain in a different way or experience just a bit more than last time before you need to step back and close the door. You may be able to see things you never saw before.

As you face your grief and live with it, the pain becomes less intense. Early on after losing your loved one, you just want to be out of your pain, no longer grieve, and have things suddenly get better – as if a stomachache or a toothache is now fixed. Now, you are forced to learn how to live with your grief. As you do this and accept that nothing will be the same as it once was, your grief can actually be transformative. You will smile again, and you will be surprised. We hope that as you are reading this now, you are at the stage in the grieving process where you can actually believe this. You will see that your loved one lives on in the behaviors, the words, and the expressions of others, and in the memories that you and others have helped create.

> *It happened one day that I had two clients back-to-back. Mom 1 had come to see me about behavioral issues with her five-year-old daughter and after our session, I left her with my secretary to schedule her next appointment while I went back to prepare for my next client. Mom 1 was still laughing with my secretary when I came into the waiting room to escort Mom 2 into my office, a*

mother whose child had died in a car accident two months earlier. Mom 2 saw Mom 1 laughing with my secretary and as soon as we entered my office, commented sadly, "I will never ever be like that. I will never laugh again." "Oh yes you will," I said. "You may not believe me now. You see, Mom 1 would give me permission to tell you that five years ago she, too, lost her older daughter in a tragic car accident." Mom 2 was able to witness with Mom 1 something that, had she not seen it, she simply would not have believed could be true. Of course Mom 1 thought of her daughter frequently, but she could also experience laughter in her life along with renewed meaning, and not only the pain of her loss. She was healing, and found a way, despite her grief, to see the positive. She was forever changed, but learned a lot in her grief journey.

The call of the future helps us get through the pain of the present and the trauma of the past.

R. Jonathan Sacks,
Judaism's Life-Changing Ideas, p. 181

Rather than waiting until we are happy to enjoy the small things, we should go and do the small things that make us happy.

Sheryl Sandberg and Adam Grant, *Option B,* p. 100

FINDING A WAY TO MAKE MEANING OUT OF LOSS

Death marks the end of your loved one's life, but not the end of your relationship with them. That is forever. The nature of your relationship to your loved one changes, but does not end. All relationships change with time. Your loved one lives on in your actions, your memories, your stories, and in that which you value and pass on. You will internalize and find ways to remember and bring meaning to your relationship with the deceased while moving forward in your journey through life. You strive not to let the loss define you as you work to put meaning back into your life. You do not have to do this journey alone; you can rely on the compassion and caring of others, although you may have to let your friends and family know what it is that you need. You will be forever changed because of the death of your loved one. It is inevitable. You will begin a journey of trying to figure out who you are now – without them. This will be a new relationship. It has to be.

> *We don't quit loving our loved one once they have died. We used to love them in their presence. Now we need to learn to love them in their absence.*
>
> David Kessler, "Interventions for Dealing with Unattended Grief," Webinar, December 22, 2021

> Maimonides said, "Death is the way of the world." We are embodied souls. We are flesh and blood. We grow old. We lose those we love. Outwardly, we struggle to maintain our composure, but inwardly we weep. Yet life goes on, and what we began, others will continue. Those we loved and lost live on in us, as we will live on in those we love. For love is as strong as death, and the good we do never dies.
>
> Adapted from R. Jonathan Sacks, "Healing the Trauma of Loss," in *Studies in Spirituality*, p. 209

While you will be forever changed by your loss, and your grief will be with you for now, you can learn to honor your loved one in your own way. Kessler (2019) discusses the importance of "meaning making" in order to help heal the pain of a loss. He suggests that by finding a way to make meaning out of your loss, you integrate this loss into life, carrying it with you as you find your "new" way of being and the healing within. While you may not have control over the "package" you are given in life, you do have control over how you choose to deal with this package. Not being able to find meaning may keep you stuck in an earlier and more intense stage of grieving. As you process the pain of your loss, you can find a place of acceptance. As you slowly change your narrative over time, you learn to love in a different and new way. This is your task within the painful journey of grief.

> *If life has a meaning, if our own life has a purpose, if there is a task we have yet to fulfil, then something within us gives us the strength to survive suffering and sorrow.*
>
> R. Jonathan Sacks, *Judaism's Life-Changing Ideas*, p. 181

> *When bad things happen to good people, our faith is challenged. That is a natural response, not a heretical one… the wrong question to ask is, "Why has this happened?" We will never know. We are not God, nor should we aspire to be. The right question is, "Given that this has happened, what then shall I do?" To this, the answer is not a thought, but a deed. It is to heal what can be healed, medically in the case of the body, psychologically in the case of the mind, spiritually in the case of the soul. Our task is to bring light to the dark places of our and other people's lives.*
>
> R. Jonathan Sacks, *Judaism's Life-Changing Ideas*, p. 106

RESILIENCE

> *After burying her husband [Col. Ilan Ramon, who died in the 2003 Columbia space shuttle disaster] and son [Capt. Asaf*

> *Ramon, who died in a 2009 IAF training accident], and then battling cancer herself, Rona Ramon, of blessed memory, said: "Mourning has no number; it will always be with us." This leads to the very difficult questions of why?*
>
> *The uncertainty led me to fulfill a dream, and learn how to grow out of the crisis. The hand of fate strikes us all, and what is left for us is the choice – how we choose to stand up and which sounds we choose to make in our world.*
>
> *Similarly, the Efrat community, after the terrorist attack that killed three of the Dee family members, is asking those same questions, and like Rona, is choosing to find the points of light in the darkness.*
>
> *We have not been broken, and we won't break.*
> *We are in pain, but united.*
> *We cry, but are undaunted.*
> *We bury our dead in the ground, and raise our flag high.*
> *The nation of Israel lives!*
>
> Oded Revivi, Mayor of Efrat, "Rising Out of Tragedy," *Jerusalem Post*, April 14, 2023

In your grieving is your ability to be resilient, to bounce back in the face of loss. You will be changed through your grief and its challenges, which can be both empowering and transformative. You may reevaluate yourself and your values – what is and is not important in your life. In gaining clarity and a new perspective, you will hopefully see strengths that you didn't know you had.

While you may deeply miss your loved one, and feel sadness, you can both grieve and find glimmers of pleasure in your everyday life and relationships.

> *Dave's death changed me in profound ways. I learned about the depths of sadness and the brutality of loss. But I also learned that when life sucks you under, you can kick against the bottom,*

break the surface, and breathe again. I learned that in the face of the void – or in the face of any challenge – you can choose joy and meaning.

Sheryl Sandberg, Commencement Speech at UC Berkeley, May 16, 2016

❧

If ever there is a tomorrow when we're not together...

There is something you must always remember.

You are braver than you believe, stronger than you seem, and smarter than you think.

But the most important thing is, even if we are apart... I'll always be with you.

A.A. Milne, *Winnie the Pooh*, 1926

Chapter 9

Relationship Changes After Loss

There are many aspects of relationships that may change after a death, as both your role and that of others will now be different. You may feel the kindness, caring, and support from family and friends that naturally draws you closer, or find others to be less responsive or understanding of your needs, leaving you feeling more distant and alone. Your loss may result in your becoming closer to – or sadly more distant from – your spouse, your siblings, your children, your parents, and other family members and friends. You may share the commonality of the pain of this loss together, and having this other person be there for you and you for them may feel tremendously comforting. It may feel reassuring to bring up the memory of your loved one, and just their presence in the room can feel good. However, it can also become an uncomfortable feeling when there had been family discord and differences of opinion with respect to treatment when your loved one was ill, when there were issues regarding the dispersion of your loved one's possessions, and now in doing things in the way you believe they would have liked.

The situation is different, and not everyone will feel the same. This can make it awkward or uncomfortable with respect to how the loved one is mentioned, or not mentioned, and must be done in such a way that is not hurtful to others. Two mourners may be in different places emotionally and have very different needs. One may feel relieved, while the other may still very much be mourning the loss. Family tensions, conflicts, and dysfunction within the family will also have an impact on the general atmosphere – both before and after a loss.

Relationships have various challenges even before a death. You may discover that the glue that held various family members together was with the person who died, and now you will each go your own separate ways, even more so than before. You, or someone else, may now choose whether or not to take on this role after a death. Reassigning, relinquishing, and redefining roles takes place over time, and might not be done overtly or in agreement with everyone. If, for example, your mom always ensured that you would get together on holidays and special occasions, with her no longer around to encourage everyone to meet up, no one may opt to fill the void. Depending on your ages, you may find that you are less close with your siblings or to your other parent or stepparent. Perhaps now holidays are celebrated differently, with or without immediate family or extended family or friends. Some may want to maintain the relationship as best as they can; others will appreciate the opportunity to have some distance from each other and are happy to now make changes or no longer be together.

Sadly, fights often take place, leaving various members not talking to each other – especially over possessions or monetary division. While not considered during your loved one's life, it is perhaps also possible that their caregiver, foreign worker, or someone else may have played a huge part in your loved one's life, and you and other family members may not agree with the remuneration as designated in the will.

DEATH OF A PARENT AS AN ADULT

No matter your age, and even as an adult, you will still be a child grieving the loss of a parent. In addition to your own grief, you may now find yourself spending time supporting or caring for the remaining parent. However, even as an adult, you as the child will grieve for all of your past, present, and future that has been taken away from you.

> *As a pediatric clinical psychologist, I attended a conference on Death and Children four months after my mom's death without a thought about my own personal loss. After all, I was an adult! In the middle of the conference, it suddenly hit me – I am still that child who lost a parent, and it didn't really matter how old I was. I was very much focused in my work on young children and their grieving, and I had not realized that I was going through many of the same issues that they were. Yes, I was a professional, and a parent, but I was still a thirty-five-year-old child.*

Losing a parent at any age means a break in the historical link between one generation and the next. There is so much information that you've shared and so much more that you often wish that you had thought to tell them or ask about, but now you will not have those answers. The opportunity to work on your relationship directly with your loved one is no longer possible, and even information that you never even thought about before, may now no longer be available. How did they manage "x" or what did they think about "y" for example, may now have to go unanswered. As the "sandwich generation," at times you were too busy raising your own children to ask for this information when they were alive. You may not have anyone else to ask; you may instinctively want to pick up the phone to share information with your parent only to have that painful reminder that this cannot happen. At some point, you may want to access genealogical data that only your parents knew regarding past family history. It may be painful to realize that your parents will not live to see your children, or grandchildren, be born, or experience other milestones such as a bar mitzva or wedding.

> *My mom died when I was in my early thirties. She was young, and I felt I was too young to lose a mom. This was heightened even more so when our son turned the age that I was when she died. For years, too, I could not imagine living past the age that she was when she died. It certainly forced me to face my own mortality. When I thankfully reached her age, I realized just how young she truly was. There were so many things I would have liked to have been able to ask her – about marriage, parenting, what we were like as children, and more. Initially, as each day ticked by and I was okay, it was a stark reminder to make the most out of every day that we are blessed to have, and to make each moment count. To look around and appreciate all that I was given and have. I definitely think it shaped my outlook on life, just how precious it is, and what I wanted to do with it. It gave me the ability to honor who she was and make her memory a blessing.*

With a death, each family member redefines themselves and, based partly on the relationship you had with your parents, it may influence how your family stays connected. Sadly, too, after a death when one person feels they were treated unfairly or poorly by the deceased parent, sorting through the will and personal possessions may add to the frustration of some family members.

The loss of your parents may now signify a loss to other family members as well. Once both parents die, you may hear yourself being referred to as an orphan for the first time.

> *I was visiting a friend who had just lost her mother, having lost her father several years ago. "It is not just that I feel orphaned," she said. "It is that I feel vulnerable. As long as even one of my parents was alive, it was as if there was a kind of buffer between me and death. Now that they are both gone, it begins to feel that it is my turn. No one to protect me. I face the Malakh haMavet (Angel of Death) directly, face to face, head on."*
>
> *We all deny our mortality, and as long as the older generation is around, we feel that they, and not we, are the ones on death's frontlines. We are insulated from death's claws by them. It is their turn and not yet ours. But once we lose our own parents, we can no longer deny our mortality. It is our turn.*
>
> *How apt are the words of the psalmist, "Ki avi ve'imi azavuni veHashem ya'asfeni – When my father and mother abandon me, the Lord will take me in" (Ps. 27:10). When our parents "abandon" us and leave this world, we are bereft in many ways, and our positions in life become precarious. We need God at those moments, and turn to Him, confident that He will "take us in."*
>
> *R. Dr. Tzvi Hersh Weinreb,* "Discovering Our Mortality," https://outorah.org/p/3069/

DEATH OF A SPOUSE OR PARTNER

No matter how prepared you think you may be for the death of your spouse, the death of your life partner or spouse is a major loss. They likely had several roles in your relationship, your family, and socially with others, and each of these will be mourned for what was and now what will be. Each role is a reminder of the life you lived together, and whether it was a late-night talk about your children or a walk together in the neighborhood, each moment of the day will be filled with multiple reminders of your relationship. Add to this all that your partner did for you personally and within the family, as well as your shared history of daily life, and you may be aware very quickly how difficult it is to no longer be a "we."

This will impact your sense of security and independence as well as your relationships with your children and other family members in ways that you may not have thought about previously. You may find yourself having to comfort your children for the loss of their parent, at a time when you are struggling with your own grief. You may question not only how your loved one could "leave" you, but also how you will cope without them. The process of moving on will not be helped by asking why, but rather, when you're ready, what you can do. Looking forward with more hope, and looking back with less pain, is a process that will take time.

> We learn from the Torah (Gen. 23:2) how Abraham was deeply affected by the loss of his wife. He not only eulogized her, but he also cried upon burying her. "*Vatomat Sara beKiryat Arba hi Ḥevron be'eretz Kena'an vayavo Avraham lispod leSara velivkota* – And Sarah died at Kiryat Arba, that is Hebron, in the land of Canaan, and Abraham went to mourn for Sarah and to weep for her."
>
> The fact that the Torah highlights that our forefather was deeply impacted by the death of his spouse not only shows the deep relationship between them, but also teaches us that this response is very appropriate.

My father-in-law spoke of the "brisket brigade," a term he coined to describe the many women who showed up at his door bearing meals after my mother-in-law died. Being considered "highly eligible" in an independent-living [retirement] community, where women far outnumbered men, he was even invited in the early days of his loss by single women to dine together. It appears that if a man's wife dies, he is often provided with meals both in his home and at the homes of others. He also may have invitations to socialize with other couples. If a woman's husband dies, however, she is more likely to be seen as capable of looking after herself at home. She may also be seen as a threat to other couples, especially the wife, and thus left out of a couple's invitation.

We simply did everything together. The children would laugh at us. Whether it was to get gas for the car, or walk to recycle bottles, we were a team. And now, the "awesome we-some" had to become an "awesome onesome." It was much more difficult than I could have imagined. Looking back now, slowly, slowly, with the help of my friends, my family, and my community, who were all there for me, they pulled me along through what felt like thick mud. When I said I was done, I had enough, and that I did not want to go on, they insisted I put one step in front of the other and continue living. Death has separated us, but it has not, and never will, end our relationship. I smile when I go to get gas and to recycle now. I remember those times – the stories, the laughter, the annoyance of which there was no shortage – and it is okay. My pain has shifted. I knew in some place in my mind that I had to go on for our children, my partner – and now I know I had to go on for me.

When an elderly person loses a spouse or a partner, they may discover that not only have they lost their loved one, but also their independence. They can no longer rely on their partner to be there, and now may be a time to reassess whether they can continue to live on their own, maintain a car, physically be able to navigate their neighborhood, and more. They may need more assistance, and may have to change their living situation and/or secure a caregiver. However, they will also likely want to be part of the decision-making process and may be resentful if you make choices on their behalf which, while for their benefit, may feel restrictive and insensitive.

DEATH OF A SIBLING

While losing a parent may be the more natural course of events, when you lose a sibling, closer to you in age, this may leave you anxious about your own mortality, perhaps for the first time. The impact of a death of your sibling will in many ways be related to just how close you were. While siblings typically share a common past history, some may speak multiple times a week and others may not be close at all. You may look towards your siblings as a source of friendship or companionship, as an ally in dealing with your parents over the years, or even as a competitor for your parents' attention and a source of resentment. There is often ambivalence in your complex relationship. In addition, the grief you feel over a sibling's death may be in some way minimized in comparison to the loss your parents may be going through. If the death was sudden and unexpected, your parents may not be able to be there for you in the way you need them; they may be painfully over-protective or withdrawn, and you may even feel partially responsible for the death or find yourself in some way acting out for attention.

> *When I went off to university, people in the dorm often asked me about my family. I have come to hate the question, "How many siblings do you have?" While it sounds like an innocuous question and is a good conversation starter, how do I answer? If I say three, that doesn't feel right. If I say two, that doesn't feel right, either. If I say I have two siblings here and one "in heaven," I have let them know I had a sibling who died. My*

response is often met with total silence from them. No one wants to talk about death, and I certainly can't, especially not with a stranger. The conversation goes from light to heavy with one quick question.

There are many different explanations given by commentators as to why Moses didn't follow God's instruction when he hit the rock instead of speaking to it. In "Losing Miriam" (*Covenant and Conversation: Numbers*), Rabbi Jonathan Sacks suggests that Moses was grieving. Moses lost control because his sister Miriam had just died. He was in mourning for his oldest sibling. It is hard to lose a parent, but in some ways, it is even harder to lose a brother or sister. They are your generation. You face your own mortality.

Miriam was more than a sister to Moses. The Israelites may have lost their water, but Moses had lost his sister, who had watched over him as a child, guided his development, supported him throughout the years, and helped him carry the burden of leadership. Bereavement leaves us deeply vulnerable. In the midst of loss, we can find it hard to control our emotions. We make mistakes. We act rashly. We suffer from momentary lapses of judgment. These are common symptoms even for ordinary humans like us. The real story, though, is about Moses the human being in an onslaught of grief, vulnerable, exposed, caught in a vortex of emotions. In Moses' anguish at the rock, we sense the loss of the elder sister without whom he felt bereft and alone.

With the death of a husband (or wife) you lose your present; with the death of a parent, you lose your past, and with the death of a child, you lose your future.

Norman Linzer, *Understanding Bereavement and Grief*, p. 256

DEATH OF A CHILD

Our Children Are Given to Us as a Gift

Rabbi Meir was a Jewish sage who lived in the time of the Mishna. He was considered one of the greatest of the *Tanna'im* of the fourth generation. His wife Bruria, one of the few women cited in the Gemara, is described as having enormous inner strength. The Midrash on the Book of Proverbs, 31 (*Eishet Ḥayil*) tells that her two sons died suddenly on a Shabbat, but she hid the fact from her husband until after Shabbat – so as not to spoil his sacred day of rest. She then found a way to tell him the sad news. Bruria consoled him by saying, "The Owner of the *pikadon,* deposit, asked for it back." She was intimating that their sons were never "theirs." They were a deposit, a gift from God for a short time, a gift that He was now retrieving.

> *After I sadly lost my own child, I was reminded it was appropriate to recite the verse, "God has given, and God has taken away; may the name of God be blessed" (Job 1:21). The Ben Ish Ḥai explains that we often only understand how much God gives us after God takes it away. It is then we value what a precious gift we had, and how much we ought to have appreciated it.*
>
> *And so I named my next son Natan, meaning "give." I learned to understand that everything we have in life is a beautiful gift from God. Whether times are good or challenging, God is there to lend us support.*
>
> Rabbanit Yemima Mizrachi, "Our Beloved Mother," *HaMizrachi Magazine,* November 2020

Parashat Shemini (Lev. 9) speaks of the death of Aaron's two sons, Nadav and Avihu. Aaron appears so shocked, so stunned by the sudden, unanticipated, and violent death, that he neither

> cries out in grief nor shouts in anger. Rather he is absolutely silent, and remains silent about this enormous loss for the remainder of his life.

There is nothing worse than losing a child. The death of your child is a loss that is incomprehensible. When we speak in the trauma world of an event that overwhelms the system, the death of a child is it. Parents are supposed to die before their children – not bury them. With the loss of your child, your assumptive world is violated as this unnatural sequence of events impacts all aspects of your family dynamics. How do you heal from such a loss? How do you move forward in your grief when life gives you constant reminders of all that you have lost?

There is a natural upsurge of sadness when your child is not there to go through the many milestones you see in your other children, your friends' children, and in your children's friends. What would your child be like now? Is this the time your child would have gone through life-cycle events such as a bar or bat mitzva, graduation, army, or wedding? How now do you celebrate their siblings' milestones?

> *The confluence of Yom HaZikaron and Yom HaAtzma'ut represent an emotional challenge for even the hardened Israeli veteran, let alone new olim. Add to that all those who have lost a loved one, either to war or terror, and the mountain is all the more difficult to climb. Even more than two decades after the murder of our son by Hamas terrorists, we find ourselves dizzy and drained after touching the lowest lows and highest highs of the previous week.*
>
> *Words alone fail to fully capture our feelings. How can you describe what it is like to bury a child? Where can you store the glowing memories of years gone by and the lost aspirations of the years to come? How can we balance the loss of a limb on*

the family tree, while at the same time embrace this brave new world of Israel that we have chosen to make our own?

Adapted from R. Stewart Weiss, "Hatikva: Hope and Faith," *Jerusalem Post Magazine*, May 5, 2023

You will constantly be challenged as a parent to face your loss, and this often happens suddenly and unexpectedly, when engaging with others. Someone, for example, may unknowingly ask you how many children you have. Once easy to answer, now there seems to be no suitable answer to give, especially to a stranger. You start to dread a casual question or simple small talk.

While one may read about the death of someone else's child, you rarely expect it to be you and the nightmare yours. The death of your child at any age, including as an adult, can be excruciatingly painful, traumatic, and sometimes sudden. Because of the tremendous attachment and love for a child, your grief will feel more intense. We are shocked to find ourselves consumed by the intensity of our sorrow and in a state of deep despair many, many months later. With their death comes a change in your parental status and role, and a loss of your hopes, dreams, and expectations for their future. It is in many ways as if your child is "frozen in time" at the age they were when they died. You have lost not only part of your child but also parts of yourself, your relationship with your partner, your family, and your future – all that could have been but now will never be.

As a grieving parent, you may be angry, perhaps blame yourself, or feel resentful, guilty, or ineffective. You may feel so distraught that you wish you could join your deceased child. You may wonder now how you can be there to look after your other children.

King David grieved the death of his son Absalom despite the fact that his son rebelled against him and sought to unseat him from the throne of Israel. When David heard that Absalom was

> dead, he was inconsolable: "And the king was deeply moved and went up to the chamber over the gate and wept. And as he went, he said, 'O my son Absalom, my son, my son Absalom! Would I had died for thee instead of you, O Absalom, my son, my son!'" (II Sam. 19:1).

Your relationship with your partner

As difficult as grieving is when you lose a child, you and your partner may grieve very differently, and this can put a tremendous strain on your relationship. One of you may need to review every detail over and over, and the other may get to the stage of not wanting to discuss the loss anymore. This leaves both frustrated, one feeling that the other doesn't care or want to listen and the other feeling annoyed at the thought of rehashing everything. Each viewing the other as insensitive, they may be at an impasse. With such intense pain and longing over the death of your child, the bond between you and your partner is stretched; intimacy may feel tentative as each parent will mourn differently, be at a different place along the grief continuum, and have little energy left over for themselves let alone anyone else. It is not at all uncommon for couples who are grieving the loss of a child to withdraw from intimacy for a long period of time. You may end up putting your relationship on the back burner, but now, more than ever before, especially when you may be in two very different places and feeling especially vulnerable, the relationship needs to be valued and nurtured. This is not easy. That said, while some marriages of bereaved parents ultimately dissolve, many become stronger. Counseling often helps each person better understand how the other grieves, and can strengthen the relationship's very foundation.

Roles often change as people determine how everyone else is looked after in this new reality. Each person will have to sort out their place and this will also take time, sometimes leaving others in a temporary state of flux. This is normal, but can be very difficult for family members to witness. As parents learn to relate to their other children while the family grieves together, and everyone starts to establish a more comfortable role for themselves, they do eventually move forward.

No matter how learned we are in the world of death, loss, and bereavement, even the most professional among us must grieve and give ourselves time. David Kessler, a well-known grief therapist, who wrote with Elizabeth Kubler-Ross, suffered the sudden loss of his twenty-year-old son. Kessler learned that in addition to the five stages of loss outlined by Kubler-Ross, there is a sixth stage, and that is making meaning out of the loss. His work is seminal, and we encourage you to read his writings, take advantage of the free offerings on his website, join his support groups, and benefit from all that he has to offer as someone who has been there.

More so than with most other losses, a parent who loses a child may feel that their child is forever with them. Some parents will want to hold onto all of their child's belongings for a very long time. Some will want to be surrounded by pictures of their child to keep their memories alive; others will find it too painful to speak of their deceased child and not want to have a daily reminder of "what was" staring at them in their home.

If there are other children, losing a child will also challenge you with respect to parenting them. Sapped of energy, steeped in grief, and finding it hard to get out of bed in the morning, you may find it not only difficult to function, but also to be there for anyone else. When you are there for your other children, both you and they may feel the loss, pressure, fear, anger, sadness, and more. Inadvertently, your children may feel they are competing for your attention.

While individual therapy can be helpful, couple and family therapy may also be very beneficial. A bereaved parents (and sibling) support group can be a particularly powerful resource. There is no one better to guide you than other families, parents, or siblings who have been there. They simply understand the issues and provide a source of comfort without pretending that all is okay when words seem too difficult to find. These families also show you that you will not only get through this, but you will also grow in ways that you could not have imagined.

PREGNANCY LOSS AND DEATH OF A NEWBORN

> *After the death of our baby daughter, I felt as if everywhere I went, I saw smiling pregnant women and baby carriages. I wanted to be happy for my friends, but I found myself sad, jealous, and even resentful. I was not at all happy, and did not like the person I had become. While yearning for another child, I was afraid that I would have to go through the unbearable pain of losing another child. It took me months to begin to sleep better. Thankfully, my husband and a close friend really pulled me through. They sat and they listened through my tears and allowed me the space I needed to share my feelings and my pain. I will be forever grateful.*

The death of a fetus or newborn child is a very painful and often unexpected tragedy for anyone unfortunate enough to experience it. Often these early deaths – be it a pregnancy termination or loss, a late miscarriage (silent birth), stillbirth, or time spent in Neonatal Intensive Care – are particularly intense and complicated. There is a loss of parenthood and often a sense of failure, self-blame, guilt (at perhaps short-lived relief), and lowered self-esteem. There is also often increased marital conflict, as each parent attempts to cope with the loss both individually and as a couple, often each with their own pace in the grieving process.

Pregnancy and infant loss are often not spoken about or even recognized. An unborn fetus, for example, is not considered to be a life. As such, Judaism does not offer any traditional rituals or support for parents who may be consumed by this sorrow. Unlike deaths at a later stage, Jewish law does not obligate parents to observe the normal burial or mourning rituals (including shiva) of a stillbirth baby or a baby who died in the first thirty days of life. Historically, stillborn babies were buried discreetly, often only with the *ḥevra kaddisha* but no family members present. The baby was named and circumcision of males was performed just prior to burial. Graves were often left unmarked, and parents did not know the location. It is only recently, in Israel for example, that after the twenty-second week of pregnancy, parents are informed of the location of the burial site and offered an opportunity to participate in the burial should they desire. This has allowed a space for grieving, and the beginning of some closure for the family.

We have said frequently throughout this book that Judaism's beautiful response to death is psychologically profound and therefore is often spoken about in comparative religion studies. Given this, at first glance, not having prescribed Jewish rituals for perinatal death may seem cruel and lacking compassion compared to other deaths. However, given the high incidence of infant mortality throughout history, encouraging ritual mourning was seen as a burden to the family. It was precisely because so many babies died (and they were already considered pure souls and in no need of ritual), that it was considered kinder to let the parents and other family members "just get on with life." Now, however, centuries later, as infant mortality has thankfully greatly diminished, perinatal loss, which is now considerably less common, is seen as much harder to bear. Judaism does recognize this, and offers many halakhic leniencies, while making little obligatory. In this way, families are for the most part encouraged to do as much or as little as they want to with respect to observing traditional mourning customs.

Early loss, however, still often goes unrecognized, and with few people knowing, the parents are often left on their own and with little sensitivity and support to relive the pregnancy, birth, and more. There are books to help guide couples with respect to ritual and loss, and no one should ever have to mourn alone.[9] Online and in-person support groups for this loss are also now more readily available, as families have understood the need to recognize and mourn the loss with others who have been through similar situations and, when possible, prior to subsequent pregnancies. One mourns these losses for months, and often years – if not forever – even when other healthy children are born. Those who have not experienced this firsthand may say things that are unhelpful and even very painful. Being told that you can have another child, that you are young, and other such dismissive statements in the midst of grief and tremendous uncertainty still have a huge impact on the healing process.

> *Many years ago, I was asked by my friend as a member of the ḥevra kaddisha to join the rabbi and the head of the ḥevra kaddisha in the burial of her miscarried baby. Prayers were said and the small wooden box was given its respectful burial in the Jewish cemetery. It was a beautiful ceremony and such a privilege to be asked to accompany this precious soul to its final resting place. I think it gave these parents a sense of peace.*

> *After nine exciting months of waiting, my mom gave birth to a stillborn baby. I was only eight years old at the time. My mom had an emergency cesarean delivery, stayed in the hospital for close to a week, and then came home empty-handed and sad. My dad told us that if it comes to a choice between the mother and the baby's life, Judaism values the mother's life over that of*

9. Avraham Stav, *As a Fleeting Dream: On Coping with Pregnancy Loss*. Jerusalem: Mosad Harav Kook, 2023

her child. This made sense, and we learned to live with the loss. It was never really discussed, although every year on the baby's date of birth my mom said to me, "Had your sister lived, she would have been x years old." She kept her memory alive, and I always felt that I had a sister whom I did not know. It was only at my mother's shiva that I learned that this baby had been buried in an unmarked grave. My mom always thought the hospital simply took the baby away. There were no details. I realized then how knowing her infant daughter had been buried in the Jewish cemetery would have given her such a tremendous sense of closure.

Back then, the feeling was that it was better she simply "forgot" about it. No one forgets a few months into the pregnancy, let alone when she knew that there was life and a heartbeat up until a few days before the full-term delivery of a stillborn. When my mom expressed concern, the doctor minimized her feelings.

Times have thankfully changed, as I saw many moms in the neonatal intensive care unit cuddling and taking as much time as they needed to say their goodbyes to their babies who had died, taking pictures, and collecting mementos such as a lock of hair or a footprint. I realized how this difficult but important process gave the parents a much-needed sense of support, so that they could begin to heal. Any ritual that validates loss for the family enables everyone to move on. Something as simple as placing moms who have a pregnancy loss in a different area of the hospital, such as gynecology, and away from mothers with healthy newborns, is not something that one can take for granted even today.

DEATH OF A GRANDCHILD

As a grandparent does not fall under the seven acknowledged mourners, and your grief may not be recognized to the full extent it perhaps should be, your loss as a grandparent may come under the category of a "disenfranchised loss" (see chapter 2). Grandparents grieve not only for the loss of their own grandchild and the special relationship they had with them, but also for the deep pain their own child experiences as a bereaved parent. This is a very painful double loss.

> *Our children told us very early about their pregnancy, and we were all filled with excitement. It was a huge shock later on when one of the tests revealed something very wrong, and while further testing was indicated, the fetus shortly thereafter was miscarried. It all felt so painful, and while we wanted to be there to support our children, we realized how sad we also felt. No one seems to talk about these events – to other young friends or among our friends. To make matters worse, our children were placed on the maternity floor, the very last place they would have chosen to be.*

RELATIONSHIPS WITH FRIENDS AND CO-WORKERS

The death of someone close to you will involve many changes on your part, both big and small, and those you interact with – family, friends, and colleagues – cannot help but be greatly impacted by your loss as well. After a death, it is easy to become isolated as you harness all your energy for your own grief work and have little left for socializing. Furthermore, life outside of your loss may feel empty and trivial. Friends, or those with whom you work, will still see humor in life and might have the expectation that you will want to participate in the same way that you did previously. At this moment, that could not be further from the truth. Work-related issues may now seem overwhelming, and it may be more difficult to focus and concentrate for any length of time, making you feel less productive. Work friends may barely acknowledge your loss, and this, too, might be painful and further isolating. They may not realize or understand that while they are avoiding bringing up your loved one for fear of upsetting you, you are thinking about your loved one almost continuously. They may be uncomfortable seeing you in your pain, yet may not know what to do or say.

> *After the death of my daughter, I truly felt that people actually crossed to the other side of the street to avoid me. It was not bad enough that I lost my precious daughter, but other moms, whose daughters were friends of my daughter, did not even come for shiva – and then when I did see them, I felt that they looked at me as if I had a contagious disease that they might catch by talking with me. I heard whispers when I entered a room. I was not imagining it. I exemplified their worst nightmare. I felt as if I was being punished twice. It was all so hurtful.*

Those friends and colleagues who seem to "get you" do understand. It will often be easier for you to be around those who are there for you, and to open up with them about your loved one and your loss. They will not necessarily know how you are feeling, so you will need to let them know what you need and what would be helpful. In addition, you may need to make sure that your expectations at the moment are realistic.

> *Many people who had not experienced loss, even some very close friends, didn't know what to say to me or my kids. Their discomfort was palpable, especially in contrast to our previous ease. If friends didn't ask how I was doing, did that mean they didn't care? If they did ask "How are you?" I took this as more of a standard greeting than a genuine question. I wanted to scream back, "My husband just died, how do you think I am?" I didn't know how to respond to pleasantries.*
>
> *At first, going back to work provided a bit of a sense of normalcy. But I quickly discovered that it wasn't business as usual. As hard as it was to bring up Dave with friends, it seemed*

even more inappropriate at work. So I did not. And they did not. Most of my interactions felt cold, distant, stilted.

I finally figured out that I could acknowledge my grief at work. I told my closest colleagues that they could ask me questions and they could talk about how they felt, too. One colleague said he was paralyzed when I was around, worried he might say the wrong thing. By ignoring the loss, those in pain isolate themselves and those who could offer comfort create distance instead. Both sides need to reach out. Speaking with empathy and honesty is a good place to start.

Adapted from Sheryl Sandberg and Adam Grant, *Option B*, p 36–40.

CHANGES FROM A SPIRITUAL AND RELIGIOUS PERSPECTIVE

It is quite possible, and even probable, that your relationship with God and faith will go through several phases as you attempt to deal with your loss. You may feel a sense of denial or disappointment in that having done everything "right," bad things still happened, and prayers seemed not to be heard or were ignored. Each person must arrive at their own place of understanding or acceptance. Perhaps you felt that God did hear your prayers, but in this situation, they could not be answered in the way that you had requested. Perhaps, too, Hashem heard your prayers and your loved one's suffering was much diminished. Your religious and spiritual beliefs will hopefully guide you to where you need to be. We hope that you have a relationship with a rabbi or other spiritual leader that goes beyond asking what halakhically is or is not acceptable, and that discussion with them can give you true comfort. It is common to have intense feelings at various times, and grappling with and working through the intensity of grief and issues around life and death may at times be quite challenging. Your search for answers, your anger, and your questioning may leave you without answers regarding your loss.

There are those who find it difficult to pray and connect with God when their grief is raw. But with time, they come to find comfort in prayer. Psalm 147 verse 3 describes God as "*Harofeh lishvurei lev* – One who heals the brokenhearted." In Psalms 30:12, King David thanks God for the transition from grief to happiness: "*Hafakhta mispedi lemaḥol li pittaḥta sakki vate'azreni simḥa* – You converted a lament into dancing for me. You have undone my sackcloth. You have girded me with gladness."

On the Shabbat following Tisha B'Av, we read the comforting words of Isaiah the prophet, "*Naḥamu naḥamu ami, yomar Elokekhem* – Comfort, comfort my people, says your God." Rabbi Sam Shor[10] shares the interpretation of the verse by the Gerrer Rebbe. The Rebbe points to an interesting passage in the Midrash Rabba. The Midrash states, "Don't read it as *Ami* (my people), rather *Imi* (with me)." The Lev Simcha explains that not only do the Jewish people feel comforted on this Shabbat of *neḥama* (comfort), but God experiences comfort as well. God is comforted in knowing that our pain is lessened, in knowing that we are healing and comforted. God is pained when we are in pain, and shares in our comfort when we heal and are comforted.

Ultimately, we hope that you can find comfort as you search to reevaluate your past, present, and future and seek to make meaning of all that has happened.

You may find that your priorities as well as your beliefs have changed, and this can feel surprising. You may have a greater appreciation for life, and recognizing just how fragile life can be, want to

10. Torah Tidbits 1429 / *Va'etchanan* 5781 July 29, https://assets.torahtidbits.com.

live each day as if it is your last. Things that were once important may feel less so, and now other people and events may assume more or less meaning. Now is a time of new beginnings, and this in itself may feel daunting. You may ask yourself how your values have changed, and how your faith is now different. Ritual can draw you closer to the inside of the synagogue, but you may have also learned that both serenity and solace could be found by praying at home or in nature. You may find that with regular synagogue attendance, your religious observance increases. You may also find that because of the loss, you want to distance yourself from ritual as it brings you increased pain. You may feel vulnerable and afraid; take your time even if you are not quite prepared for this journey.

Chapter 10

Suicide

While halakha clearly and unequivocally prohibits intentional, willful suicide, Judaism now recognizes, with a greater understanding of mental illness, that there may have been mitigating circumstances such that causing their own death was not an individual's rational intent. Desperate people sometimes do desperate things. They may see no other way to handle a situation, and feel they have no better solution to their pain. It may mean that they can only envision their life filled with pain, but it does not necessarily mean that they actually want to die. Do we therefore really know with 100 percent certainty that someone truly, until the very last moment, wanted to end their life or just end their pain?

It is possible that we will never know, and therefore, whenever possible, people are given the benefit of the doubt. All efforts are made to find any leniencies in determining how the death is viewed. Judaism recognizes that individuals may have this deep conflict, or may be mentally ill, unstable, or may not see an alternative, but that perhaps at the very end they would have chosen to change their mind. One always hopes that there will be a change of heart, that someone will reach out for help, or will see another way that may not have been obvious or relevant previously. Things are not always as they may seem and even with a last-minute change of heart, it may sadly be too late. It is perhaps for this reason that while halakha clearly prohibits an act of deliberate suicide, Judaism, in its compassion, has rigorous criteria that must be met in order to determine that a death was truly a *result* of suicide. In looking for extenuating circumstances the individual is always given the benefit of the doubt. While death may appear to be the result of self-directed injurious behavior, with the intent to die, perhaps the goal was simply to no longer be in pain. These are not necessarily the same.

Few things are as uncomfortable as the stigma of suicide. There may be a sense of embarrassment over the situation, or that it may be seen by others as a deliberate and selfish act, one of rejection and abandonment of those left behind to mourn. The latter may feel helpless and betrayed, wondering if they had missed any signs or could have prevented it. Suicide leaves others to try and make sense out of the situation, to search for understanding in a sea of guilt. It is not easy to acknowledge the fact that everyone is responsible for their own choices and cannot be responsible for those of others – especially grown adults.

This is an important concept in your path back to healing. You can only influence certain situations and, just as in any other loss, there is much that you cannot control, and perhaps will never understand. While you may imagine a different outcome *if only* you had noticed "the signs," there may not have been any, or the deceased may have gone out of their way to hide their feelings. Anger, guilt, and questioning how they could have done what they did, why they didn't let others know that they were unhappy, and why they broke the family apart, may all be questions that will forever be left unanswered.

My client paid me in cash, after paying in previous weeks by check. Having broken up with her boyfriend, closing her bank account, and canceling her session for the following week, I suspected she was planning to take her life. She did not deny this when confronted and while I said I was there for her, she said she was done with life and would not agree to meet with me again. My colleagues said there was nothing I could do if indeed she was determined to take her life. By some miracle, my client went home and discovered her mother had been diagnosed that day with cancer. She now felt she had a reason and purpose that required her to live, and changed her mind. While we spoke once after that, she never returned to therapy and informed me that she was okay.

As a young clinician, I came face to face with the helplessness that families and friends have described when they have sought counseling as a result of suicide. My story ended well but others have replayed scenarios to see what they may have missed, grappled with lies told to ensure that a planned attempt was not foiled, and describe painful anger, sadness, frustration, and guilt. Other clients have been comforted by the probability that what others may have attributed to suicide, in deeper discussion was most likely an accident.

A shiva house after a suspected suicide can feel intrusive, with people (and sometimes the media) indirectly or even directly asking what happened and wanting information. I felt it was no one's business to ask me this question, which seemed only to satisfy their curiosity. For the most part though, I came to recognize that now more than ever, I needed their loving support. Shiva gave me that structure and helped me reframe how I saw things. My other children's friends who were in and out of the house, and also shocked and grieving, were all very supportive of each other.

My daughter took her life, and I believe that she is in a better place for her. She was so deeply depressed and wanted to be out of her misery for so long, and attempted it many times. This world was too harsh for her. She never felt she belonged, and was suffering daily. As sad as I am, I feel a sense of relief for her.

As a senior responder of United Hatzalah's Psychotrauma and Crisis Response Unit, I have been called to the scene of many suicides. All deaths are difficult, but with a death by suicide there is always a sense of shock and sadness, regardless of whether the person was seventeen or seventy years old. Whether a person is old, physically unwell, terminally ill, or has had a history of mental health issues, it is very painful for those left behind. As trained first responders, we arrive early on the scene and provide support for the whole family as well as the medics. We help by being there to offer empathy, to listen, to help people process and work through trauma, and to provide a calm presence. We help those in need connect with resources and strengthen families, and to mobilize their support network of friends and others both within and outside their community. We know that the days and weeks ahead will not be at all easy, but by being involved early on, we can have a significant impact in preventing the long-term effects of trauma.

Chapter 11

The Aftermath of Terrorism

Terrorism is the intentional harming through sudden, unexpected, random acts of violence aimed at maximizing the number of casualties and creating generalized anxiety and fear. Not only are those killed and injured, along with their family and friends, greatly impacted, but the goal of terrorism is also to instill terror within the community and the country at large. No place has dealt with more conventional and non-conventional threats to its safety than Israel. Ever since its inception, and as a nation we have all experienced a sense of deep collective grief and loss. Perhaps as a result of this, and living under tremendous uncertainty, Israelis have learned to unite, live for the moment, and make the most out of life – knowing just how precious life is. Nonetheless, such loss leaves in its wake so many people around the world who are affected not just by the actual deaths themselves, but by the horrors of terrorism as well.

Nothing that can be said can begin to take away the anguish and the pain of these moments. Grief is the price we pay for love.
Queen Elizabeth II's message to New York after the 9/11 terror attack

GRIEF IN A TIME OF WAR

As we were about to go to press, war broke out in Israel. On Simḥat Torah, October 7th, 2023, fifty years almost to the day since the Yom Kippur War, at six thirty in the morning, sirens began blaring throughout Israel. Many Shabbat observers and others assumed the siren in their area was simply a false alarm. Within minutes, however, it became obvious that we were being attacked from all vantage points. Areas of southern Israel adjacent to Gaza were stormed by a barrage of rockets while the many kibbutzim along the perimeter of Israel were ambushed by Hamas terrorists infiltrating the country by land, sea, and air. Missiles were sent from the north and south, and in no time, some 1,200 people, including babies and the elderly were brutally killed, more than four thousand people were wounded, and at least 240 people abducted and taken hostage. Entire families were wiped out, and communities completely burned and destroyed in the most horrific ways possible. It was a pogrom of unimaginable magnitude. Too graphic to describe here, we will simply state that since the Holocaust, one could not imagine atrocities as were experienced in this one day. The citizens of Israel and ultimately the world were left in a state of shock and disbelief.

The suffering inflicted on the residents of the pastoral communities, the army bases, and the young people at the Supernova music festival is still being revealed. Stories of incredible bravery continue to come to light. As in cases of post-traumatic stress syndrome, it is possible that more time will pass before the full impact is felt.

> *Beyond those who suffered the horrors firsthand or witnessed them up close, all citizens of Israel have been affected and are suffering from trauma. This has been compounded by the massive Hamas rocket attacks launched on wide areas of the country. And for many, there is also the worry for the welfare of soldiers, loved ones, serving on the frontlines.*
>
> *From the depths of the horrors, something positive emerged. There is a feeling of national solidarity and togetherness that is almost palpable. It is omnipresent. Israel took a beating, but it is bouncing back with the help of its characteristic resilience.*
>
> "Israeli Solidarity," Editorial, *Jerusalem Post*, October 22, 2023

We cannot even begin to process the enormity of the effect of the infiltration and barbaric attack of over six thousand Hamas terrorists into Israel. The impact was devastating not just in Israel, but also throughout the entire Jewish world. People were left grieving on so many levels – for their loved ones, both soldiers and civilians, who were murdered that day or in the days that followed, and for an assumptive world that was completely turned upside down and destroyed. Israel had never lost so many people in one day since the founding of the state. Due to the sudden and unexpected attack, many were killed and left maimed or in a state of shock and disbelief as the extent of the attack was revealed. People lost their possessions and their homes, their communities, and their sense of safety and security, and were dealing with the ongoing struggle to find their place in this new reality. In the rest of the world, antisemitism rose to an all-time high, leaving people anxious and in shock. Jews removed both their *kippot* and *mezuzot* in a topsy-turvy world that seemed both unfriendly and unsafe.

In the immediate crisis, there was initially little assistance and much confusion and fear as to what was happening. Furthermore, because it was Shabbat and Simḥat Torah, many in the

Orthodox community were without telephone or media exposure and were therefore unaware of the gravity of the situation and the horrific nature of the attack. Once the situation became clearer, the army and other emergency services' rapid response was dramatic and, in many cases, heroic.

On a moment-by-moment basis, not only did people fear for the safety of the hostages and those missing, but families had no knowledge at all as to whether their loved ones were alive or not, and under what conditions they were being treated. Many people were grieving multiple losses – of more than one family member, comrades-in-arms, entire neighborhoods and communities, and so much more. The participants at the music festival came from all over Israel and even abroad, and their injuries and deaths affected people in all parts of the country.

Many people were forced to wait endless days, weeks, and more to hear about the status of their loved ones, which was unknown. Were they taken hostage, missing, or murdered? This wait was very difficult, with people trying to be hopeful but also realistic given the absolute heinous nature of the attack.

> *My family in South Africa asked me to describe the feeling in Israel now.*
>
> *I said, "There is a heavy feeling everywhere. It's like one giant shiva house. And to make it worse, we are not only all grieving, but we also are scared, anxious, and suspicious all the time."*

> *I don't even know how to comprehend it. I've just heard that my friend from a kibbutz in the south is in the hospital with a bullet in her lung, having had several other bullets removed. Her spouse and infant were killed in the horrible attack on October 7th. One of her children is still hospitalized with serious injuries.*

> *Another child has been released from hospital but has no home to go back to as their house was burned to the ground. This child is recovering but going through this trauma with the extended family for support.*

Emergency first-aid response teams such as Magen David Adom, United Hatzalah, Zaka, and the Fire Department provided vital services in the first hours and days after the attack. They worked alongside the army to help rescue and transport the injured to hospitals and brought the deceased to the morgue to be identified. Due to the dangerous security situation and the poor condition of the victims, with at times only partial remains being found, identification was extremely time-consuming and required great care and expertise. Pathologists from other countries as well as Israeli archaeologists with expertise in locating human remains were called in to assist the Israeli medical and rabbinical teams. Through DNA sampling, once death could be confirmed, the families were informed, the bodies released, and plans made for burial. Judaism's sensitivity and respect for the deceased meant that this process was expedited as much as possible, with people working around the clock in order to ensure that burial was not delayed any more than was absolutely necessary. It was only then that one could possibly even begin to attain some closure. Although the custom in Israel is to bury someone directly in the ground, due to the nature of the deaths, the deceased were typically placed in coffins. As so many people died in such a short period of time, a request was made for volunteers to work with the *ḥevra kaddisha* to help dig graves and bury the dead. During the early days after war broke out, burial in Israel of bodies from other countries was halted. The bodies would be buried locally, with the expectation that they would be exhumed and reburied in Israel as soon as the situation allowed.

The Israeli army maintains their own *ḥevra kaddisha* for both men and women. They also have a team that informs the families of soldiers of a death, and a group of trained professionals who assist them in the year of mourning and beyond.

With respect to the civilian population, members of the Psychotrauma and Crisis Unit of United Hatzalah were on call to provide emotional first aid and support. They assisted ambulance teams, others involved in transporting the deceased, as well as journalists and politicians who were exposed firsthand to the tragedy or later saw unedited footage of the massacre. Various members worked with the relocated families, and the mental health community offered support for many in need from almost the beginning of the war.

BURIAL AND SHIVA

Burial and shiva for many of the civilians murdered on October 7th took place not in their home communities or vicinity, but rather in other locations due to continued safety concerns. As many family members and friends were seriously wounded or killed, the call went out on social media to help embrace the mourners by attending the burials and shiva. Typically, a funeral and shiva are attended primarily by close friends and family members who all know the deceased or their family. After the massacre, an entire country was in mourning, and this was reflected on a national level in the attendance at burials and shiva by people unknown to the families in solidarity with the bereaved. On the day of the funerals, large numbers of people lined the streets, many bearing flags to show their support. When soldiers were unable to leave their base due to the call of duty, they sent representatives – spouses and other family members in their place to comfort the mourners. Due to the nature of the deaths, the media was often present, and at times, broadcasts were shown live.

Many of the people who tragically lost family members also lost their homes, and some were evacuated due to safety concerns. In relocating people, when possible, communities were kept together in order to be able to comfort and be of support to each other. Private individuals as well as hotels and guest houses graciously opened their doors to welcome those displaced and to offer a safe place to live and grieve. This meant that many families were sitting shiva in places relatively unfamiliar to them. This in itself was unsettling. Strangers who often felt at a loss as to what they could do to help, nonetheless came together in the most amazing ways imaginable, to give comfort and provide food and other necessities. While shiva usually has set visiting hours, during the war, people came to comfort the bereaved whenever they were able to get away from the army or place of work, both day and night.

DIGNITY IN DEATH

Jewish law is careful to ensure dignity in death. For this reason, all remains are gathered and buried. Due to the horrific nature of the deaths on October 7th, it was not possible to collect the remains from all of the vehicles. The decision was made by Zaka, with the proper rabbinic authority, for the first time ever to bury all of the vehicles that contained ashes and blood, to preserve the dignity of those who were killed in their cars.

Comforting the Mourners
Rabbi Shai Piron wrote this prayer for bereaved families for Yom HaZikaron, 2015. It was republished and recited at memorials after the Simḥat Torah massacre in October 2023. The uniqueness of this prayer is its emphasis on the challenges faced by the mourners and those who seek to comfort them[11]:

Please my God, at a time when we remember those who are gone, rest your divine spirit on parents and widows, orphans, brothers and sisters, and friends.

11. See Appendix for original Hebrew prayer.

Brighten their days, fix their dreams, give them strength to live, to be. Sow in them seeds of hope, moments of joy.

May they know how to balance between memory and mourning, between building and destruction, and give us wisdom to be there for them as a help and support.

May we know how to distinguish between the power of a word and the power of silence.

May we find a way to choose correctly between closeness and distance, between need and withdrawal.

May there be peace in the land. "May there be peace within your walls, and tranquility within your citadels" (Ps. 122:7).

In the land may there be life and everlasting peace.

May the one who creates peace on high bring peace to us and among us. And let us say: Amen.[12]

SOLIDARITY

The support for the hundreds of thousands of soldiers in compulsory and reserve service during this still ongoing war has been amazing. Citizens from both Israel and abroad have been donating money and collecting a full range of supplies for army bases and outposts. Given that people initially were unable to leave their posts, it was a given that more equipment and supplies would be needed. Both men and women stepped away from their studies, work, and other family responsibilities to report to duty with very short notice. In addition, flights from abroad were packed with reservists wanting to come back to serve and defend their country. Citizens also stepped up to entertain and feed the troops; restaurants and gourmet chefs have koshered their kitchens in order to send meals to the various army units; people have baked everything from *ḥallot* to cookies and

12. Translated into English by G. Junger. See Appendix for prayer in Hebrew.

full-course meals; and teams heading to bases to provide a barbeque or pizzas have helped to keep up the spirits of those on prolonged army duty. In addition, entertainment of all kinds has gone to army bases to help boost morale. Information was posted on social media with respect to what was needed by soldiers and where to deliver it. Municipalities and synagogues also organized activities, day care, babysitting, and other support for the families of the soldiers. While schools were closed, teenagers volunteered to help look after younger children and assist older children with Zoom classes.

In addition to supporting soldiers and their families, there was an awareness that businesses in the north and south of Israel were facing financial difficulties, or were going to have to close due to the security situation, relocations, lack of tourism, and army reserve duty. As a result, people found creative ways to support these businesses. Flower growers who could not provide for wedding halls and other cancelled events began selling to the public. Fresh fruit and vegetables that normally would have been exported were brought to the center of the country and sold. With the lack of a workforce, many farmers were left with produce in the field which if not picked, would spoil. Hi-tech workers, students, and hospital employees, among others, organized groups to help pick these fruits and vegetables. The growers were deeply touched by the spirit of volunteerism from all around the country. People from around the world also showed their solidarity by coming to help in many different capacities.

> *As a commander in the IDF, I had been given permission to send some soldiers out for a short break to visit their families. I went over to one of the men and said, "Go home to your wife and your kids. Take a break for a day and come back tomorrow." The soldier responded, "I'm fine, my wife is fine. We're doing ok. Put me at the bottom of the list and let that guy over there get the break, not me." I went to the one he pointed to, and that soldier responded,*

"I don't need to go. I'm a single guy, no wife, no kids waiting for me. Put me at the bottom of the list. That guy over there, he has a wife, he has kids, ask him to go home." This type of behavior reminds me of the midrash that describes two brothers who had each inherited half of their father's farm. One of the brothers was married and had a large family; the other brother was single.

One night during harvest time, the single brother thought, "How can I sleep when my brother has so many mouths to feed?" He got up, gathered bushels, and quietly brought them over to his brother's barn.

Meanwhile, his brother also could not sleep. "How can I enjoy my produce and not be concerned with my brother? He is alone in the world, without a wife or children." So, he got up and quietly brought over bushels to his brother's barn.

The next morning, each brother was surprised to find that what they had given away had been replenished. This happened night after night. Then one night it happened. The brothers met during their evening adventure. And there, they embraced. God looked upon this expression of brotherhood and said, "On this spot of mutual love I wish to dwell. Here My Holy Temple will be built."

As the midrash expresses, the space between the brothers' fields is where the Beit HaMikdash was built; and the love between these soldiers is that same brotherly love.

Rav Ilay Ofran, Facebook post, October 14, 2023

THE FIRST MONTH

As a country, this war was traumatic on so many levels – whether for a child who clung to his parents for fear when hearing a siren, or a parent trying to work with no daycare and having to run with several kids in the middle of the night to a shelter. Soldiers on missions were unable to carry their cell phones. As a result, families were left for days and longer with no knowledge at all about their loved one's safety and well-being.

The medical and mental health community was also under tremendous strain, working day and night under difficult conditions. Everyone was trying to simply make it through a very difficult time, aware that daily life was completely disrupted and in no way normal. In addition, antisemitism around the world increased and left people feeling vulnerable and anxious.

Almost from the beginning of the war, people were encouraged to talk about and share their experiences and to seek professional care, if appropriate. In the early or acute stage, in spite of the sudden and unexpected nature of the massacre and the trauma incurred by everyone, leaving a country in a state of national mourning, the incredible resilience and togetherness of Israel's citizens was very evident. As time passed and the situation became more chronic, grieving, while very much present, would in many ways be delayed, given the ongoing nature of the war. How do you grieve your fallen comrade when you have to go back into the battlefield? How do you visit the families of mourners when you yourself are injured and in the hospital?

RESILIENCE

When death is sudden, unexpected, violent, or involves children, we are challenged to the extreme to work with the multitude of losses and move forward in some way. After the first several hours, help arrived through the army, police, and private citizens. For several months afterwards, the goal of the Iron Swords War was to eradicate Hamas, get our hostages back, protect our beloved country, and restore its security at a time when its very existence was being threatened to the core. Only after the war ends will the difficulties of this enormous tragedy be properly addressed, and the most humane Jewish rituals of faith can begin to help with the healing process.

President Herzog's Message of Hope

It's been almost a month since our country underwent a serious change. For almost a month, we have been in a war like no other. Almost a month has passed since that cursed day when the sun rose, the flowers blossomed, and butchers slaughtered, slaughtered, and slaughtered – women and men, elderly and infants, from kibbutzim and communities, cities and towns…

The pain of the families of the hostages and the missing is simply unfathomable. My conversations with them are the most painful conversations I have held in all of my life…

Our spirit cannot be broken.… This spirit is you – my sisters and brothers – the people of Israel. Israeli society is our true secret weapon. You are my greatest hope, our greatest hope. Am Yisrael Ḥai!…

Above all, we have national resilience and unending strength. And with us at every moment, we have the power of hope.…

Our hope is not lost, the two-thousand-year-old hope, to be a free people in our country, the land of Zion and Jerusalem.

Excerpted from President Isaac Herzog's Address
to the Nation, *Jerusalem Post*, November 3, 2023

My brother and his family live on Kibbutz Kfar Aza. They survived the terrible attack, but they lost his in-laws and many friends and neighbors on October 7th. They stayed at a hotel in the center of the country and joined their family and friends who were sitting shiva.

I had no words of comfort to offer these people who had lost so much. But before leaving the shiva, I held my brother's hand and said, "Our parents were Holocaust survivors and they rose from the ashes. So will you. And you will rebuild – just as our parents did."

SHELOSHIM DURING WARTIME

It is relevant that in a Jewish state, the passing of thirty days from the Simḥat Torah massacre was marked both on the Hebrew and secular calendar. This particular *sheloshim* was a national rather than a personal memorial. The day was marked by municipal ceremonies throughout the country. Memorial candles were lit, speeches were made by family members, and a minute of silence was observed. Given the situation, prayers were said for the release of the hostages and the welfare of the soldiers, and the Israeli anthem, *HaTikva*, was sung. Smaller, more intimate neighborhood memorials were also held for people to honor their loved ones. In various communities across the world as well, memorial ceremonies were held in solidarity with Israel. In addition, individuals and families marked the *sheloshim* from the actual day of burial, which was often several days later than the official ceremonies. *Kaddish* for all but parents traditionally ended after this thirty-day period.

> *The Jewish laws of mourning are structured so that by the sheloshim, life starts returning to normal.*
>
> *Life in Israel, however, has not begun to return to normal a month after the slaughter.*
>
> *Normal in Israel is happy and vibrant and joyful and optimistic. A month after October 7th, the country has slipped into a certain wartime routine, but the national sense of grief, bereavement, and deep, deep sadness has not dissipated.*
>
> *It's everywhere. It's on the television. It's in the papers. It's in conversations around the Shabbat table. It's on people's faces in the supermarket. It's on everyone's mind, and it's in everyone's heart. You can feel it.*
>
> Adapted from Herb Keinon, "As Resolute as on Day One," November 10, 2023, p. 13

HELPING CHILDREN DEAL WITH DEATH AFTER A WAR

In this war, every child and adult has been affected. At the very least, they may have felt the effect of disrupted schooling when schools were closed, or they had to return to Zoom after their prolonged and difficult experience of remote learning during COVID-19. In addition, many children may have heard multiple sirens and had to run frantically to a safe area. Some children, along with their parent(s), travelled to other countries to get away from the war. They may have had difficulty re-integrating upon their return.

Tragically, other children were taken hostage or lost their lives in a horrific manner. This has had a major impact on their parents, siblings, schoolmates, and other children. In addition, whole families have suddenly been torn apart, leaving children to grow up without one or both parents, siblings, and other family members and friends. Children who have experienced trauma need support from their loved ones. While it is important to be truthful, there is no need to overwhelm a child with too many details. Because so many family members have been called up to army reserve duty, and others have been displaced, children may have found themselves without the comfort of their home and the stability that family would typically provide. They may have no school at all, be in unfamiliar surroundings with children and adults they don't know, or attend different frameworks, all the while facing these new challenges with little warning or preparation. While resilient, children may nonetheless need time and help to navigate these experiences, both from adults who now typically will be in their lives, as well as from professionals. If attending funerals, for example, they may be exposed to more drama than they could have imagined. Shivas too, once more private, may involve the greater community. While they will carry these losses with them forever, the goal is to enable each child to cope in the here and now, and as they get older and have more questions, to feel supported by the community around them.

SPIRITUALITY AND JEWISH IDENTITY

It is not unusual during challenging times for people to turn to prayer and religious observance. What we are witnessing now as a result of October 7th is not only a surge in Jewish identity, but also a desire to take on Jewish rituals. There have been requests from soldiers in the field, both religious and secular, for tzitzit (four-cornered fringed garments) and *siddurim* (prayer books). This demand was so great that volunteers stepped in to try and meet the need for the request of sixty thousand pairs of tzitzit, and Koren Publishers waged a campaign to provide over ten thousand *siddurim* and *ḥumashim* for soldiers on the frontlines. Men who had not put on tefillin (phylacteries) since their bar mitzva began to lay tefillin again, and women took upon themselves to light Shabbat candles – and sometimes extra ones for the hostages – and additional prayers were said both at that time and in the synagogues.

> *Omer Barak, an Israeli author posted, "As part of the soul-searching I have done at this time, I came to realize that in the past I refused to say the words, 'I am Jewish.' In every lecture I gave abroad, I would say that I am an Israeli, that I was born Jewish, but that there is nothing Jewish about me. Now, for the first time in my life, I realized that I can't escape it, and I realize that I don't want to, either. I am proud of my Judaism. I am ashamed that I denied it.... Today I lit candles with my children for the first time in my life. I prayed for the hostages. For the soldiers. For us."*
>
> Adapted from Yedidya Meir, "Am I the Child with a Cap?" *B'Sheva,* November 9, 2023

MAKING MEANING OUT OF LOSS

The devastation of the Simḥat Torah massacre shocked both Israel and the world to its core. While the entire Jewish world is grieving the tremendous physical, emotional, and communal losses incurred in this war, it is clear that after October 7th, 2023, nothing will ever be the same. As a result of both the individual and collective trauma endured, we will all need time to recover from both our physical wounds and our emotional pain. However, just as the individual does after a devastating loss, we will heal as a society and ultimately grow from this catastrophic period. This national rehabilitation will serve as a time of renewal and opportunity for growth. While never having wished for this disaster to have taken place, perhaps now we can embrace the unity that has resulted and find a way to show greater appreciation for our similarities while respecting our differences. Over the generations, the Jewish people have shown tremendous resilience, and we pray that with time we, too, will move forward as a nation.

In a world so shattered, it is impossible in the moment to imagine just what our future will look like. As we look back at history, using the Holocaust as a model, we know that lives will be rebuilt, and people will search to make meaning out of their loss. This is in part our Jewish journey from death through healing. As a community we give each other tremendous strength and this, our resilience, gives us hope, *tikva*. Some day we will write a revision to this chapter, but for now, as we attempt to move forward, we pray that all who have been impacted by this horrific tragedy will be comforted.

> *Shai Ḥermesh came back to Kfar Aza to collect whatever he could from the rubble that was once his home. His son Omer was killed on October 7th; he and the rest of his family survived. He told the soldiers who had come to assist him, "I believe we will also get through this, and we will return and rebuild Kfar Aza again."*
>
> *Yediot Aḥaronot*, November 16, 2023

POST-TRAUMATIC STRESS DISORDER (PTSD)

There are sadly many who may be considered "lightly injured" due to minimal or no physical harm, yet are grieving and impacted greatly by a world turned upside down. They are traumatized by the images, noises, smells, and so much more that ruins their day and destroys their nights. They remain hypervigilant, on guard against anything at all suspicious, jump at a loud sound, sleep poorly, have issues relating to others or holding down a job, avoid certain situations, and may expect the worst at every turn. If this constellation of symptoms lasts beyond a month or so, one begins to see not just Acute Stress Disorder but rather Post-Traumatic Stress Disorder. In addition, those who have a history of previous trauma and have then gone on to experience another event or a prolonged war, may now experience more complex post-traumatic stress (C-PTSD).

Those experiencing unrelenting difficulty around the loss of a loved one or have persistent symptoms of stress are encouraged to seek therapy. Know that you are not alone, and that by sharing your pain with others, you will lighten your burden. As social beings, we need connection in order to heal.

Trauma carries with it so many associated losses. While many are in the present, some relate to previous traumas – both great and minor. Grief is cumulative, as we have said often, and past adverse experiences will directly impact how one copes in the here and now. Trauma takes away our relaxed or laissez-faire attitude that "everything will be okay." It is hard to "just notice" and be curious, when you become programmed to always imagine or expect the worst. While the average person does not think about what catastrophic events can and will happen, when one has experienced sudden, unexpected, and violent traumatic experiences, they expect the worst-case scenario at all times. As Jews, many of us experience a transgenerational trauma, with deep wounds from the Holocaust that have recently been reignited with the horrors of the war.

With terrorism and other traumatic events, both adults and children may be greatly impacted by their own losses, as well as by those of others around them. They may feel the stress and absorb the fear of their loved ones, without quite knowing why. Adults, for example, may be listening to the news constantly, without awareness that children in the background are exposed but have little understanding of horrific scenes being repeated, the sounds of sirens, and the concomitant chaos. These may lead to a sense of disorientation, difficulty focusing and concentrating, somatic complaints, irritability, sleep issues, increased anxiety, and tremendous sadness in both adults and children alike.

The mental health community recognizes, because of the prolonged nature of the war in Israel, that we are not yet in the state of "post trauma" in terms of making a final diagnosis for many of the country's citizens. People who experienced an acute stressful event such as those on the southern kibbutzim or at the Supernova festival on October 7th, or soldiers who were involved in combat operations or released hostages, may be suffering from PTSD as a result of these discrete stressful experiences. For many others, such as the families of the hostages or residents of areas still under continuous bombardment, the stressors are ongoing. It is perhaps inaccurate to diagnose PTSD in individuals for whom the stress is chronic and persistent. Here it may be more appropriate to refer to it as a prolonged stress reaction or disorder.

Anyone with concerns is encouraged to reach out to a professional. Both individuals and families may benefit from therapy at various stages of absorbing the magnitude of the many losses. Children too will require reassurance that all is okay in their world at a time when adults are having difficulty coping themselves. With effective counseling, everyone can learn to move past these issues.

> *Twenty years on, I still have PTSD. There are triggers out there. There are very specific things that I cannot deal with: fireworks are the absolute worst. Sudden loud crashes and bangs, a host of other things.*
>
> *However, thanks to my counseling, I have techniques to help me get through those moments.*
>
> *What I have learned from my brush with death is that I have a level of empathy and understanding of how people behave when they have been through extreme trauma. I understand how to listen to them, how to get them to open up to me, how important it is for the world to hear their stories. I continue to be drawn to them, even though logic dictates I should run screaming in the opposite direction.*
>
> *However, there is another lesson I've learned. There is no logic to traumatic events. They are, by definition, destabilizing. You can't ever really overcome them, but you can learn to handle them, with the right support.*
>
> *For me, that support has come in a multitude of ways, including by seeing how many good people there are in the world even when you have seen evil right before your eyes.*
>
> Adapted from Kelly Hartog, "Twenty Years On: The Lessons I Learned from the Terror Attack in Kenya," *Jerusalem Post*, November 27, 2022

SURVIVOR GUILT

With some injuries and deaths, especially those that are more traumatic or of a life-threatening nature (pandemic, suicide, the death of a soldier, terror attacks, or a parent who outlives their child), for those remaining behind, there may be a sense of guilt that you survived whereas others did not. You may feel that you could have done more or even prevented the death, or that it should have been you who died and not the deceased. You may question why you escaped death while others did not.

Ask yourself, if your loved one were here now, what would you want them to know? This may give you some insight into some of the more difficult aspects around your grief. Perhaps ask, too, what you think they might want you to know. Sometimes it's very hard to feel joy when you are here and your loved one is not. The inner voice saying, "It should have been me" may tear at your heart, but would they want you to live that way – unhappy, sad, and wishing that your life had ended instead? Perhaps you may be able to see the situation as one where you ask yourself why you were granted the gift of life, and use this to bring meaning and purpose into your days going forward. At some point, you may be able to look back at the loss, perhaps with regret but without a sense of guilt, and with hope for the future.

The flood changed Noah. After a year on the ark, Noah was commanded by God to leave. We assume that Noah would be ready to get out of the ark. But Noah was hesitant. Why? Elie Wiesel offers a poignant insight. He calls Noah "the first survivor." The world had experienced a Holocaust, and Noah was reluctant to walk out of the ark because the entire world, as he knew it, had been destroyed, and that was difficult for him to face. The Torah tells us that Noah's reaction to the flood was to plant. Planting after a great destruction is surely a meaningful response. It represents hope and belief in the future. But what did Noah plant? He planted a vineyard, drank the wine, and became drunk. Noah could not face the fact that everybody except himself and his immediate family was destroyed by the flood. He was unable to face reality. It is possible that when the impact of the flood and the great loss of life began to sink in, Noah may have become depressed. He turned to wine to numb his emotional pain.

Rabbi Lance Sussman suggests that one possibility for Noah's actions is that he developed the first reported case of Post-Traumatic Stress Disorder, or survivor's guilt. This phenomenon can occur in a variety of life-threatening situations, including car accidents, wars, and natural disasters, but it also can work its way into very personal tragedies, affecting friends and family of those who died by suicide. Survivors may find themselves wondering why they lived through the event. Survivor's guilt can have a serious impact on an individual's functioning. Following a trauma, people may also experience feelings of regret. The rehashing of the events could further exacerbate the feelings of guilt, particularly if people feel their own actions – or inaction – may have worsened the consequences. Noah could not live with the guilt of survival. It takes courage to rebuild a shattered world.

If we find ourselves in Noah's position, feeling alone, angry, or guilty about our life circumstances, it's helpful to have coping mechanisms in place ahead of time or to seek professional help. It's challenging to push through a traumatic experience, but finding healthy ways to cope with emotions is essential.

Adapted from Dr. Bill Sutker, "Noah 5780 –
Did Noah Have PTSD?"
Kehillat Chaverim, North Dallas, USA, 2015

Chapter 12

The Impact of Social Media on Death and the Grieving Process

Social media has had a huge impact – both positive and negative – on just about every aspect of death, mourning, and the grieving process. Bad news travels fast, and in the digital age even more so. Expediting information-gathering and transmission at the time of a death are helpful in enabling police to access information or for family to gather quickly. However, this information may inadvertently first be seen by and disseminated to various individuals long before it is heard by those most directly impacted. This may result in those most relevant to the deceased being informed from unofficial sources that their loved one was killed or injured. Examples include the sharing of graphic identifying photos sent from the scene of a fatal car accident or terror attack, or information regarding the death of a soldier being shared through social media prior to notification of any next of kin.

Notably in the time of the COVID-19 pandemic, social media offered the advantage of allowing others to participate from afar in the dying process, the funeral, and the ensuing shiva. This will be explored in more detail in the discussion about COVID-19 (see chapter 14), but it has without doubt served as a model for influencing current death practices, especially for those wanting to participate in Jewish life events while living at a distance. During the war in Israel, Zoom and other social media platforms served as a way for people to find emotional support during a traumatic time. Social media also enabled first responders to get immediate assistance for handling ongoing events, and for charitable endeavors to best help communities, soldiers, and others. Unfortunately, social media has also had a negative impact, spreading fake news, which both causes unnecessary panic and leads to the need for correcting misconceptions. Sadly, in the first hours of the Simḥat Torah massacre, for example, people were inadvertently and directly exposed to graphic material that unfortunately caused further traumatization.

As social media has become more advanced, one is now forced to deal with such ethical issues as how, what, and even if one should post online. Whether through Facebook, X (Twitter), Instagram, WhatsApp, or Telegram, as well as other forms of social media, anything from the initial death announcement to the funeral service, offering condolences, or telling stories of the deceased can and will be viewed by a multitude of people. Some families and funeral homes now offer a memorial page to enable guests to write a tribute on their website. One has to question whether posting will be helpful or hurtful now as well as in the future, given that much that is said may remain forever in the public domain. Also, while it may make sense today, will the family's wishes be respected, and will they change over time?

Another issue that has more recently been discussed is the digital legacy or footprint that is left behind after a death. While once not even an issue for discussion as part of advanced-care planning, expressing wishes for preserving one's digital immortality may be of utmost importance not just for future generations in general, but also in helping with the entire grieving process. With respect to their photographs, videos, music, social media profile, blog, or address book, does the dying individual want to leave details as to how and who may access this? What, for example, happens to the deceased's Facebook page, their computer, or cell phone, which may be loaded with personal information? If a mobile device or computer is password protected, can anyone access and share it? Who determines what gets preserved? Additionally, is it appropriate to put up information that may describe the dying process in great detail, how one can take their life, and more? Will this information be helpful or harmful, and who will monitor it to ensure that vulnerable individuals do not access it? Something seemingly as minor as a Facebook reminder to wish someone a happy birthday or to notify them about an upcoming event when they have died may be very painful. Does one remove this information or leave it up as a memorial?

> *After my wife's death, I debated what to do with regards to her Facebook page. On the one hand, since she was no longer with us, it made sense to close it down. Who needs that painful reminder? On the other hand, as a beloved teacher for so many years, perhaps having this space for students to leave their thoughts gave them the opportunity to share their grief. In the end, I decided to leave it up. Although the messages people send on her birthday feel jarring, the memories people share give me comfort.*

Can and how does an account become inactive, and is this easy information to access? What are the privacy issues and ethics involved in assuring that digital information is dealt with appropriately for family members and other beneficiaries? With cyberbullying impacting our youth as well as adults, what are the ramifications of inappropriate access?

As with much of social media, there are both pros and cons. The internet can be invaluable for providing one-on-one or group support, helping people to explore self-help options, mourn safely within a public forum, and feel as if they are part of a community. However, risks also need to be assessed, and laws formulated that protect both the individual and the public. In order to ensure that safety is guaranteed in this complex and ever-growing arena, open discussion is essential with both children and adults alike.

Chapter 13

Children and Death

HELPING CHILDREN DEAL WITH DEATH

It is our natural instinct as adults to protect our children from death. Yet, death in many ways is not new to a child. Children see death from a very early age as part of the natural life cycle. They see a wilted flower, a crumbled leaf, have stepped on bugs, have seen a dead bird on the road, or sadly have been privy to world news and events around them. By the time a child experiences a more painful loss, they have typically begun to formulate some concept of death. How your child perceives a death is dependent on their age and stage of development, in addition to their relationship with the person who died. This in turn will impact how you as a parent (or grandparent or loving other) deal with that child. Each child will respond differently. Entire books are written with respect to children and death. We will attempt here to give only a brief overview.

SPEAKING WITH YOUR CHILDREN ABOUT DEATH

While going through the shock and sadness of your own personal loss, you may also have to help your children, grandchildren, or other children cope simultaneously with their loss. Where do you even begin, and what do you say at a time when no words may feel adequate and, more than ever before, you may want to shield them from the harsh realities of death, especially when death is sudden or traumatic?

Ideally, whoever tells your child about the death will be a close family member – a parent, a grandparent, an older sibling, or a favorite teacher or rabbi. This should be done as soon as possible, so that your child does not hear the news from someone else (which in this day of social media, for older children, can happen within minutes). Hopefully this is done in a familiar and safe environment, such as at home, where questions can be asked and your child comforted; but at times, this unfortunately will not be possible.

Speaking to a child about death is only the first step. Sadly, adults so deeply entrenched in their own grief may well be oblivious to the pain of their children. If children are quiet and not outwardly expressive regarding their feelings, it is also easy to mistakenly assume that they are okay, when in reality they may not be. Early on, you may find it helpful to ask a close friend or family member to be there for your child when you are unable to be physically or emotionally present. This may include the time of the funeral, shiva, and various moments in the months that follow.

When speaking with children, it is important to keep the discussion as simple, age- and stage-appropriate, open, honest, and straightforward as possible. You want to be able to tell them what they need to know without extraneous and irrelevant details that can be confusing to them. Letting them know that you are there for them should they have more questions later on and reassuring them that all feelings are normal are both important. They need to be able to express their concerns around the death, and have their questions answered over time. They may initially feel sad or upset – or feel nothing at all. You should reassure them that all – or no – feelings are okay, and that they may feel differently at different times. You can also share how *you* feel, if you think it relevant. Perhaps you were surprised by the suddenness, or felt sad. Children will often return for more information after they absorb the initial shock of the death. It is best to take your cues from them and answer their questions when you can. For some children, "I don't know, what do you think?" may be the most helpful way to begin this process. Just like adults, children need time to understand what happened, express their feelings, and commemorate the loss in a meaningful way.

It is important to use language that will not be misunderstood and inadvertently cause your child to be more fearful. Using words and expressions such as "went to sleep," "went on a trip," "were sick," "passed away" (to where?), "are lost" (will they be found?), "are no longer with us" (who are they with?), "went to visit God," or "needed to help Hashem" (God took my loved one, will I have to go too?) as a way to soften the truth may inadvertently cause more confusion. Instead, statements such as, "they were very old" or "they were very sick and died" can be more helpful, but not all deaths are easy to explain or will make sense. By being present for your child, making eye contact and openly listening to their concerns, you let them know that you are helping to keep them safe and that they are not alone. This is key for just about any child who may be worried about who will be there to care for and about them, given this very recent death. Children want to know that they are not alone, they are safe, and that someone will look after their needs. They also need to know that nothing they said or did caused the death, it is in no way their fault, and that nothing they could have said or done could have prevented the death or brought their loved one back. Children often carry guilt because they fear they caused the death of a parent or sibling, even though it is almost always not the case.

Children may feel anger at being left behind or that the deceased "left." They may be fearful that they, too, and others they love will also die, and may have a sense of increased anxiety with respect to the future, wondering who will look after them. If the death is of another child, they may ask if this could happen to them too, and might feel that their sense of safety and security is threatened. Children look to an adult to provide stability and strength. While perhaps uncomfortable, these feelings are weighty and need exploration in order for the child to ultimately grieve "appropriately" and feel supported as they move forward in life.

That said, depending on their developmental stage, they may not see death as real or permanent, and as such may wonder where their loved one is and when they will return. With their concept of time rather limited, they may expect this to be very soon. To a young child with "magical thinking," people appear and disappear, "bad people" or "superheroes" come and go, and the concept of finality may mean very little.

As an adult, you may find that some of your children's feelings or questions seem odd to you, as they have very different concerns than you would ever have imagined. Your goal in being there for them will be, in part, to encourage their questions and provide reassurance.

> *I remember sitting down and telling my six-year-old very bright and articulate son that his beloved grandmother, who had been very sick, had died. Towards the end, we had prepared him that she would not recover, and we took pictures of them together in the hospital. He told me he had two questions. Focused on the*

fact that she would be in a coffin, he wanted to know if she would have a pillow for her head and would she be comfortable? He then wanted to know who would make sure to cut her fingernails. I let him know that the coffin was silk lined and there was a small pillow, and that when you die, your fingernails and hair no longer grow. These answers appeared to satisfy him. From the perspective of a six-year-old, these questions were so appropriate – yet not at all what I would have anticipated.

After my mother died, my granddaughter asked, "Is Great Granny in heaven? What does it look like? Is she with Hashem?" I was hesitant because I didn't know what the correct answer was, or what was appropriate to say to a child. In the end, it was easier for me to say, "Go ask Saba."

THE FUNERAL AND CEMETERY

Parents frequently ask if their child should attend a funeral. While there are no clear-cut answers, attendance is very much related to the age and stage of a child, their relationship to the deceased, and whether or not they actually want to attend. The emotional maturity of the child is more relevant than their actual age, and this may influence their desire to be there or not. That said, we have seen young children who want to attend, and teenagers who do not. Respecting your child's wishes is important. No one should be forced to attend a funeral.

As an adult, you may need to hear their fears in order to better understand their concerns, and in order to explain what they think they may see and how this may differ from reality. It is important to explain in detail what will happen, and to let your children know that an adult (and not necessarily you) will be there for them, and that if at any time they are not comfortable, they can walk away with that adult.

Children need to know in advance both what they may see or hear. They may never have been to a funeral, a cemetery, seen *kriya,* heard a eulogy or prayers, or experienced adults upset and crying. They will need to know that their loved one will be wrapped in a shroud or be placed in a casket, and that when earth is shoveled onto either, it may sound louder than they might expect. Being told that it is okay to feel sad, regardless of age, and that their loved one will be lovingly enveloped in earth may help reassure them. Let them know that they can help pick out a rock and place it on top of the grave. These all help to explain what for a child can be a sad or strange situation. Some children may opt to go to the funeral, but not be present for the burial itself, and they need to know that this, too, is okay. Should a child choose not to attend at all, they can still be an active participant, and have their feelings recognized and validated by drawing pictures, sharing their memories, or writing a special story.

THE WEEK OF SHIVA

With so many adults present in a shiva house, it is easy to inadvertently ignore the children who are present, thinking that they simply don't belong in the adult conversation, or even in the room. Children may take things in, misunderstand conversations, or find the crowds of people overwhelming – without understanding the depth of what happened. Any child may belong in a shiva house if they would like to be there, and be there with you. Children bring life to the shiva house, reminding mourners that the mundane tasks of life continue and have meaning. Being around a shiva enables children to have the opportunity to experience support from others and better come to terms with the loss.

When children are the mourners, they come to realize that people will be there to take care of them, and that they are not alone.

Children do not need to be around the entire time, and if it feels appropriate, they may benefit from having a playdate with other children. Again, assuming that this is the child's first shiva, there will be much that will need to be explained and your child's questions and desire to talk of their loved one should be encouraged. Depending on the age of your child, their peer group may also want to be visiting the shiva house, and this should also be encouraged.

When children are the mourners, they need to have their friends around them. It is not uncommon for teenagers to create a separate circle and seek the company and comfort of their friends. As an adult watching, it may be hard not to pass judgment on what you might consider to be inappropriate behavior in a house of mourning. Young people mourn differently than adults. They may be laughing, joking, and discussing anything but the deceased.

For those who are misplaced from their homes, as happened during the war in Israel, when families sat shiva in hotels and other places, children may grieve the missing family member as well as their familiar and comforting surroundings.

It is easy for children to be "forgotten grievers," especially if they are quietly playing on the sideline, or acting out, and the adults in their world may not recognize this or be able to be there for them.

Children are not "little adults." They do not grieve continuously, but rather in spurts, often needing to take breaks. One minute they are devastated, and the next they are happily involved with their friends. Not appearing consistently or intensely sad, adults may assume that the children are doing fine, when in fact they may not be. Play often provides a structure for how a child works through the issues at hand. Don't be surprised if your child seems oblivious to what is going on around them, and then seemingly out of the blue asks a question or demonstrates that they are working on a loss through play, conversations, or artwork. Children are not indifferent, but simply "take breaks" in both their assimilation of information and in the grieving process. Often, adults don't realize that when others have long forgotten the death, a grieving child may only just be beginning to face their painful journey. Sadly, it is at this time that they may be told to "be strong" and not be encouraged to express their feelings.

> *For months after my mom died, when I carpooled the children to Hebrew School, driving past the cemetery where she was buried, I'd often say to the kids, "Say hi to Nanny." It was a lighthearted way of encouraging and ensuring a continued connection and the kids would happily say, "Hi, Nanny." They never seemed to question it. This greeting shouted out from a passing car seemed to teach them an important lesson that it was okay to maintain a connection with someone who was no longer physically present, and even "speak" to them in their own way.*

During special family times, such as anniversaries of the death and holidays, a child's pain may feel almost too much to bear. While those special recipes once helped your child celebrate the joy of being together, this, along with the empty chair at the Shabbat table, for example, can be a constant reminder of what was. Visits to the home of others, a trip to the park, class events, and many other daily activities serve as reminders of what is *now* as compared to what *was*. These all can leave your child with pain that may be invisible to others.

As a child gets older, they may revisit their early grief. Grief in general is cumulative; the more one experiences, the greater the impact of each loss. It is important to achieve closure for each of the child's previous losses.

Household schedules, routines, and rules provide a much-needed structure for everyone at such a difficult time, but often get tossed aside. Providing a sense of discipline and guidance when the rest of the world feels out of control and unstable are essential for a child's security, but it may feel like an impossibility.

School, homework, bath and bedtime, meals, and playdates all can give children a sense of welcome familiarity and normalcy, which help aid in the healing process. The Jewish home in general has a weekly routine, and elements that can remain the same will be helpful to children and adults alike.

THE RETURN TO SCHOOL

You will want to inform the daycare, babysitter, or school as well as your child's teachers that there has been a death in the family before your child goes back. If your child is not in a Jewish educational institution, it might be appropriate to explain Jewish mourning rituals to the relevant staff. For children who have experienced a loss of any kind, the return to school may be upsetting and frightening. The school, teacher, and rabbi can provide a good support system for your child and the family, both while still at home and upon the return to school. They may arrange for other children to visit, and teachers and staff may visit themselves.

After a death, your child may be overwhelmed by many emotions and most likely won't know what to say to their friends. Their friends, not ever having experienced such a loss, and not wanting to make things worse by not knowing what to say, or wanting to bring up a difficult discussion, may stay away.

A bereft child may suddenly appear different to their classmates. They may be upset, have difficulty concentrating, and while once dependable, now appear to be forgetful and preoccupied. Feeling very much alone, they may sense that there is no one for them to talk to. Somatic complaints, numbness, anger, bully-like or obnoxious behavior, mood swings, indifference, poor school performance, and pervasive sadness may all be seen.

That said, the school can help prepare your child's classmates, answer their questions, and enable them to be supportive and receive support as well. Some children will now be saying *Kaddish* in daily minyanim, and everyone will need to know how best to help out. The teacher and broader support staff can be the eyes and ears with respect to how your child is doing, and be there to provide guidance as needed.

> *We got the call that my brother died, and it was as if time stood still. I will never forget the look on my parents' faces. I cannot believe that six months have passed already. Sometimes I think my parents forget that I am even here, and that I am their child too. I feel as if I could disappear, and they would never even notice. I am trying so hard to not bother them and to be the best son I can be. My rabbi at school has been helpful. He told me that his father died when he was my age, and I think he understands me. He told me how sad he was and how alone he felt, but that it did get better. He has suggested that I talk to God, and told me that it is okay to be angry with God and tell Him just how I feel. He promised that God would rather I talk to Him than be silent. He said that it certainly helped him with his grief. I think it's helping me to feel a bit better.*

SYMPTOMS OF GRIEF IN CHILDREN AND ADOLESCENTS

Children under three years of age

- Regression in development – speech/sleeping/eating/bedwetting/toileting
- Increased temper tantrums
- Sadness/irritability/excessive crying
- Anxiety and fearfulness – fear of the dark, strangers, being left alone
- Attachment concerns/increased dependency and clinging/withdrawal from others

TIP: Providing a sense of safety and security through verbal reassurance and physical comfort is key at this age, as in all stages. Children of this age need adults to fill in the words for their feelings of confusion and abandonment.

Preschool-age children

- Regression in development
- Eating issues
- Toileting issues/bladder and bowel "accidents"
- Hyperactivity/hypoactivity and lethargy
- Temper tantrums/anger outbursts with little or no provocation
- Excessive crying/sadness
- Social withdrawal/overdependence on others
- Sleep disturbance and nightmares
- Somatic complaints
- Fear of loud noises

TIP: Daily comforting, bedtime routines, and rituals such as saying the *Shema*, avoiding unnecessary separations, and letting them know when you need to leave and when you will return can be reassuring and helpful. Encourage children to express their feelings of loss and sadness – through play and art, but verbally as well.

School-age children

- Poor school performance
- Difficulty in focusing/ concentration

- Refusal to go to school
- Increased attention-seeking behavior
- Hyperactivity/hypoactivity/aggressivity
- Lethargy and fatigue
- Temper tantrums/anger outbursts with little or no provocation/irritability
- Excessive crying/sadness/depression
- Increase in anxiety
- Social withdrawal/overdependence on others/whining and clinginess
- Sleep disturbance and nightmares
- Somatic complaints – headaches/stomachaches and other physical symptoms
- Fear of loud noises

TIP: These children have a better understanding of the finality of death, and will have many questions. They will need a great deal of reassurance that they and others around them are okay and will be there for them. Rituals and routine provide structure and are often comforting.

Adolescents

- Increased sadness/depression
- Increase in anxiety, feelings of helplessness and lack of control
- Decline in academic performance
- Social withdrawal/overdependence on others
- Sleep disturbance and nightmares
- Somatic complaints – headaches/stomachaches
- Truancy/resistance to authority

- Increased risk-taking behavior
- Lying/stealing
- Experimentation with drugs and alcohol
- Suicidal ideation/suicidal attempts

TIP: Adolescence is a time of increased peer group importance. No longer children but not yet adults, being available to offer a listening ear and asking them what could be helpful lets them know that you are there for them. Wanting but not having a sense of control can feel very overwhelming. It's okay if you share your feelings with them, but don't overwhelm them with your concerns. Your goal is to enable them to draw on their strengths at such a difficult time and reestablish a sense of trust in a world of uncertainty.

THERAPY

The grieving process is not an easy one, and this is especially true for children who at times, and for various reasons (being young, small, and quiet), may be unacknowledged grievers. Trying to please grownups by being "super" well-behaved, some children look like they are doing well when they are not. If your child acts out, they are more likely to get the attention of others, and this may be seen both at home and in school. That said, with time, assuming the loss has been addressed, children in general do well.

Very young children may initially regress in toileting, eating, sleep, and other behaviors. A somewhat older child may be less talkative, feel they have to go out of their way to please adults or act as if everything is okay, appear disinterested in death, and avoid interactions with others for fear that something will also happen to them. A child may "appear fine" so as not to upset the adults in their world who are already dealing with a lot. Other children may ask the same questions over and over again, as they attempt to make sense out of the death.

Older children and adolescents may question their own health and may fear that others, including themselves, may soon die as well. Lack of predictability around the time of illness and death for someone who already feels so out of control by simply being a teenager, in a world now filled with even more uncertainty, may feel very overwhelming. Loss may leave the adolescent feeling alone, isolated, and unsupported. Some teenagers may now be more willing to take risks and act out in ways that put them in danger. Others may try to take on the role of the deceased parent or attempt to replace the person who died, enjoying the parentified role and change in family status. Adolescents may joke and make light of their feelings, act tough, and at times seem impervious to their pain.

> *There are many areas that our group of bereaved teenagers addressed. One adolescent said, "I had a hard time returning to the shul where my dad davened. His empty seat felt so painful." Another spoke of her pain when asked how many brothers and sisters she had. There was no longer an answer that she could give that felt okay.*

> *When I smell my mom's perfume on someone, in a flash I am thinking of her and the mornings when she would kiss me when I went off to school as she was getting ready for work.*

Some children simply want to be recognized and have it acknowledged that they exist and are important. Their message of "don't forget about me" may be lost at this difficult time. Whereas the grieving adult or the younger child more readily elicits help, adolescents may inadvertently be ignored. Needless to say, the possible reactions are many, and the symptoms of grief described in adults may all be seen in children to varying degrees.

Parents going through their own loss are often caught up in their own grief and may not be able to talk about how their children are feeling. It is important to get help for your child if you cannot be there for them, and if they need someone outside of the family to talk with. Children may try to protect their parents and find it hard to share how they are truly feeling. If you have lost someone, you may very much appreciate the help of your older children and inadvertently "parentify" them, putting pressure on them to act more maturely. Some children might make decisions based on what they think their deceased parent would have wanted or approved of.

At some point, children and adolescents do move on. They discover that they are focusing again, and school grades may start to improve. Friendships begin to have meaning, and the normal process of separating from the family as they struggle towards independence slowly begins again. Crying and pervasive sadness diminish and sleeping and eating start to improve.

WHAT IS NORMAL GRIEVING FOR A CHILD?

Children need to know that their feelings are "normal," and that it is okay to feel sad. Grief is a normal but potentially very intense process, and with it will come a host of uncomfortable feelings such as anger, sadness, and much more. They need to know that you are there for them and will talk about whatever they need to talk about, whenever they need to talk. Now, more than ever, may be the time to take your child out on a date with you, go for a walk, or have a chat over a board game, Reading and cooking together, as well as car rides, will give you an opportunity for discussions to come up naturally.

It can be difficult to assess when grieving is no longer considered normal, and you may want to reach out to a professional at any stage if you are concerned. One of the best parameters is to assess behavior change over time. One would want to see that the frequency, intensity, and duration of symptoms of grief diminish with time. So, while one would expect to see regression in developmental milestones or other behaviors, one would hope that with time, the issues begin to improve and a child's behavior for the most part returns to what it was like before the death.

If one sees persistent depression, severe anxiety, increased aggressivity, a refusal or inability to talk about their loved one, somatic complaints that seem unremitting, suicidal ideation or gestures, school issues, and other symptoms that seem to persist beyond what one might expect or is comfortable with, please reach out to a professional. Very young children through adolescents each grieve in their developmentally appropriate or inappropriate way, and will need additional warm, loving, and consistent support from others, along with information and reassurance that they will be okay.

HOLIDAYS AND CHILDREN

You may ask yourself how you and your family can possibly survive the holidays while bearing such a painful loss. It seems as if there are reminders everywhere – home, school, the grocery store, synagogue, and even the park. You may all feel inwardly very down when the rest of the world appears in holiday mode. Even if it is not true, everyone seems to be making plans around you, and acts almost celebratory in comparison. You and your children might want to forget that the outside world exists, as it may all feel too much. As a family, you could each be thinking the other is fine or not have the energy to engage in conversation to even find out.

Now may actually be one of those times where it is important to reevaluate your priorities as a family and focus on what is truly important or whatever you need to attend to. If something is unnecessary and causes increased stress, skip it. If it gives you or the children comfort, then consider it. You will need to let people know what your children need and what is helpful, and seek out those people who will be supportive and help bring special meaning to your family.

Family traditions and rituals might have to change to accommodate your recent loss. If certain foods, for example, are a very painful reminder of a loved one, now could be the time to change the menu. If everyone has always had their special seat, ask your children how they feel about trying out a new place at the table. Children may experience the emotional presence of their loved one along with their physical absence, which can be both painful and confusing. Addressing this as well as examining the entire holiday and finding a way to make it work for everyone will be an important goal. While one family member may want to accept an invite, another will desperately want to remain at home, with or without other guests. You may all need to make choices and compromises that you can be comfortable with in order to try to accommodate everyone. You, too, can decide which tasks are necessary to accomplish and which are not, what you would like to change and why, and delegate the responsibility to complete what must be done. Your children should be included in the tough decision-making so that their voices can also be heard.

Holidays, anniversaries of the loss, and other meaningful occasions may also provide you with the opportunity to do something special with your child as a way to honor your loved one. Whether you memorialize your loved one through donating to their favorite charity, plant a tree, write a poem, create a real or virtual photo montage or album, or visit the cemetery, you can do whatever you both need to in order to get through the difficult moment. Determine in advance what you will do on your own and as part of the family to help you cope and bring meaning back into your lives. This may be the year when you want to reach out to others and spend time at a hospital or local soup kitchen, or read on a regular basis to an elderly neighbor. There are many projects of various kinds that can provide just the involvement with the outside world that you would want – and if not this year, there is always next year.

It is important to acknowledge that special occasions will feel different than they once did. How can they not? Now, more than ever, you may wish to be reunited with your loved one – but this is not to be. Getting through these difficult events will take tremendous creative energy on your part. Whether and how you decide to celebrate these times is indeed your choice and that of the family, and may change from year to year. Children receive permission to grieve from adults and those willing to express their feelings of grief. Taking it one moment at a time really can help, and if you feel that you or your child is experiencing difficulty with this loss, seek professional support and advice. You may think that looking for help is an acknowledgement of weakness. We prefer to see it as the first step towards a more positive future – and an attestation of strength, love, and support.

> *Years ago, when working with a young mom who was dying and about to leave behind her eight- and ten-year-old children, we made a recording for each child and left each a special box of items with a letter to be opened when they were older. It was very meaningful for the children and at the time, it gave mom an opportunity to work on something for the children when she felt up to it that would help give them a little piece of who she was and what she wanted them to remember about her. Leaving a voice recording would also help the children connect to their mom and remember her voice.*

Chapter 14

COVID-19 and Loss Within the Jewish Community

August 4, 2021 – Today the worldwide covid case count surpassed two hundred million.

Reuters

February 22, 2022 – Israel on Monday night passed 10,000 corona-related deaths since the pandemic started two years ago. Two hundred and twenty eight of those occurred in the last seven days.

Shira Silkoff, "10,001 Dead of Corona," *Jerusalem Post,* February 22, 2022, p. 7

April 14, 2022 – Global COVID-19 cases surpassed five hundred million. About 6.5 million deaths since the pandemic began. The

> *United States reported highest number of deaths, followed by Russia, Brazil, and India.*
>
> Adapted from B. Kavya and Aparupa Mazumder, *Reuters,* as quoted in the *Jerusalem Post,* April 15, 2022, p. 8

❧

> *May 13, 2022 – death of one million people in the United States from COVID-19.*
>
> *Reuters*

❧

> *June 11, 2023 – Today the worldwide coronavirus case count was 690,149,669, with 6,890,211 deaths worldwide and 662,648,340 recovered.*
>
> COVID, Coronavirus statistics, *Worldometer*

COVID-19 was one of the most impactful events of the twenty-first century. This global pandemic not only changed many practices both religious and otherwise, but left us with many lessons to learn along the way. (As of this writing, the virus has mutated into many variants and there are still numerous cases worldwide, appearing daily. While far from over, COVID-19 is now typically seen as less virulent.) The pandemic not only had a far-reaching effect on how we were able to mourn, but it has continued to affect our lives due to the lack of closure experienced by so many people. Jewish mourning rituals provide structure and comfort, and having been prevented from utilizing these left many people feeling unsettled until this day when they look back at their losses. It is with this in mind that we have chosen to include a chapter on COVID-19 and loss.

Judaism's halakhic response and commentary throughout history to various pandemics was surprisingly relevant to

COVID-19, which began in late 2019/early 2020. Issues such as how to conduct oneself so as to remain healthy by maintaining social segregation, shuttering synagogues, and self-quarantine procedures, as well as concerns regarding death and dying, have all been addressed in detail and are considered meaningful until today.

> *During the Passover Seder of April 2020, quarantine in Israel forced people to celebrate alone and in the absence of close family and loved ones. In reciting the traditional question, "Why is this night different from all other nights?" the irony of the retelling of the biblical Passover narrative of the ten plagues was sadly not lost on anyone.*
>
> *Mid-May 2020 – Israel – restrictions and closures have lessened, though everyone is required to wear a mask in public, be physically distanced two meters apart, and pay close attention to hand hygiene. People are just beginning to return to school, stores which have remained closed are starting to open, and the numbers of infections are being closely watched to ensure that they remain low. Work, when possible, until now has been "from home," restaurants are not yet opened, and synagogues which were generally closed entirely have recently allowed first up to ten, then nineteen, and now fifty people to pray together, outside and socially distanced. Israel has fared much better than other parts of the world and this is believed to be in part due to early and extremely strict physical isolation efforts. That said, there is a tentativeness in the air for many, given the novelty of the virus and the uncertainty of its behavior. With a heatwave driving temperatures up, people vacillate between concern with respect to crowds as restrictions get lifted and a deep hope that the virus will be driven out permanently by summer. Nonetheless, some people anxiously await and attempt to prepare for a possible second wave of COVID-19,*

> *which is expected by the fall or winter, in time to possibly coincide with the Jewish New Year.*
>
> B.L. Ludman, "COVID-19 and Its Impact on Loss within the Jewish Community," *ADEC Connects*, June 7, 2020

COVID-19 affected every aspect of life and death within the Jewish community. With its multiple challenges on so many different levels, the pandemic forced the Jewish world to recognize, reorganize, and reexamine synagogue attendance, as well as many other losses – both big and small – along the painful continuum of illness, death, and bereavement. These multifaceted concerns had resultant enormous implications for traditional Jewish practice.

THE INITIAL IMPACT OF THE PANDEMIC ON THE JEWISH COMMUNITY

Most people did not expect to deal all at once with the sudden onset of a pandemic, the lack of normalcy, economic hardship, and instability. In addition there was complete uncertainty with respect to physical, emotional, and financial well-being, both in the present, as well as in anticipation of further loss. Stigma and embarrassment about possibly contracting and giving someone COVID-19, as well as feeling threatened by others and their actions, added to the feeling of shame and loss. People experienced both individual and collective grief with issues so overwhelming that they created ongoing anxiety, fear, guilt, and sadness for just about everyone. With tremendous confusion, constantly changing rules, and prolonged isolation after a suspected exposure, there was an increase in anxiety, feelings of helplessness hopelessness, and depression, leading to more people requesting medication. Globally there was tremendous illness and loss from COVID-19 and proportionally the Jewish community worldwide was hard hit, especially in the early days. This was attributed in part to the nature of traditional religious practice especially among the Orthodox and ultra-Orthodox communities, who came together in large groups at least three times a day, seven days a week, for communal public prayer.

In addition, multiple life-cycle ritual ceremonies such as *brit mila*, bar and bat mitzva celebrations, weddings, and funerals frequently involved hundreds and even thousands of attendees who, by the very nature of the event and the tremendous warmth within the community, prayed and danced in close proximity to each other. Furthermore, the height of contagion occurred between Purim and Pesaḥ, a time that typically involved even larger festive gatherings than usual. Sadly, information regarding the infectious nature of the virus, isolation procedures, and hygiene techniques were not disseminated fast enough in the ultra-Orthodox Jewish communities throughout the world. With little access to such information, for many, it was sadly too late. By the time COVID-19 was declared a pandemic, large clusters of people, including several members within individual families, were already seriously affected.

SEPARATION OF PATIENTS FROM THEIR FAMILIES

Due to the rapid spread of this novel coronavirus, crisis management involved quick and extensive isolation and social distancing for all patients and their families, both with and without a COVID-19 diagnosis. With border closures and flights canceled, patients were painfully separated from their loved ones both near and far, and left alone at the worst imaginable time, and ultimately for some, at the end of their lives. Within a very short timeline, the mitzva of visiting and comforting the sick (*bikkur ḥolim*) became impossible.

> *When my father got sick with COVID-19, I could not visit him. Only my brother, who had already been sick and recovered, was allowed to see him. At my father's funeral, I regretted that I had not seen him at all in his last weeks of life.*

In addition, sudden, unexpected deterioration of patients with multiple organ failure led to much confusion and even death, without the physical and emotional presence of family members or a rabbi. *Viddui* (confession prayer) and other prayers, as well as end-of-life discussions, could not take place as patients advanced quickly toward death, further exacerbating the distress of patients, families, and the medical personnel involved. Healthcare workers had to cope with very long hours in Personal Protective Equipment (PPE), informing family members about more serious illness, with increased demands, tremendous uncertainty, and horrific loss. Being overworked, understaffed, and underpaid all helped contribute to exhaustion and compassion fatigue.

Yet, in spite of this, there were many positives, and the resilience within the Jewish community was remarkable. Knowing how the presence of family has always been very critical to patient care, Israeli hospitals, on the forefront in addressing these concerns, were among the first, globally, to respond to the psychosocial impact of hospitalization without family being present. Hospital teams introduced PPE with photos of the faces of the medical staff visibly pasted on the front of their uniforms for patients to see, used audio-visual technology or phone conversations whenever possible to enable bedside communication between the patient and his family, and most importantly, allowed a loved one, properly gowned and protected, to be in the ICU near the time of death.

THE EFFECT OF COVID-19 ON JEWISH MOURNING RITUALS

Declaration of death, tahara, and burial

As discussed previously, one of the most beautiful aspects of Judaism's approach to death is its focus on ritual. In normal times, these rituals lovingly embrace the mourner and gently guide them step by step, from the time of death, through the funeral, shiva, *sheloshim,* and first year of mourning. This is done at a pace that parallels and promotes psychological healing. With COVID-19, this was painfully altered in every possible way, shaking the entire Jewish community to its core for a very long time.

Declaration of death, subsequent care of the deceased, and physical preparation of the body for burial, all of which hold a very important and meaningful place in Jewish ritual, required changes, as protocols both in hospitals and funeral homes were continuously evolving. To avoid the possibility of contagion to all those involved, the *ḥevra kaddisha* was at times required by law to perform the most minimal ritual preparation (*tahara*) of the body, and sometimes none at all. Whenever possible, the *ḥevra kaddisha,* maintaining a safe distance from one another, correctly donning and removing their difficult to attain but mandatory PPE and taking additional precautionary measures, worked much longer hours, given the increase in numbers of deaths occurring daily. Furthermore, while Jewish ritual practice usually included watching (*shemira*) over the body from the time of death until burial, and identification by a family member prior to burial, given the possibility of infection, this, too, was modified.

> *I am grateful for the words of a wise and spiritual friend who suggested, "The souls of those who passed away now with abbreviated burials and shivas were so pure they ascended directly to heaven and did not require traditional mourning rituals." These words will be a source of comfort and understanding for me, as will the memory of my beloved mother.*
>
> Ellen Bachner Greenberg, "Mourning My Mother During COVID-19," Aish.com, July 20, 2020

With Jewish burial, the time between death and interment has always been kept as brief as possible, with the deceased often buried within twenty-four hours of death. During COVID-19, the *ḥevra kaddisha* had to handle up to ten times as many deaths as before. Given the tremendous amount of paperwork and manpower involved, with so many deaths and multiple funerals a day, burials were either expedited or suffered inevitable delays. Furthermore, for those wishing to have their loved one buried in Israel, even greater coordination was required, making the process all the more difficult. Restrictions and increased costs on international air travel with reduced access and availability, along with more stringent requirements, greatly complicated interment. At times, this necessitated temporary burial outside of Israel, with reburial later. This meant rending garments (*kriya*) for a second time, and observing another full day of shiva, both of which took a great emotional toll on the grieving family.

> *There were the nearly insurmountable logistics of moving my father's body to Israel. One airline was completely shut down. Another, which had flights from New York, didn't accept cargo. Then we heard about a specially scheduled flight from California that was bringing much needed COVID-19 supplies to Israel, and the airline had room for two caskets. My father's was one of them.*
>
> Adapted from R. Shmuley Boteach, "Nearing an End to My Year of Kaddish," *Jerusalem Post*, February 8, 2021

Funerals during COVID-19

Funerals, too, changed dramatically during COVID-19. Once large, with possibly hundreds or thousands of attendees, at the height of the pandemic funeral homes were closed, indoor gatherings and eulogies were forbidden, and services were limited to a minimal graveside prayer. Now restricted to ten people, the minimum requirement for a minyan, people were spaced at least two meters apart and wearing masks. When counting the members of the

PPE-clad burial society and immediate family, this initially did not allow for others to be present. While in some places it was later raised to fifty attendees, it still felt highly restrictive given that in the recent past, it was not unusual to have many hundreds and more in attendance. With funeral attendance often prohibited, and access restricted due to concerns about the health and welfare of attendees, global lockdowns, closed airspace and more, funerals, at this point, often took place with only very immediate family present, if at all, in the cemetery.

It is customary in Jewish burial for those present to fill in much of the grave with soil. This was often abandoned during the pandemic, in order to keep mourners safe from physical contact and minimize time spent at the cemetery. At times, with so many people being buried in a day, the graves were not filled in until later. For those in attendance, in order to limit exposure to others, the burial ceremony itself was often abbreviated, with little or no opportunity to eulogize the deceased, or say goodbye in any meaningful way. Jewish burial procedures place so much emphasis on honoring the deceased by helping escort them to their final resting place. The inability to do this was considered a tremendous loss and was very painful for both mourners and others who wanted to be there to offer support.

> *My mother died during the global pandemic. The funeral was limited to a handful of people. Even then, many of my mother's family and close friends were scared to attend. Fearful of leaving their homes and being in contact with other people, we followed all the government regulations, but my feeling was that it wasn't "meḥubad," honorable, for my mother to leave the world this way. She was such a social person with so many friends. Under different circumstances, there would have been a hundred people seeing her off.*

Comforting the bereaved – such a hallmark of Jewish practice – with so many restrictions, began to include or be replaced by "virtual" mourning as grieving practices moved online. For families unable to travel, or who had no other option, this virtual attendance offered at least some comfort by enabling them to "be there" from a distance. With the global pandemic, the concept of a Zoom or livestreamed funerals became the only way that mourners could bid a final farewell to their loved ones. In spite of its limitations, being able to attend from afar has been carried over to post-COVID times as a viable option that allows participants to be part of the funeral when distance, illness, and other factors prevent physical presence.

While allowing for "attendance" when no other option was available, virtual funerals were not without their drawbacks. Some mourners felt that it was difficult enough not to be involved in the funeral process, and looking on from a distance (often from their living room and in a different country) felt even more removed, painful, and surreal. Added to this was the inability to tear *kriya* in the physical presence of the deceased and with other mourners. Not witnessing the sights and sounds of a burial firsthand made the acknowledgement and acceptance of the loss more complex and difficult to fully comprehend. Not being able to attend a funeral and be physically present at the burial robs you of the feeling of finality.

> *The announcement that the funeral was on Zoom made it sound like people should not come to the cemetery. As a result, there was no minyan. Others who were in the cemetery for their own losses, and not mine, joined us to help make our minyan.*

Shiva

With the focus primarily on the deceased before the funeral, after the funeral the emphasis now shifts to that of comforting the mourner. While under normal circumstances, mourners would be comforted and taken care of by attendees both at the cemetery and again when returning home, this, too, underwent change during the COVID-19 pandemic. Mourners, if they were able to attend the funeral in person, often returned home to an empty house and to immediate family only. Instead of being served a meal of consolation as they prepared to settle in for shiva, they often found themselves on their own.

As we have discussed, sitting together with other mourners, and being comforted in person by friends, family, and other members of the community, is a very important part of the healing process. With COVID-19, shiva bore little resemblance to pre-pandemic days.

In the very early stages of COVID-19 (early to mid-March 2020), when there were still shiva visits, hand sanitizer was often a prominent feature in the room. People felt awkward and refrained from getting close or embracing. If they did engage in physical contact, both mourner and visitors were often uneasy and anxious to the point where even a harmless cough drew much unwanted attention.

While in these very early days, shiva visits were made wearing masks, with some requesting a pre-sign-up arrangement, as numbers climbed and restrictions increased, visits often stopped altogether. Though some were still able to have visitors outdoors, visits in large part moved online or were conducted by telephone.

Mourners felt very lonely and isolated. In a time when they desperately needed the comforting embrace of others and the sharing of treasured memories, they were left to sit, eat, mourn, and pray almost completely alone. Family members in a different city or country were unable to comfort each other physically and were often left to grieve alone in their own home. There they remained without the stories, photos, and visits by others, or the ability to share their experiences in being together.

In a typical shiva house, there would have been family and friends, many who knew the deceased well, and those who didn't – but knew the mourner and came to give comfort and hear about the special person who died. Many visitors too, would have brought full meals or comforting snacks. The mourners, not having to worry about their basic needs, would have been cared for by the community that in normal times would have provided this gentle form of embrace. The mourners and others present would have given visitors insight into the life of their loved one, and in return felt nourished emotionally. There would have been tears and there may have been laughter, all of which in an exhausting week would have helped the mourner begin to heal and gain closure at such a difficult time.

Now bereft during this pandemic, most mourners missed the opportunity to experience any of this, with visitation being limited or suspended altogether. It often felt surreal and, in many cases, with no visiting the sick, no funeral, and no shiva, for some, the death itself did not feel at all real.

As with funerals that were unable to be "in person," the possibility of "virtual" shiva became more commonplace, as a space and place was made for mourning and grief to move online. (This practice has also continued in some cases post-COVID-19, as a way for those unable to attend to participate in some way.) Zoom shivas slowly became more sophisticated; often someone would be assigned to set up and monitor the technology as well as moderate the virtual event, taking the pressure off of the mourner.

While for some a virtual shiva session may have been better than nothing, for others it was perceived as intrusive and unsatisfying. There were difficulties in being let into the Zoom call by a host, difficulty hearing, sound delays, issues with poor bandwidth, people interrupting or speaking too loudly or too much, and often multiple people speaking simultaneously. In addition, people not muting themselves and saying things that were both irrelevant and irreverent were an added distraction. Another issue that was stressful to mourners was the need to relay the same difficult stories surrounding the loss repeatedly, as every few minutes new people continued to join the prolonged online "visit." When visitors are seated together in a shiva house, there is a more natural flow with visitors coming and going and often staying for a brief period.

In a Zoom shiva, people often did not know what to say, when to say it, when to stay quiet, and when to leave. Seeing only the face and possibly shoulders, nonverbal cues and posture were harder to assess. While in a natural conversation – face to face – it is normal to look away, gaze-averting in a Zoom call could have been interpreted as a sign of disinterest. It was not easy to direct conversation to the mourner and achieve the feeling of being physically and emotionally present. The mourner, too, often felt forced to be "on," thus having to serve as moderator and needing to elicit conversation and maintain an exhausting focus with those who joined at random times.

As difficult as in-person shiva is, virtual shiva can feel both empty and draining. Sadly, with an inability to travel or to gather in person, with few other choices, this frequently became the only option and an accepted norm.

COMFORTING THE MOURNER – *NIḤUM AVEILIM* DURING COVID-19

> *The halakhic guidelines regarding comforting mourners is that you don't speak unless the mourner initiates conversation. It is possible to comfort someone without speaking, simply by being with them. How does this work if you are participating in a Zoom shiva, or if your face is masked and it's difficult to convey your feelings? Despite my best intentions, I found it very difficult and frustrating to offer support to people grieving during the height of the pandemic. Many people were afraid*

of having visitors or limited the visits to certain times. Many older people found it difficult to understand me with a mask on. I asked myself if it was correct to go when I found the experience so frustrating. I reminded myself that many of these people were not able physically to be near their loved ones at the end, and probably needed even more understanding and support. It was easier when people accepted visitors outside, but there were challenges, such as the weather, noise, and other distractions.

I went to visit a woman in my community whose husband died. Although many places had lifted the restriction to wear masks, I was wearing a mask, knowing there would be a lot of people present in a small place. The woman asked me if I would take down my mask as she found it difficult to hear me. I had mixed feelings. I wanted to respect the wishes of the mourner, especially in her home, but I wanted to keep myself safe. Was it a fair, legitimate request of hers to make?

Our family held three Zoom shivas for our family and friends from all over the world. It was very organized and surprisingly comforting. We were five mourners – myself, my siblings, and my father. Since there were travel restrictions, we could otherwise never all be together.

Unfortunately, during COVID-19, both mourners and the greater community were by necessity removed from and deprived of the outpouring of comfort, which was so integral to the healing process. With no community interfacing with the mourner, and being there to help mark the rituals, make the meals, cover the mirrors, dote on and protect the mourner, it was almost as if the death did not happen. When the door is not left ajar (as it normally would be), and no one walks in, who would notice the absence of leather shoes, the unkempt beard, the shirt torn just prior to the funeral, and the desolation? Who would be there to honor the deceased and elevate them through the sharing of stories and help validate this loss, made all the more painful due to the circumstances? At times, the situation felt so unreal that one was rocked by a sense of disorientation and disbelief. Finally, with so many funerals in the community taking place within such a short period of time, and synagogues closed or limited in attendance, finding the emotional space to grieve each person's loss along with their own COVID-19 losses was almost impossible.

Israel was ahead of most countries with respect to its vaccination program and in loosening COVID-19 restrictions. As the warm weather returned, in-person shiva visits started up again, albeit with limited numbers of attendees, physically distanced and with face masks.

MEMORIALIZING A LOVED ONE

With the goal of attempting to connect mourners and those providing consolation, during the pandemic technology offered many advantages. Some mourners honored and memorialized their loved one through shared photo albums, montages, and time capsules and family and friends could put up their memories and stories on social media or through funeral homes. These were seen as very beneficial and were continued long past the week of shiva.

FINDING A MINYAN TO SAY *KADDISH*

For mourners wanting to say *Kaddish* three times a day, arranging a minyan was very challenging. In a typical shiva, people naturally visit around the time of prayers, so that they can help constitute a minyan so the mourner/s can say *Kaddish*. With no visitation during the pandemic, some were able to participate in a Zoom minyan and say *Kaddish*, while others had to abandon the idea of a minyan and the opportunity to say *Kaddish* altogether. For those fortunate enough to live in an enclave of several Jewish families, the concept of a balcony, courtyard, or park minyan provided a sense of community for its participants and enabled neighbors to acknowledge the loss. The flexibility and informality of these minyanim held great appeal even after pandemic restrictions were lifted.

> *I felt deeply and passionately over the past eleven months, amid the challenges of the coronavirus, that it was my responsibility to say Kaddish three times a day for my father without missing any prayer. Even in normal times, it takes an effort to motivate oneself to go to services three times a day to say Kaddish. In Orthodox neighborhoods, it is normally easy to find a minyan. In 2020, however, the global pandemic turned organizing a minyan into a monumental challenge. Religious services were banned in some places, or the number of congregants was limited by the secular local or state authorities. If a synagogue was open, you often needed a reservation to attend, and then had to wear a mask and have your temperature checked. Consequently, my commitment to say Kaddish forced me, more often than not, to organize my own minyanim. It was miraculous that at the end of the eleven-month period of saying Kaddish I had not missed a Kaddish. The challenge sometimes felt absolutely overwhelming, and the pressure was, at times, almost too much to handle.*
>
> *When my father died, a leading Orthodox rabbi told me I had no obligation to say Kaddish, that it isn't that important compared to studying Torah in somebody's name, given the pandemic. The word "mishna" has the same Hebrew letters as "neshama," which means soul, so he argued that learning Mishna*

> *for a parent is more important than Kaddish. [Nonetheless], I'm going to say it for my father. Nothing, God willing, will stop me.*
>
> *From the day of my father's burial nearly a year ago, my entire life revolved around Kaddish. As time went on, I became a nudnik [nuisance]. The minyan became more challenging. Eventually, even friends don't want to be around you, for fear of being asked to be the tenth man at the minyan.*
>
> *It may seem hard to believe that a rabbi living in a Jewish neighborhood in New Jersey and working in the heart of New York City would have difficulty finding a minyan, but that is one of the many adverse consequences of trying to carry on during a pandemic. Most of the hundreds of prayer services I arranged were outdoors, with everyone masked and socially distant. We all wanted to stay safe. I pulled random Jews off the street to daven on sidewalks. I prayed in grocery stores and restaurants. I prayed outside of kosher butcher shops and a few times even in gas stations. We were praying in the freezing cold, snow, ice, wind, and rain. One of the greatest miracles of our minyan – aside from its very existence – was that, to our knowledge, thank God, not one person got sick. We had no coronavirus outbreaks. My year of Kaddish is over. I feel a chasm in my soul, not to mention in my daily routine.*
>
> Adapted from R. Shmuley Boteach, "Iran, Mike Pompeo Dominate My Father's Last Kaddish," *Jerusalem Post*, April 19, 2021

SHELOSHIM

During the first month after burial (*sheloshim*), there are typically many signs of ritual mourning that are observed as the mourner transitions back into society. Most notable, in addition to reciting *Kaddish* with a minyan three times a day, is the unshaven beard (for men) and not attending social gatherings. Given that during the pandemic synagogue attendance was at times not possible, and social gatherings were limited or did not take place at all, mourners were often not recognized as such.

> *A big part of avelut in general is not participating in social events and semaḥot. What does my mourning look like when nobody is making semaḥot or parties, and there are no movies or concerts? On the one hand, it is easier in that there is no issue regarding attending or not, deciding whether or not my partner would go without me, or if we just go to the ḥuppa and then leave. Do I stay for the kiddush after davening? There is no shul, so there is no question. On the other hand, these were important things. They made me think about my loved one and about grief. Not having to make these decisions as I had to do previously has made me wonder how much more difficult it will be to move on.*

UNVEILING THE TOMBSTONE

The unveiling of a tombstone, which may occur from the end of the *sheloshim* until the first *yahrzeit*, marks a very important milestone in the grieving process. When tombstones were unveiled during COVID-19, people often experienced a sense of *deja vu* – in their limited ability to honor their loved one with others present because of restrictions. For many attendees, if they did get to the cemetery, they continued to remain masked and at a distance. For others, the unveiling continued to remain private and not shared.

> *My sister died and all the airlines had canceled their flights. The skies were closed. How could I not be there? But I was completely unable to go. I could only watch the funeral on Zoom and had to sit shiva far away from my sister's family. It was terrible. For the first yahrzeit, I flew to see her grave. I had to test before flying and then quarantine upon arrival. It was something I needed to*

do for my sister's family as well as myself. The death was not a reality until I saw the actual grave and tombstone.

My aunt died right before Pesaḥ at the onset of the pandemic. The funeral numbers were limited. I did not attend, and I longed to give my cousins and uncle a hug. I attended the sheloshim and we rubbed elbows. But still no hug. Not until the first yahrzeit was I able to hug my uncle and cousins. Their year of mourning was made even more difficult by the distance we all had to keep between us in order to keep safe.

ADAPTING TO RESTRICTIONS

One of the most devastating aspects of COVID-19 was the tremendous isolation that was imposed on the world. As a result, at a time when people were going through a loss, they felt even more alone in their sadness and pain. With friends not able to be there in person to share their grief, the burden of the loss on family was even greater than "normal" times. When the sense of connectedness got severed in relationships with others, it became that much more difficult to feel part of greater society and life in general. At times, too, it was just too hard to listen at a distance and share the pain when someone was not there to literally hold your hand. This led one to suffer in solitude, making the grieving process all the more complicated. The pandemic, at times, did not allow for people to publicly grieve, but left them stuck and retreating. In addition to these grieving individuals were the extended families, communities, the nation, and the world that also carried the burden of each loss.

For some, their sense of self in a topsy-turvy world was threatened and their sense of reality disrupted. Given that the usual experiences around grief and rituals for healing were simply not available, for many the grieving process felt unreal, began later, or didn't happen at all.

As noted previously, the physical presence of others is fundamental in Jewish life, as are established mourning rituals that provide a sense of comfort, security, and routine. While physical and social distance are the antithesis of the character of Judaism, in the interim, the goal was to learn how to stay emotionally and socially connected, while remaining physically apart and separated. Being comforted by the community and feeling their support, albeit without touch and at a distance, was an important part of the healing process.

The community learned to change their conception and terminology from that of "social distancing" to that of "physical separation." This involved working on being socially and emotionally very present and connected, while still protecting everyone from the risk of contagion. When one could not visit either the sick or bereaved, it was important to access other forms of communication and means of connectedness. Although it was not always easy to assess when and how it was helpful for families and patients to visit virtually in the ICU, as well as to create their own alternatives for being present virtually at either a funeral or shiva, these brought comfort. Offering to walk with loved ones at a distance, when done safely and with the emotional and physical well-being of all in mind, was in the end a precious gift during such difficult times.

In summary, COVID-19 forced both individuals and communities to create new rituals. People close and far acknowledged that they cared through phone calls, video chats, email messages, sending meals, and, when possible, their presence. They each helped during a time when almost everything felt fragile, and nothing felt at all normal. This lack of stability and great uncertainty led to increased anxiety, which made it more difficult for mourners to move forward. That said, the Jewish community was and continues to be very resilient. The opportunity for post-traumatic growth has led to tremendous acts of kindness.

> *When the shul re-opened with masks, the rabbi invited all those who had lost a loved one during COVID to attend a shiur after the service. The deceased were mentioned by name, as well as their connection to the community member. It allowed those mourning to have some public recognition of their loss, and community members, who had not seen each other for a long time, to offer condolences.*

LESSONS LEARNED

While halakha makes a sharp separation between mourning and celebration, as with just about everything in Judaism, we manage to carry both joy and sorrow in our hearts simultaneously as we go through life. Happy that the pandemic is (mostly) over, or at least controllable with vaccinations, we nonetheless carry the pain of the tremendous suffering incurred from both its physical and psychological losses. As such, it now behooves the Jewish community to examine the impact of changes that took place in the three years of COVID-19. This will be particularly relevant not just for adults, but also for our children, who have to bear the precious legacy of the community's actions. The impact of loss on children of all ages as a result of the pandemic must be seriously explored. Some young children, during a very formative time in their life, because of masking, did not see nor experience the faces of other children or adults except when they were in their own home. They knew only a period of their life with COVID-19 and were kept away from their loved ones for fear of infecting their elders.

The essence of Jewish education entails constantly encouraging our children to ask questions. What values have taken on greater appreciation and new meaning, and what have each of us, including our children, learned from this? How should we live our lives differently now because of the pandemic? What are our life goals? Have we reevaluated our purpose in life?

> *We began to appreciate our family more intensely, for as we agonized over those who had tragically succumbed to the disease, we understood in a very real way that life is short and must never be taken for granted.*
>
> R. Stewart Weiss, "Rabbi Strangelove, or How I Learned to Stop Worrying and Love the Lockdown," *Jerusalem Post,* January 28, 2022, p. 33

❧

> *I learned after my sister died during the pandemic that, for the most part, I no longer needed to do what I didn't want to do. If I didn't want to go somewhere, or be with people who did not make me feel good, why should I? Life is short; why should I do something, "just because"? This was very liberating.*

With COVID-19, there were many missed opportunities. For some, important conversations never happened. While many wish they had asked their loved one more about their life and what they had hoped for in death, with the pandemic, this opportunity was often denied. COVID-19 patients were isolated from family and caregivers, which made joint decision-making difficult, if not completely impossible. This often led to regret and remorse.

The pandemic shocked everyone, and somehow asking serious questions about what they would want their life to look like if they got sick felt surreal and too close to home. For some, talking about death felt intrusive and, as with the superstitious belief that it would bring an "*ayin hara*" (evil eye), death might come sooner if it were brought up.

The world has painfully been reminded just how fragile life can be. We understand that people can get very sick very quickly. Therefore, it is important to prepare advanced directives and make your desires known to both your family – and ultimately, medical staff.

While grief is experienced by each person in their own way, and there is clearly no one "right" way in which to grieve, the pandemic brought new challenges that were especially difficult for the bereaved. It's only natural that when our loved ones are ill or dying, we want to be there for them in every way, to honor them and say our goodbyes, and in turn be with those who can help us in our grieving process. Digital communication, as well as other measures described above, while not a substitute for face-to-face communication, played an important role, and its impact needs to be evaluated now that life has returned to "normal."

Given the sudden, traumatic, and unexpected events during COVID-19 and lack of closure in so many areas, one would expect mourning to be more intense and exhausting. Was it? With losses felt very deeply in all spheres of life, and the grieving period perhaps more prolonged and complicated than one would have expected, one might want to evaluate the nature of any long-term consequences of loss during COVID-19. It is essential for those who work with those who were most affected by the pandemic to try to anticipate some of the issues that may continue to evolve in order to best help those in need.

Finally, attempting to make sense in such a chaotic time may have entailed a greater search for meaning and purpose. How did one derive God's comfort and that of others in such an anxious and sad world? A multitude of feelings were, and will continue to be, addressed, as one looks to honor their loved ones and feel a deeper connection.

As we reach out and ask those who may still be struggling with loss, as well as the effects of "long COVID," what could be helpful for them at this time, we might be surprised to discover that the answer is not what we might expect. Finally in this post-COVID world, it is important as a community to validate that it is truly okay to not be okay, as we strive to offer help, caring, and our renewed presence in each other's lives.

POST-TRAUMATIC GROWTH AFTER COVID-19

While a pandemic death is so devastating, how you are able to make meaning out of the loss itself is what will enable you to grow. Finding gratitude for the times you spent with your loved one, honoring them and their memory, and, with time, finding hope even in your pain will change you and allow you to grieve with more love than hurt. It will take time.

Chapter 15

The World Beyond the Grave

THE WORLD TO COME – *OLAM HABA*

The term *Olam HaBa* (literally, the World to Come) in contrast to *Olam HaZeh* (this world) refers to the hereafter, the afterlife, which begins with the termination of our life on earth. *Olam HaBa* seems to encompass the two basic concepts of the "Coming of the Messiah" and the "Resurrection of the Dead."

> *For most religions throughout history, life after death has proved more real than life itself. That is where the gods live, thought the Egyptians. That is where our ancestors are alive, believed the Greeks and Romans and many primitive tribes. That is where you find justice, thought many Christians. That is where you find paradise, thought many Muslims. Life after death and the resurrection of the dead are fundamental, non-negotiable principles of Jewish faith, but Tanakh is conspicuously quiet about them. It is focused on finding God in this life, on this planet,*

> *notwithstanding our mortality. "The dead do not praise God," says the Psalm (115:17). God is to be found in life itself with all its hazards and dangers, bereavements and grief. We may be no more than "dust and ashes" (Gen. 18:27), as Abraham said, but life itself is a never-ending stream, "living water." It is this that the rite of the Red Heifer [which purifies one from being in contact with death] symbolizes.*
>
> Adapted from R. Jonathan Sacks, "Healing the Trauma of Loss," in *Studies in Spirituality*, p. 209

Maimonides denies that humanity can have a clear picture of the afterlife, and compares earth-bound creatures with the blind person who cannot learn to appreciate colors merely by being given a verbal description. Flesh-and-blood people cannot have any precise conception of the pure, spiritual bliss of the world beyond. Thus, says Maimonides, the faithful should not concern themselves with the details.

While many of us are curious about the world beyond the grave, most would say we have no idea of what it entails. Judaism alludes to that world, but directs us to concentrate on life and not death, suggesting that when the time comes, we will have the opportunity to make this our focus. In the words of Rabbi Joshua ben Chanania (Nidda 70b): "When they come to life again, we will consult about the matter."

> "I have put before you life and death, blessing and curse.
> Choose life..."
>
> Deut. 30:19

> *...The major impact of Olam HaBa is on my life here and now, not in the sense of re-righting the scales of justice, but rather as a paradigm for this very life. What the concept of revivification, resurrection, [and] afterlife says to me is that you can fall down*

> *and rise up again. You can hit [rock] bottom and turn around. You can suffer depression and reversal – and spring back. Life inevitably has its swings, and just as some sort of physical life and the life of the soul can come back after death, so can life on this earth. It is no coincidence that in the Shemoneh Esreh, the blessing for resurrection incorporates concepts of lifting the fallen, healing the sick, [and] freeing the trapped: It is the blessing not only of life after death, but [also] of optimism for better times in this life. Not only can God restore life after death, but the Holy Blessed One can [also] lift us up, over and over again. And not only God, but [also] you, I, can restore, renew, refashion our lives.*
>
> *For that alone, a belief in life after death is worth holding on to. Besides, the rabbis say, who does not believe in it will find no place in the World to Come. I'm not willing to take any chances. I believe. I believe.*
>
> Blu Greenberg, "Is There Life After Death?" *Wrestling with the Angel: Jewish Insights on Death and Mourning,* p. 313

RESURRECTION OF THE DEAD – *TEḤIYAT HAMEITIM*

Judaism believes in the resurrection of the dead (*Teḥiyat HaMeitim*). The second blessing of the *Amida,* referred to as *Gevurot* – God's might – says: "Blessed are you, O Eternal, Who resurrects the dead." The Talmud says that three keys belong only to God: The key of life, the key of death, and the key of rain. The giving of life is in God's hands, as is the taking of life.

As part of the morning blessings, we thank God for restoring our strength to us each morning with a pure soul with the prayer. *Alokai Neshama,* "My God, the soul You placed within me is pure. You created it, You fashioned it, You breathed it into me, You safeguard it within me, and eventually You will take it from me, and restore it to me in Time to Come. As long as the soul is within me, I gratefully thank You, Hashem, my God and the God of my forefathers, Master of all works, Lord of all souls. Blessed are You, Hashem, who restores souls to dead bodies."

The end of the prayer above refers to God as He who restores souls, both to those who wake up each morning and in the future time of *Teḥiyat HaMeitim.*

The belief in *Teḥiyat HaMeitim,* resurrection of the dead, was codified by Maimonides as the last of his Thirteen Principles of Jewish faith. This concept is also found in the *siddur* in the hymn of *Yigdal*: "God will revive the dead in His full kindness, may His name be blessed and praised forever."

Although *Teḥiyat HaMeitim* is never mentioned in the Torah, this concept appears in the later prophets and writings. The vision of Ezekiel of the Valley of the Dry Bones that came to life again is a vision of hope. Rabbi Joseph B. Soloveitchik explains that *Teḥiyat HaMeitim* gives credence to the core belief that there will be a rectification of the evil and pain that has been suffered by so many in this world. *Teḥiyat HaMeitim* is not meant to be an act that merely highlights God's power to perform miraculous and wondrous deeds. Rather, it is a fulfillment of God's goodness to make right that which is wrong; it is a moral and ethical act on God's part ultimately to bring justice and wholeness to where there has been pain and brokenness.

Death is not forever. Praying for *Teḥiyat HaMeitim* can give a person comfort and hope.

> *Belief that those who died will one day live again is one of Judaism's great principles of hope… Jews kept hope alive; hope kept the Jewish people alive.*
>
> R. Jonathan Sacks, Commentary on *Koren Shalem Siddur*, p. 110

People who have experienced "near death" have described a sense of peace and calm and welcome, as well as images or words from loved ones who have passed on. It may give people comfort to know that they will be reunited with their loved ones at a future time.

When Miriam Peretz was asked after the loss of her two eldest sons and her husband, how she could be happy and bring happiness to others, she responded, "I believe with full faith that the day will come when the Messiah will arrive, and then I'll see [them] again."[13]

DEATH AS A TRANSITION TO ANOTHER LIFE

> *If the soul is immortal, then death cannot be considered a final act. If the life of the soul is to be continued, then death, however bitter, is deprived of its treacherous power of casting mourners into a lifetime of agonizing hopelessness over an irretrievable loss. Terrible though it is, death is a threshold to a new world – the "World to Come."*
>
> R. Maurice Lamm, *The Jewish Way in Death and Mourning*, p. 232

God made life such that nothing "dies" forever. He created nature's life and death cycles and seasons to teach us that physical death and rebirth mirror a spiritual dormancy and

13. Smadar Shir, *Miriam's Song* (Gefen Publishing House, 2016), 271.

> rebirth. This keeps us from thinking that death ends our existence. Instead, it marks our transition to a more wonderful life beyond.
>
> R. Aryeh Kaplan, *Sefer Yetzirah – The Book of Creation. Understanding the Afterlife in This Life*, p. 31

An analogy that conveys the hope and confidence in the afterlife is the tale of twins awaiting birth in the mother's womb. It was written by Rabbi Yechiel Michel Tucazinsky for his work on the laws of mourning.[14]

> *Twins are talking to each other in the womb. They begin to wonder as they continue to get lower, what will happen next. Their whole world has been in the interior of the womb. One brother says, "After our 'death,' there will be a great new world." The other brother replies, "There is no basis for this belief. There is only this world and nothing beyond. It will be the end. There is no world to come." Suddenly, the water inside the womb bursts, and the believing brother exits the womb. The other brother begins to cry. Hearing agitation, shouting, and cries, he thinks, "I was right, it is over." Outside, though, at that very moment, those same shouts are actually the shouts of joy, congratulations, and mazal tov. A new baby has just been born.*
>
> *For this baby who came out, a new world has opened up.*
>
> *As we separate and "die" from the womb, only to be born to life, so we separate and die from our world, only to be reborn to life eternal. The exit from the womb is the birth of the body. The exit from the body is the birth of the soul. As the womb requires a gestation period of nine months, the world requires a residence of seventy or eighty years. As the womb is a prozdor,*

14. Gesher HaḤaim, 1947 (Hebrew).

an anteroom preparatory to life, so our present existence is a prozdor to the world beyond.

R. Maurice Lamm, *The Jewish Way in Death and Mourning*, p. 234

The story of the twins in the womb is one I frequently share with both my religious and secular clients. Often they approach me as a religious therapist and say, "You have faith, it's easier for you. I see death as very final, black and nothingness." I ask if I can share a parable, which offers hope and choice. It serves as a reminder that none of us knows what exists beyond our current state of being. In the same way that the twins may question if anything exists beyond the womb, we may question if anything exists beyond life as we know it in this world. We can believe that there is nothing beyond the grave, but Judaism gives us the opportunity to believe that there may be everything. I choose to believe that like the baby born into a new world, we, too, will be pleasantly surprised.

At the memorial service for nineteen-year-old Gedalia Natan Kastner, his father spoke these words: "We live in a world that is described as a corridor, a preparatory room, a place where we are sort of practicing before meriting the next world. In other words, there is life after life. In Judaism, there is no such concept as dying followed by darkness, and that's the end of the ballgame. We believe that there exists a world out there in all its glory and peacefulness, in which one can enjoy a high level of spiritual living – one that is impossible to know in this world.

But it emphatically does exist – it is vital to believe that Gadi is now in such a place."

Adapted from Dr. Bernie Kastner, *Understanding the Afterlife in This Life*, p. 36

"All of Israel have a share in the World to Come, as it is stated: 'And Your people are *tzaddikim* (righteous)' (Is. 60:21). They shall inherit the land forever. They are the branch of My planting, the work of My hands, in which I take pride" (Sanhedrin 90a).

Judaism teaches that everyone is ensured a place or portion in *Olam HaBa*. Its nature, however, depends on one's conduct in this world. What we do with our share and what it will look like when we come to the next world are dependent on our deeds in this world.

Chapter 16

Healing After Loss

> *David Kessler reminds us that we knew how to love the people we've lost when they were physically present, and the work for us now is to love them in their absence.*
>
> R. Howes, "The Grief We Hold"

For a while after your loved one's death, people will ask you how you are doing. It is a difficult question that may feel irrelevant and irreverent, and often adds more pressure to your grieving process. A question such as "How are you doing *right now* or *today*?" may feel a bit easier to answer. After a while, and probably long before you feel ready to no longer be asked, people may stop asking how you are as they assume it's been "long enough," whatever that means. At some time, though, you might start to ask yourself, "How *am* I doing?" It is definitely relative, and you will certainly have upsurges in grief that make you wonder if you'll ever feel better. That said, you may begin to notice that you have more good moments, or hours, or even days. You may wonder just why and what made the day or parts of it feel okay.

As you slowly process your grief, you may begin to notice that you feel lighter. Every waking moment is not consumed by your loss. In fact, there will be times when you are not thinking about it at all, or if you do think about it, you feel calm and okay with it. You may discover that slowly you have begun to return to activities that you once participated in, that socializing to some extent feels good, that physically you feel less achy and a bit healthier, and emotionally you no longer feel that you are grieving in the same way as before. You may find that you have a capacity to hear and are interested in learning about how others are doing, and that your ability to focus and concentrate, while not yet what it was before your loss, has improved. Yes, the symptoms of grief that we spoke about seem to be slowly subsiding. You feel less overwhelmed and anxious, have more joy in your life, and guilt and other unpleasant feelings, along with the painful memories, seem to be receding just a bit more.

> *With a loss comes a huge hole. A hole in your life that can never be filled. A person you loved is gone. Gone forever. You continue to live, but that hole is never filled. What can happen, though, is that next to that hole a seed can be planted. A seed that may be the birth of another child, a new partner, or a new relationship. This new sapling will never fill the hole or take its place, but it can provide love and healing as it grows next to it. And this in itself, while feeling both frightening and exciting, engenders hope.*

It feels as if you are finding a place for your loss and are more accepting of what was and what is. While at one time your goal was to get through that minute or hour, now you are more future-focused and are finding meaning in your life. You hold your loved one in a special and healthy place in your heart. Remember that closet we spoke of? Now you allow yourself to open and close the door with more ease, for longer, and with less pain. You hold onto all that you treasured in your relationship with your loved one, you appreciate all that you shared and valued, and take these special memories of your loved one with you as you continue on with life's journey.

We don't have a choice over the package that we each are given in life, but we do have a choice as to what we do with that package. How will you allow your loss to affect you, and in what way do you want it to define who you are? In what ways will you grow because of it, or be stuck in your loss and remain angry with the world? This is a choice that only you will be able to make. How do you choose to put meaning into or make meaning out of your life? This, too, is a choice.

MAKING MEANING OUT OF LOSS

> *We live life looking forward, but we understand it only looking back.*
>
> R. Jonathan Sacks, *Judaism's Life-Changing Ideas*, p. 39

We know that, with the exception of death, there are few certainties in life. Depending on how your loved one died, you may have sadly learned that you may only regret what you don't do and say, and not what you do. Life can be short, and definitely shorter than we may have anticipated. When our loved ones are snatched away without so much as a goodbye, we learn to put our affairs in order, say goodnight with love to those we care about every day, and not to procrastinate with respect to things that are important. It also helps us to focus on what is truly important and let go of the smaller things in life, or those things that we cannot change. We may appreciate life and those we care about just a bit more – and this is so important. We learn that out of something bad can come something good and meaningful, and this helps us cope, move forward, and make meaning out of our lives. This is post-traumatic growth.

One of the best gifts I received after helping prepare a body for burial was the greater appreciation I had for my family when I returned home. For a short while I could recognize what was important – my beloved family. Nothing else was really important. In my own professional work, it is unlikely, too, that I would have delved as deeply or worked with clients on loss, death, and bereavement, had it not been for my own personal losses. In fact, with almost every client, I was able to reframe for them various death and non-death losses and the impact they may have had in their everyday life. Nevertheless, in a million years I would happily trade this appreciation and self-growth for the return of my loved ones. but that is not to be at this time. I have learned to tell my loved ones at the end of every phone call that I love them. I want as little unfinished business as possible.

Thoughts shared by a member of the *ḥevra kaddisha*

Sherwin Pomerantz wrote on the thirty-ninth yahrzeit of his daughter, "The length of our days is not guaranteed. As such, we need to do as much as we can to make every day meaningful. We should strive to bring joy to others, to greet everyone with a smile, and to make everyone with whom we come in contact feel that they are the most important people in the world. We are on this earth for too short a period of time to waste that time on anger, disappointment, and frustration."

"The good things are under our control – they are waiting for people to make them happen. The good things strengthen us in order to enable us to deal with the bad things that will inevitably occur."

Sherwin Pomerantz, "On My Daughter's 39th Yahrzeit," *Jerusalem Post*, Nov. 21, 2022

LIFE IS A JOURNEY

Life is a journey. When you start out, you never really know just what your final destination will be, who will join you along the way, how you will get there, or what detours you will take. You may never reach your final destination as planned. If you take the right path, you may get closer. You may see your life as both infinite and finite. It ultimately ends in some way, and you go on to your next destination, whatever that may be. Sometimes you may get so caught up in reaching your destination that you forget to live in the moment and enjoy all of the gifts along the way.

As you make your own personal journey, you are given the opportunity to search within yourself to make your trip the most memorable and meaningful one it can be. You adopt values that reflect who you are and who you want to be. While acknowledging that no one is perfect, you can learn to achieve greater self-acceptance. This will both enlighten you and lighten your load as you make your personal journey, enabling you to achieve a greater understanding of what is really important.

As you go through the grieving process and ultimately heal, you will learn that, in spite of your deep pain, you hopefully have noticed the blessings and cherished the moments. You have faced your fears, and many may no longer matter. You have taken life one step at a time, and one day at a time. Life today is your journey. It will be what you have chosen to make of it and that in itself is your ultimate healing.

Appendix

A CONTEMPORARY PRAYER FOR THE END OF RECITING *KADDISH* FOR A FATHER BY RABBI BENJAMIN LAU

(See Chapter 6, page 177)

To be recited after the last *Kaddish* at the end of eleven months of mourning:

אָבִינוּ שֶׁבַּשָּׁמַיִם
זָכִיתִי לְהַשְׁלִים אֲמִירַת קַדִּישׁ לְעִלּוּי נִשְׁמַת אָבִי-מוֹרִי,
מֵאָז עֲלִיָּתוֹ לְגִנְזֵי מְרוֹמִים וְעַד עַתָּה.
הִשְׁתַּדַּלְתִּי לְכַבֵּד אֶת אָבִי בַּשָּׁנָה הַזֹּאת בְּכָל נַפְשִׁי וּבְכָל מְאוֹדִי,
וְעַתָּה עוֹמֵד אֲנִי לְפָנֶיךָ נִרְגָּשׁ וְאוֹמֵר: עָשִׂיתִי כְּכָל אֲשֶׁר צִוִּיתָנוּ.
לָעֵת הַזֹּאת, בְּעָמְדִי לְפָנֶיךָ בִּשְׁעַת מִנְחָה,
אֶשָּׂא תְּחִנָּה לִפְנֵי כִּסֵּא כְבוֹדֶךָ שֶׁיַּעֲלוּ כָּל תְּפִלּוֹתַי לְפָנֶיךָ לְרָצוֹן
וְתֵיטִיב לְאָבִי, הֲרֵינִי כַּפָּרַת מִשְׁכָּבוֹ, אֶת מְקוֹמוֹ בְּעוֹלָם שֶׁכֻּלּוֹ טוֹב,
בְּקֶרֶב כָּל הַבְּרוּאִים שֶׁהֵאִירוּ אֶת פָּנֶיךָ בְּעוֹלָמְךָ.
לָכֵן בַּעַל הָרַחֲמִים יַסְתִּירֵהוּ בְּסֵתֶר כְּנָפָיו לְעוֹלָמִים,
וְיִצְרֹר בִּצְרוֹר הַחַיִּים אֶת נִשְׁמָתוֹ.
ה׳ הוּא נַחֲלָתוֹ,
וְיָנוּחַ בְּשָׁלוֹם עַל מִשְׁכָּבוֹ, וְנֹאמַר אָמֵן.

Our Father in Heaven,
I have been privileged to complete the recitation of Kaddish
to elevate the soul of my father and teacher,
from the time when he was taken to the Heavens until now.
I tried to honor my father during the course of this year
with all my heart and all my might.
And now I stand before You filled with emotion, and say:
I did all that You commanded me to do.
At this time, as I stand before You
during the afternoon prayer,
I raise my voice in supplication before the throne of Your glory,
and ask that all of my prayers will go up to You
and be acceptable to You.
And grant my father his place in a world that is all good,
among all the created beings
who shined favorably upon You in Your world.
Therefore, God of mercy,
shelter him in the shadow of Your wings forever,
and bind his soul in the bond of everlasting life.
God is his inheritance.
May he rest in peace and let us say: Amen.

A CONTEMPORARY PRAYER FOR THE END OF RECITING *KADDISH* FOR A MOTHER

(See Chapter 6, page 177)

To be recited after the last *Kaddish* at the end of eleven months of mourning:

אָבִינוּ שֶׁבַּשָּׁמַיִם
זָכִיתִי לְהַשְׁלִים אֲמִירַת קַדִּישׁ לְעִלּוּי נִשְׁמַת אִמִּי-מוֹרָתִי,
מֵאָז עֲלִיָּתָהּ לְגִנְזֵי מְרוֹמִים וְעַד עַתָּה.
הִשְׁתַּדַּלְתִּי לְכַבֵּד אֶת אִמִּי בַּשָּׁנָה הַזֹּאת בְּכָל נַפְשִׁי וּבְכָל מְאוֹדִי,

וְעַתָּה עוֹמֵד אֲנִי לְפָנֶיךָ נִרְגָּשׁ וְאוֹמֵר: עָשִׂיתִי כְּכָל אֲשֶׁר צִוִּיתָנוּ.
לָעֵת הַזֹּאת, בְּעָמְדִי לְפָנֶיךָ בִּשְׁעַת מִנְחָה,
אֶשָּׂא תְּחִנָּה לִפְנֵי כִּסֵּא כְבוֹדֶךָ שֶׁיַּעֲלוּ כָּל תְּפִלּוֹתַי לְפָנֶיךָ לְרָצוֹן
וְתֵיטִיב לְאִמִּי, הֲרֵינִי כַּפָּרַת מִשְׁכָּבָהּ, אֶת מְקוֹמָהּ בְּעוֹלָם שֶׁכֻּלּוֹ טוֹב
בְּקֶרֶב כָּל הַבְּרוּאִים שֶׁהֵאִירוּ אֶת פָּנֶיךָ בְּעוֹלָמְךָ.
לָכֵן בַּעַל הָרַחֲמִים יַסְתִּירֶהָ בְּסֵתֶר כְּנָפָיו לְעוֹלָמִים,
וְיִצְרֹר בִּצְרוֹר הַחַיִּים אֶת נִשְׁמָתָהּ.
ה' הוּא נַחֲלָתָהּ,
וְתָנוּחַ בְּשָׁלוֹם עַל מִשְׁכָּבָהּ, וְנֹאמַר אָמֵן.

Our Father in Heaven,
I have been privileged to complete the recitation of Kaddish
to elevate the soul of my mother and teacher,
from the time when she was taken to the Heavens until now.
I tried to honor my mother during the course of this year
with all my heart and all my might.
And now I stand before You filled with emotion, and say:
I did all that You commanded me to do.
At this time, as I stand before You
during the afternoon prayer,
I raise my voice in supplication before the throne of Your glory,
and ask that all of my prayers will go up to You
and be acceptable to You.
And grant my mother her place in a world that is all good,
among all the created beings
who shined favorably upon You in Your world.
Therefore, God of mercy,
shelter her in the shadow of Your wings forever,
and bind her soul in the bond of everlasting life.
God is her inheritance.
May she rest in peace and let us say: Amen.

PRAYER FOR BEREAVED FAMILIES BY RABBI SHAI PIRON

אנא אלי בשעה בה אנו זוכרים את ההולכים, השרה שכינתך על הורים ואלמנות, יתומים, אחים ואחיות, חברים וחברות.

האר את ימיהם, תקן את חלומותיהם, תן בהם כוח לחיות, להיות, נטע בהם תקווה, רסיסים של שמחה, יהי רצון שיידעו לאזן, בין זיכרון לאבל, בין בניין לחורבן ותן בנו תבונה להיות להם לעזר, למשענת.

שנדע להבחין בין כוחה של מילה לכוחה של שתיקה, שנמצא דרך לבחור נכונה, בין קרבה לריחוק, בין דרישה לפרישה, ויבוא שלום בארץ, "שלום בחילך, שלווה בארמנותייך" (תהלים קכב:ז).

וחיים ושלום מן העולם ועד העולם ישרו בארץ, ועושה השלום יעשה שלום עלינו ובתוכנו, ונאמר אמן.

Please my God, at a time when we remember those who are gone, rest your divine spirit on parents and widows, orphans, brothers and sisters, and friends.

Brighten their days, fix their dreams, give them strength to live, to be. Sow in them seeds of hope, moments of joy.

May they know how to balance between memory and mourning, between building and destruction, and give us wisdom to be there for them as a help and support.

May we know how to distinguish between the power of a word and the power of silence.

May we find a way to choose correctly between closeness and distance, between need and withdrawal.

May there be peace in the land. "May there be peace within your walls, and tranquility within your citadels" (Ps. 122:7).

In the land may there be life and everlasting peace.

May the one who creates peace on high bring peace to us and among us. And let us say: Amen.[15]

---

15. Translated into English by G. Junger.

References

American Psychiatric Association. *Diagnostic and Statistical Manual of Mental Disorders,* 2022. Fifth edition, Text Revision (DSM-5-TR). American Psychiatric Association Publishing. https://www.psychiatry.org/psychiatrists/practice/dsm

Angel, M. *The Orphaned Adult: Confronting the Death of a Parent.* Human Sciences Press, 1987.

Bowlby, J. *Attachment and Loss.* New York: Basic Books, 1980.

Boss, P., and Yeats, J. R. "Ambiguous Loss: A Complicated Type of Grief When Loved Ones Disappear." *Cruse Bereavement Care Bereavement Journal.org* (2014), vol. 33, no. 2, pp. 63–68.

Brody, S. "How to Build Consensus on Divisive Issues: Four Lessons from the Terminally Ill Patient Law." *HaMizrachi Magazine.* Tisha B'Av 5783/2023, vol. 6, no. 3, p. 21.

Callanan, M., and Kelley, P. *Final Gifts.* New York: Bantam Books, 1997.

Doka, K., ed. *Disenfranchised Grief: Recognizing Hidden Sorrow.* Lexington, MA: Lexington Books, 1989.

Fisher, J. "What Does It Mean to Grieve?" Online Webinar, Academy of Therapy Wisdom, May 17, 2022.

Greenberg, B. 1995. "Is There Life after Death?" In Riemer, J. ed., *Wrestling with the Angel: Jewish Insights on Death and Mourning*. p. 313. New York: Schocken Books.

Hoffman, L.A. "Kissed by God." *New Jersey Jewish News* (*Ḥukkat*–Numbers 19:1–22:1), June 16, 2010.

Howes, R. "The Grief We Hold: Loving in the Midst of Loss." *Psychotherapy Networker Magazine* (March/April 2021), Psychotherapynetworker.org.

Kaplan, R. Aryeh. *Sefer Yetzirah – The Book of Creation* as quoted in Kastner, Bernie. *Understanding the Afterlife in This Life*, p. 31.

Kastner, Bernie. *Understanding the Afterlife in This Life*. Devora Publishing Company, 2007.

Kessler, D. "What No One Tells You About Grief Healing with David Kessler." YouTube, October 4, 2022, https://www.youtube.com/watch?v=M51dSkAVnb4.

Kessler, D. "The Sixth Stage of Grief: Why Meaning Making Is More Important Than Ever." Online Webinar. May 8, 2022, https://www.youtube.com/watch?v=nVhsSX-gOCo.

Kessler, D. "Interventions for Dealing with Unattended Grief." Online Webinar. December 22 , 2021.https://catalog.pesi.com.

Kessler, D. "Grief Counseling and Treatment in a Pandemic of Loss." The Grief Summit. Online Webinar. April 29–30, 2021. https://catalog.pesi.com.

Kessler, D. *Finding Meaning: The Sixth Stage of Grief*. New York: Scribner, 2019.

Kessler, D. *The Needs of the Dying*. New York: Harper. 2007.

Kirzner, Y. *Making Sense of Suffering.* New Jersey: Mesorah Publications. 2002.

Lamm, M. *The Jewish Way in Death and Mourning.* New York: Jonathan David Publishers, Inc. 2000.

Ludman, B.L. *Life's Journey: Exploring Relationships – Resolving Conflicts.* Jerusalem: Devora Publishing, 2011.

(The following articles by Dr. Batya L. Ludman are accessible through the website drbatyaludman.com –Selected Recent Publications)

Aftermath of terrorism

Ludman, B.L. "Coping with the In-Between." *Jerusalem Post Magazine,* November 10, 2023, pp. 32–33.

Ludman, B.L. "Coping with Stress and Trauma While Israel Is at War, Part II." *Jerusalem Post Magazine,* October 20, 2023, pp. 23–25.

Ludman, B.L. "Yes, We Are at War – Let's Help Each Other." *Jerusalem Post Magazine,* October 13, 2023, pp 18–20.

Dating and remarriage

Ludman, B.L. "The Second Time Around." *Jerusalem Post Magazine,* June 23, 2017, p. 29.

Ludman, B.L. "Psychologically Speaking: Mom Wants to Re-Marry." *Jerusalem Post (Up Front),* April 27, 2007, p. 39.

End-of-life discussions

Ludman, B.L. "The Doctor Is In: Important Conversations." *Jerusalem Post Magazine,* September 4, 2020, p. 36.

Ludman, B.L. "That's No Way to Say Goodbye." *Jerusalem Post Magazine,* May 16, 2014, p. 23.

Impact of COVID-19

Ludman, B.L. "The Doctor Is In: A Year Gone Awry: Thoughts on 2020 and the Year Ahead." *Jerusalem Post Magazine,* February 19, 2021, p. 41.

Ludman, B.L. "COVID-19 and Its Impact on Loss Within the Jewish Community." Association for Death Education and Counseling. The Thanatology Association. Cited in *ADEC Connects*. June 7, 2020.

Loss – general

Ludman, B.L. "When There Is No Right Answer: When Loss Begets More Loss." *Jerusalem Post Magazine,* July 5, 2019, p. 6.

Ludman, B.L. "Lessons Learned from a Beloved Woman." *Jerusalem Post Magazine,* July 31, 2015, p. 25.

Loss – children

Ludman, B.L. "Grief and Loss through the Eyes of a Young Child." *Jerusalem Post Magazine* November 23, 2018, p. 24.

Ludman, B.L. "Delivering Difficult News to Children." *Jerusalem Post Magazine* January 10, 2014, p. 25.

Loss – adult sibling

Ludman, B.L. "Psychologically Speaking: Adult Sibling Loss." *Jerusalem Post (Up Front),* July 18, 2008, pp. 36–37.

Serious illness

Ludman, B.L. "Plan for the Worst but Hope for the Best." *Jerusalem Post Magazine,* August 2, 2019, p. 18.

Ludman, B.L. "When Life Throws You a Curveball." *Jerusalem Post Magazine,* May 17, 2013, p. 24.

Ludman, B.L. "Psychology: Serious Illness – The Trauma of Diagnosis and Treatment." *Jerusalem Post Magazine,* October 15, 2010, p. 38.

Transmission of values – ethical wills

Ludman, B.L. "Shrouds Don't Have Pockets." *Jerusalem Post Magazine,* February 19, 2016, p. 25.

Ludman, B.L. "A Month Since the Swissair Disaster: Some Brief Personal Reflections. *The Nova Scotia Psychologist* 12, no. 4 (1998): 18–19.

Picoult, J. *Wish You Were Here.* London: Hodder & Stoughton, 2021.

Picoult, J. *The Storyteller.* London: Hodder & Stoughton, 2013.

Pomerantz, S. "On My Daughter's 39th Yahrzeit." *Jerusalem Post,* November 21, 2022.

Rando, T.A. *Clinical Interventions in Anticipatory Grief.* Handout for Workshop, December 4–5, 1996, Halifax, N.S. Canada.

Rando, T.A. *How to Go On Living When Someone You Love Dies.* New York: Bantam Books. 1991.

Sacks, J. "Between Hope and Humanity." In *Covenant and Conversation: Leviticus,* 153–156. Jerusalem: Maggid Books, 2015.

Sacks, J. *Studies in Spirituality.* Jerusalem: Maggid Books, 2021.

Sacks, J. *Judaism's Life-Changing Ideas.* Jerusalem: Maggid Books, 2020.

Sacks, J. "Losing Miriam." In *Covenant and Conversation: Numbers,* 271–275. Jerusalem: Maggid Books, 2017.

Sacks, J. "Refusing Comfort, Keeping Hope." In *Covenant and Conversation: Genesis,* 253–257. Jerusalem: Maggid Books, 2009.

Sacks, J. "When the 'I' Is Silent." In *Covenant and Conversation: Genesis,* 191–193. Jerusalem: Maggid Books, 2009.

Sandberg, S., and A. Grant. *Option B: Facing Adversity, Building Resilience, and Finding Joy.* New York: Alfred A. Knopf, 2017.

Shir, S., *Miriam's Song. The Story of Miriam Peretz*. Jerusalem: Gefen Publishing House Ltd., 2016.

Smiles, S., "Life and Death." *Mishpacha Magazine*, Nov. 29, 2022, https://mishpacha.com/life-and-death/.

Stav, A., *As a Fleeting Dream: On Coping with Pregnancy Loss*. Jerusalem: Mosad Harav Kook, 2023.

Solomon, R.L., *The Ex Talk*. Berkley, 2021.

Wolpe, D.J. "Message for the Grieving." *Jerusalem Post Magazine*. April 29, 2022.

Wolpe, D.J. "Why Stones Instead of Flowers?" In J. Riemer, ed., *Wrestling with the Angel: Jewish Insights on Death and Mourning*, 128–130. New York: Schocken Books, 1995.

Selected Support Organizations and Helplines

DEATH EDUCATION

Association for Death Education and Counseling

This organization promotes death education and counseling-related resources and provides a network for professionals.
www.adec.org

Ematai

A team of rabbinical and medical experts who help navigate the healthcare journey and respond to health-care dilemmas related to death and dying. They offer a living will, and a conversation primer for end-of-life decision making.
www.ematai.org

Option18.org – an initiative through Ematai – educates about posthumous organ donation.

Life's Door – Tishkofet

An Israeli-based organization that incorporates quality of life in empowering patients, their families, and health-care professionals facing issues around illness and loss. They provide guidance around health care and end-of-life decision making through the document *Conversation Project: A Conversation That Can Change Your Whole Life.* Forms for completing advanced medical directives in the USA and medical power of attorney in Israel may be found on their website.
www.lifesdoor.org

Ministry of Health (Israel)

A document regarding end-of-life decisions and medical wishes and management can be downloaded through the Ministry of Health and reviewed with a lawyer.
Ministry of Health – Advance Medical Directives Center
www.health.gov.il
Kol Habriyut *5400, Landline: +972-8-6241010; E-mail: Call.Habriut@moh.health.gov.il

Tzohar Ad Meah Va'Esrim (Ad 120)

This organization provides answers to ethical and halakhic questions with help in decision making by a team of rabbis and social workers.
https://ad120.tzohar.org.il/en/about
or call the Hotline in Israel at *9253

GRIEF SUPPORT

David Kessler – Online information about grief and group support

grief.com
tenderheartssupport.com

aboutgrief.com
grieving.com
parentsforever.com
griefsuicide.com
www.mygrief.ca

Gila's Way, Saving Lives

Providing educational programming regarding mental health awareness and suicide prevention.
gilasway.com
info@rabbihammer.com

GUIDANCE FOR BURIALS AND FUNERALS

ITIM : Resources and Advocacy for Jewish Life

Provides guidelines for burial in Israel and offers assistance with funeral arrangements, burial options, and parental rights with respect to burial of stillborns and newborns.
www.itim.org.il

National Association of Chevra Kadisha (NASCK)

This organization offers guidance on Jewish burial, mourning, and halakhic living wills across the United States and Canada. It assists the *ḥevrot kaddisha* in defining and ensuring respect for the deceased according to Jewish law and acts as an educational resource for promoting Jewish burial.

It offers the EMES (Emergency Medical Education Sign-up) Card and details for downloading a smartphone app with emergency contacts, relevant medical information, and a shortened version of a halakhic living will.
nasck.org

The Jewish Funeral Directors of America, Inc.

They offer guidance on Jewish funerals.
Telephone: 703-391-8400
Toll Free 1-888-477-5567
jfda@iccfa.com

JEWISH FERTILITY SUPPORT AND PREGNANCY LOSS

I Was Supposed to Have a Baby (IWSTHAB)

A social media community to support Jewish individuals and families who are suffering through primary and secondary infertility, pregnancy loss, infant death, surrogacy, adoption and pregnancy after loss.
info@ iwasssupposedtohaveababy.org

HELPLINES IN ISRAEL

ERAN

Twenty-four-hour hotline providing lifesaving emotional first-aid services for suicide, grief, and loss in Israel.
SMS: +972-52-999-3544
en.eran.org.il
Phone: 1201

Natal

Provides assistance for Israelis suffering from PTSD due to terror and war.
Helpline 1-800-363-363
natal.org.il

Glossary

Ad me'ah ve'esrim – "[May you/he/she live] until one hundred and twenty." Used as a wish or blessing for long life. Refers to the length of Moses's life.

Adar – Hebrew month when Purim is celebrated.

Adar I / Adar II – In a Hebrew leap year there are two months of Adar: Adar I (Adar Alef) and Adar II (Adar Bet).

ADI card – An ADI donor card in Israel testifies to the willingness of the holder to donate their organs or tissues after death, to patients waiting for transplant.

advance funeral planning – Preplanning with a funeral professional regarding funeral decisions and prepayment of plot and funeral costs.

advanced healthcare directive – A legal document that guides a family and health-care team with respect to future medical decisions, should one be unable to make them.

Akeda – The offering of Issac upon the altar.

aliya – 1. Moving to Israel. 2. The honor of being called up to the Torah.

Amida – The central silent prayer included in every prayer service.

Am Yisrael Ḥai – The people of Israel live.

ambiguous loss – A physical loss when a body is missing and death cannot be confirmed or a psychological loss when the person is physically present but psychologically absent.

amud – A podium for prayers.

aninut – An *onen* is a person whose immediate relative has died and is yet to be buried. The state of being an *onen* is called *aninut*.

anticipatory loss – The grief a person may feel in the days, months, and years before the death actually occurs.

arikhut yamim – A long life.

Ashkenazim – Jews who lived in the Rhineland valley and in France before their migration to Slavic lands (Poland, Lithuania, and Russia) in the eleventh to thirteenth centuries, and their descendants.

azkara – A memorial service.

avel (pl. ***aveilim***) – The mourner or mourners.

avelut – The period of mourning.

ayin hara – Literally, the "evil eye"; causing something negative to occur by discussing it.

Baraita – The oral traditions of Jewish law that were not included in the Mishna.

barukh Hashem – Literally, "blessed be God"; used more often as "Thank God," an expression of gratitude.

bar mitzva – Celebration for a Jewish boy at thirteen years old on reaching the age of observing commandments.

bat mitzva – Celebration for a Jewish girl at twelve years old on reaching the age of observing commandments.

Beit HaMikdash – The Holy Temple in Jerusalem.

bereavement – A state of grief, after the death of a loved one.

bikkur ḥolim – The act of visiting the sick.

Birkat Kohanim – A blessing recited by the *kohanim* (priests) in the Temple and today in the synagogue.

bli neder – Literally, "without a promise." A phrase used when intending to do something, but not promising to do it.

brit mila – Circumcision.

Bubbie – Grandmother in Yiddish.

burial – The placement of a dead body into a grave.

cognitive abilities – Skills required to perform a task, such as information processing, attention, and memory.

Complex Post-Traumatic Stress Disorder (C-PTSD) – A form of Post-Traumatic Stress Disorder that results from experiencing ongoing trauma such as prolonged abuse or war.

Complicated Grief Disorder – A proposed disorder for those considered impaired by persistent and intense symptoms of grief, lasting for at least a year after the initial loss.

COVID-19 – A worldwide infectious virus identified in December 2019 and deemed a pandemic.

CPR – Cardiopulmonary resuscitation; an emergency procedure done after a cardiac arrest in order to restore blood circulation and breathing.

daven, davening – Pray, praying.

death notice – A posted announcement which provides information regarding funeral, shiva, and prayer times.

delayed grief – Grief that is pushed off or delayed for a significant amount of time after the death.

disenfranchised grief – Grief that is not socially acknowledged and therefore not publicly mourned.

double burial (*kevurat makhpela*) – Burial of two bodies in the same burial plot, one on top of the other.

derasha – A sermon.

dvar Torah – Speech containing words of Torah.

eishet ḥayil – A woman of valor.

E-l Maleh Raḥamim – A Jewish prayer for the soul of a person who has died, usually recited at the graveside during the burial service and at memorial services during the year.

Emergency Medical Service (EMS) – An emergency service that provides urgent treatment, stabilization on location, and hospital transport when appropriate.

emergent – Requiring immediate assessment and medical treatment.

enduring power of attorney – A document enabling decision making on someone else's behalf when that person can no longer make their own decisions.

Erev – The day preceding the Sabbath or a holiday.

eulogy – A tribute or speech delivered at a funeral.

funeral home – A place that provides preparation of the deceased for burial and funeral services for the deceased and their family.

haftara – A series of selections from the books of Prophets that is read in the synagogue following the Torah reading each Sabbath and on Jewish festivals.

ḥag – A Jewish holiday.

halakha (pl. halakhot) – Jewish law.

Hallel – A prayer from Psalms recited on Jewish holidays and other festive days.

HaMakom – 1. Literally, "the place." 2. One of the names of God.

Hanukka – A Jewish holiday celebrated for eight days, commemorating the rededication of the Second Temple.

Hareini kaparat mishkavo/mishkava – I am an atonement for his/her resting place. Added when speaking of the deceased during the first year of a parent's passing.

Hashem – Literally, "the name"; used to refer to God.

hashkava (***ashkava***) – Memorial prayer in the Sephardic ritual.

Hatarat Nedarim – The annulment of vows or oaths.

HaTikva – The Israeli national anthem.

ḥesed – Kindness or benevolence.

ḥesed shel emet – Literally, true kindness. Any aspect of dealing with the deceased is considered true kindness.

ḥesed ve'emet – Kindness and truth.

Ḥeshvan – The Hebrew month in which there are no Jewish holidays.

hesped (pl. ***hespedim***) – Eulogy, eulogies.

ḥevra kaddisha – Jewish burial society.

ḥiyuv – Literally "obligation." Refers to someone who is in mourning and must say *Kaddish*.

Ḥol HaMoed – The intermediate days within the holidays of Sukkot and Passover.

hospice unit – A place that provides emotional and medical care for the terminally ill and their families.

ḥuppa – 1. The Jewish wedding canopy. 2. Jewish marriage ceremony.

IDF – Acronym for the Israel Defense Forces.

in-ground or field burial (*kevurat sadeh*) – The interment of the deceased, with or without a casket, into the earth.

intensive care unit (ICU) – A hospital unit which provides life support and critical care for those who are severely ill or injured.

interment – The act of burial.

intubated – Inserting a tube into the trachea in order to keep the airway open, enabling air to get into the lungs.

Isru Ḥag – The day after each of the three pilgrimage festivals: Passover, Shavuot, and Sukkot.

Jerusalem Talmud – Commentary on the Mishna originating in the Land of Israel.

Jewish law – Rules, ordinances, commandments, and practices that structure Jewish life.

Kabbalat Shabbat – The prayer service recited on Friday evening to usher in the Sabbath.

Kaddish – A prayer recited by the mourners in a quorum in praise of God.

kever – A grave.

kibbutz (pl. **kibbutzim**) – A collective community.

kibbud horim – The commandment to honor your parents.

Kiddush – 1. A blessing over wine to sanctify the Sabbath or Jewish holiday. 2. A celebratory gathering after prayer services with refreshments.

kippa (pl. **kippot**) – A skullcap or yarmulke.

Kislev – The Hebrew month when Hanukka is celebrated.

kohanim (sing. ***kohen***) – The priests who once served in the Temple of Jerusalem, descendants of Aaron the high priest. Today *kohanim* have the privilege of being called for the first *aliya* to say the blessing over the Torah during religious services. There is also the privilege of saying the priestly blessing.

kriya – The custom for the mourners to tear their garments just prior to the funeral.

layered tier burial (***kevurat komot***) – Multilayer burial within a structure either within a wall or terraced into the earth.

levaya – 1. Literally "to accompany." 2. Hebrew for funeral.

Levite – From the tribe of Levi.

likut atzamot – Bone gathering.

living will – A legal document stating your wishes with respect to medical decisions when you are unable to make decisions for yourself.

Maarat HaMakhpela – The cave of the Patriarchs. The Jewish forefathers and foremothers are buried there – Abraham, Sarah, Isaac, Rebecca, Jacob, and Leah.

Magen David Adom – Israel's national emergency medical ambulance and blood bank service.

matzeva – The Hebrew term for monument or tombstone.

meal of consolation – The meal served to the mourners upon their return from the cemetery.

memorial candle – 1. A candle lit in memory of the deceased that stays lit for twenty-four hours. 2. A candle lit at the beginning of shiva that lasts through the week.

mezuza (pl. ***mezuzot***) – A parchment with the *Shema* prayer that is placed on the doors of a Jewish home.

Midrash – A form of biblical commentary.

minhag (pl. ***minhagim***) – A Jewish custom.

minyan (pl. **minyanim**) – A quorum of ten adults needed in order to recite certain prayers.

misheberakh – A public prayer recited in the synagogue for a person in need of healing or protection.

mishloaḥ manot – Gifts of food given to others on Purim.

Mishna – The written collection of the oral Jewish law.

mitzva (pl. **mitzvot**) – A Torah commandment or good deed.

Modah Ani – A prayer said first thing in the morning thanking God.

mora lehalakha – A female halakhic advisor.

morgue – A place where bodies are kept prior to identification or burial.

Mourner's *Kaddish* – A prayer recited by the mourners in a quorum in praise of God.

mourners – As defined by Jewish law, a person who has lost a parent, spouse, sibling or child.

naḥat ruaḥ – Satisfaction or peace of mind.

nefilat apayim – Literally "falling on one's face." Part of the weekday *Taḥanun* prayer service.

neshama – Soul.

niḥum aveilim – The comforting of mourners.

obituary – A written death notice of the deceased including a short biography and often funeral and shiva details.

October 7th, 2023 – The date of the Simḥat Torah massacre in Israel and the beginning of the Swords of Iron War.

Olam HaBa – Literally, the World to Come. The world after death.

Olam HaZeh – Literally, this world. The present physical world as opposed to the World to Come.

oleh (pl. ***olim***) – An immigrant to Israel.

onen – A person whose immediate relative has died but has yet to be buried.

organ donation – The donation of organs or tissues prior to death or posthumously (see ADI card).

pallbearers – The individuals at a funeral who help carry or otherwise escort the body to the burial site.

palliative care – Emotional and medical care focusing on pain relief and quality of life for seriously and terminally ill patients.

parasha, parashat – A portion of the Torah; the weekly Torah portion.

pasuk – A verse in the Torah.

pasul – Unfit for Jewish ceremonial use.

personal protective equipment (PPE) – Clothing and accessories worn to protect against infection or injury.

Pesaḥ Sheni – Literally, the second Passover. The fourteenth of Iyar, one month after the celebration of Passover.

Pirkei Avot – "Chapters of the Fathers." Ethical teachings from the Rabbis of the Mishna.

post-traumatic growth – Positive psychological change experienced after a challenging or life-changing event.

prearranged burial – Preplanning and prepayment for burial.

probated – The legal process of ensuring that a will is valid.

Prolonged Grief Disorder (PGD) – Also know as Complicated Grief Disorder, a proposed disorder for those considered impaired by persistent and intense symptoms of grief, lasting for at least a year after the initial loss.

prozdor – A vestibule or corridor.

psalmist – The author of an individual psalm.

Psalms – The book of the Bible traditionally ascribed to King David with hymns, poems, and songs.

Purim – The Jewish holiday which celebrates the saving of the Jewish people from annihilation by the wicked Haman.

Purim Katan – When Purim is celebrated in a leap year in Adar Bet, the date of Purim in Adar Alef is called *Purim Katan*.

rabbi – A Jewish spiritual leader and teacher.

rabbinic tradition – The interpretation of the Torah by the Rabbis.

refua shelema – A wish for a complete recovery from illness.

reinterment – The exhumation and reburying of a dead body after it had previously been buried elsewhere.

resurrect, resurrection – The restoration of a dead person to life.

resuscitation – The act of reviving someone from a state of unconsciousness or death.

Rosh Ḥodesh – The first day(s) of a Jewish month.

saba – The Hebrew word for grandfather.

sefer Torah – A Torah scroll.

segula – A charm, remedy, or protection. An action that will lead to a change in one's fortune or destiny.

Sephardim – Spanish Jews who were expelled from Spain after 1492 and found their way to the countries of North Africa and the Middle East.

seuda – A festive meal.

Seudat Amen – A meal where people join together in order to make blessings and answer Amen.

seudat havra'a – The first meal the mourner(s) eats following the burial of a close relative. It usually consists of round foods.

shaliaḥ tzibur – A person who leads the congregation in prayers.

Shavuot – A Jewish holiday that commemorates the giving of the Torah on Mount Sinai.

Shekhina – The presence of God.

Shema – The Jewish prayer that stresses the monotheistic essence of Judaism.

Shemini Atzeret – A Jewish holiday celebrated on the eighth day of Sukkot.

shemira – The Jewish custom of watching over the body of the deceased from death to burial.

sheva berakhot – The seven blessings for the new couple at a Jewish wedding. These blessings are also recited at the festive meals during the week after a Jewish wedding.

shevarim – One of the shofar blasts made up of three broken notes, which sounds like crying.

shiur – A lecture or talk on any Torah topic.

shiva – The seven-day mourning period for an immediate relative.

sheloshim – The thirty-day period of mourning after the burial.

shenat avelut – The year of mourning for a deceased parent.

shofar – A ram's horn blown on the holiday of Rosh HaShana.

shomer (masculine), ***shomeret*** (feminine) – The person who watches over the body from death to burial.

shroud – The garment in which the deceased is clothed for burial.

shul – A synagogue.

Shulḥan Arukh – The "Code of Jewish Law" authored by Rabbi Joseph Karo in 1563.

siddur (pl. ***siddurim***) – The Hebrew prayer book.

Simḥat Torah – The Jewish holiday celebrated on the last day of Sukkot when the yearly Torah cycle is completed.

sukka – A temporary hut constructed for use during the Sukkot holiday.

Sukkot – The Jewish holiday commemorating the booths the Jewish people dwelled in while they were in the desert for forty years.

survivor's guilt – Emotional stress experienced by someone after surviving an incident when others did not.

takhrikhim – See shroud.

tahara – Cleansing and preparation of the body for Jewish burial.

tallit – A shawl with fringed corners worn during prayer.

Talmud – The source of Jewish religious law consisting of the Mishna and Gemara.

talmudic period – From 70 AD to 640 AD.

Tanakh – The Hebrew Bible consisting of twenty-four books.

Taḥanun – A prayer which contains confession of sins and petition for God's mercy.

Tanna'im – Rabbinic sages whose views are recorded in the Mishna.

Teḥiyat HaMeitim – The future resurrection of the dead.

tefilla (pl. ***tefillot***) – Prayer.

tefillin – Phylacteries. Black leather boxes containing parchment scrolls with biblical texts bound on the arm and placed on the head.

Tehillim – Psalms, often recited during times of difficulty and crisis.

teshuva – Literally "return"; refers to the act of repentance.

thanatologist – A person trained in death education, grief, and loss.

three weeks – The time between the Seventeenth of Tamuz and Tisha B'Av when national mourning practices are observed.

tikva – The Hebrew word for hope.

Tisha B'Av – The ninth of the month of Av. A fast day which commemorates the destruction of both Temples in Jerusalem.

Tu BiShvat – The Jewish holiday that celebrates the New Year for the trees.

tzaddik (pl. ***tzaddikim***) – A righteous person.

tzedaka – 1. Giving charity. 2. The box or container for collecting money designated for charity.

Tzidduk Hadin – A prayer recited at a Jewish funeral after the grave has been filled, affirming that the divine judgment is righteous.

tzror (***tzror haḥayim***) – The bond of life.

Unetaneh Tokef – A dramatic poem recited on the High Holidays that speaks to the seriousness of the Day of Judgment.

United Hatzalah – An Israeli volunteer emergency medical service.

viddui – The confession prayer which can be recited before one departs from the world.

will – A document regarding the distribution of a person's money and property after their death.

yahrzeit – The anniversary of the death of a parent or other relative.

Yigdal – A prayer or hymn expressing the faith of Israel in God.

yipui koaḥ mitmashekh – Durable power of attorney; a legal document in which a person appoints another person to be responsible for medical, personal, and financial matters should his judgment become impaired.

Yizkor – Literally "remember"; a memorial prayer recited in the synagogue four times a year, on Yom Kippur and the festivals, asking God to remember our loved ones who have passed away.

***Yizkor* candle** – Hebrew, *ner neshama*. A memorial candle lit in memory of the dead that burns for twenty-four hours.

Yom HaAtzma'ut – Israel's Independence Day.

Yom HaZikaron – Israel's Memorial Day for fallen soldiers and victims of terror.

Yom Kippur – The Jewish Day of Atonement in which one fasts and asks for forgiveness.

Zaka – The Hebrew initials for *Zihui Korbanot Ason,* Disaster Victim Identification. Zaka volunteers collect the remains of the dead so they may be buried according to Jewish law.

zikhrono livrakha (male), ***zikhrona livrakha*** (female) – May his or her memory be for a blessing.

Zion – A synonym for the Jewish people or the Jewish homeland.

Zohar – A work of Jewish mystical thought.

Index

About the Authors

DR. BATYA L. LUDMAN, a licensed clinical psychologist with advanced certification in thanatology (death education and counseling), works extensively with trauma and loss. She has served on the *ḥevra kaddisha*, worked, for example, with the American and Israeli communities after 9/11, and is a senior responder with United Hatzalah's Psychotrauma and Crisis Response Unit. She maintains a private practice, working with individuals, families, and communities around loss, most recently in the aftermath of October 7th. She received her doctorate from the Ferkauf Graduate School of Psychology at Yeshiva University and held faculty positions at the Mount Sinai School of Medicine, City University of New York (CUNY), and Dalhousie University in Nova Scotia, Canada. She served on the executive of both the Nova Scotia psychological association and licensing board, and currently sits on the advisory board for The Israel Association of Mental Health Professionals. She is published extensively in the professional and lay literature and writes a column for the *Jerusalem Post*. Dr. Ludman is the author of *Life's Journey: Exploring Relationships – Resolving Conflicts.*

GINA JUNGER made aliya from the U.S. in 1983. She studied at Bar-Ilan University and has been involved in Torah adult education since 1995. She is a lecturer of Jewish studies at Matan HaSharon – Women's Institute for Torah Studies. Gina is a dynamic educator who brings her unique approach to imparting Jewish values to students of all ages.

Batya Ludman (on the left) and Gina Junger

Maggid Books
The best of contemporary Jewish thought from
Koren Publishers Jerusalem Ltd.